Quantitative Methods *in*
PROJECT MANAGEMENT

JOHN C. GOODPASTURE, PMP

J.ROSS
PUBLISHING

Copyright ©2004 by J. Ross Publishing, Inc.

ISBN 1-932159-15-0

Printed and bound in the U.S.A. Printed on acid-free paper
10 9 8 7 6 5 4 3 2 1

Library of Congress Cataloging-in-Publication Data

Goodpasture, John C., 1943-
  Quantitative methods in project management / John C. Goodpasture.
    p. cm.
Includes bibliographical references.
  ISBN 1-932159-15-0 (alk. paper)
  1. Project management—Planning—Mathematical models. I. Title.
  HD69.P75G667 2003
  658.4′04—dc22

                       2003015723

    Direct all inquiries to J. Ross Publishing, Inc., 6501 Park of Commerce Blvd., Suite 200, Boca Raton, Florida 33487.

Phone: (561) 869-3900
Fax: (561) 892-0700
Web: www.jrosspub.com

DEDICATION

This book is dedicated to my wife, Ann,
for her unlimited patience and encouragement,
without which this project could never have been completed.

TABLE OF CONTENTS

PREFACE

This book is about quantitative methods in project management. Quantitative methods provide the basis for calculating value, setting up the project metrics that will be the measures of success, and helping the project manager understand the numerical values of risks to be addressed. *Quantitative Methods in Project Management* is for the project professional and day-to-day practitioner. Although grounded in theory, the objective of this book is to convey usable concepts and techniques that are workable every day in project life. Throughout the chapters, you will find sufficient introductory material set in a project manager's context to understand and apply the ideas without recourse to formal instruction. In Chapter 1, the concept that *business value is the motivator for projects* is addressed. A framework, called the "project balance sheet," is introduced and a loose workflow of quantitative skills is described.

Chapter 2 provides an introduction to probability and statistics. Really successful project managers apply these concepts routinely to set achievable expectations and manage risk. Probability and statistics are essential to "underpromising and overdelivering." Chapter 3 covers estimating methods, of which there are several, and the work breakdown structure. Good estimates cover all the scope, and all the scope is defined in the work breakdown structure. Quantitative decision making is addressed in Chapter 4. Therein, we tee-up the idea that good decisions are the outcome of decision policy implemented with rational decision making supported by risk-adjusted numerical analysis. Decision trees and tables are the tools of decision analysis. Risk adjustments in budgeting are exactly the topic of Chapter 5, wherein capital budgeting is discussed. Capital budgeting is, in effect, cash budgeting, and cash is the real source of value in business, despite the popular focus on earnings. So Chapter 5 is key material for the informed project manager.

Most project managers face a profit and loss (P&L) statement in day-to-day life. P&Ls are expense statements, largely a product of the company's cost accounting system, and are provided routinely to managers. However, the P&L does not convey value, only expense. Consequently, the P&L must be coupled with the project management "earned value" system to provide the numerical basis for understanding accumulating value. Expense accounting is the topic of Chapter 6. In Chapter 7, quantitative time management is addressed. Of course, time and cost are correlated: an increase in time is often the driver for an increase in cost. However, there are many quantitative aspects to time management that are discussed apart from cost management. Special topics in quantitative project management are covered in Chapter 8, including hypothesis testing, regression analysis, probability–impact analysis, Six Sigma, and QFD analysis. Six Sigma is a coined term that refers to a determined effort to reduce errors, which is variance, in the products and services delivered to customers. As some practitioners of Six Sigma like to say: "Our customers experience the variance, not the mean." In Chapter 9, a short treatment of project contracting is provided. Project contracting is a risk-management tool, and Chapter 9 examines the numbers and provides insight about incentive contracts as a risk-control tool.

ACKNOWLEDGMENTS

I would like to acknowledge the many people who assisted me with this book, including Ginger Levin, who got me started; Drew Gierman, who answered all my questions and guided me through the process at J. Ross Publishing; and Dr. David T. Hulett, founder of Hulett Associates in Los Angeles, who has been of inestimable value over many years by assisting me in the art and science of risk management. I am indebted to my many associates at Harris Corporation and Lanier Worldwide, Inc. who have provided opportunities and performance critiques as I have worked my way through myriad projects and programs.

John C. Goodpasture
Alpharetta, Georgia

ACKNOWLEDGMENTS

ABOUT THE AUTHOR

John C. Goodpasture, PMP, is a certified Project Management Professional with broad practical experience in executive management, project management, system engineering, and operations analysis. With engineering degrees from Georgia Tech and the University of Maryland, and as founder of his own firm, Square Peg Consulting, he is a sought after authority for management and engineering in the customized application and delivery of project management, business process analysis, and training of project practitioners.

Past assignments include program manager for certain information processing systems at the National Security Agency of the Department of Defense, strategic Project Office Director, director of a system engineering program office with responsibility for multimillion-dollar software systems at aerospace and communications firm Harris Corporation, vice president of a document archive and imaging operations group at a Fortune 500 company, and president and founder of Square Peg Consulting, Inc.

As a project manager and system engineer, John has conceptualized and reduced to practice unique techniques in his field, many of which are described in numerous symposium papers and magazine articles published on the subject of project management. In his 2001 book, *Managing Projects for Value,* John proposed the unique idea of the project balance sheet to explain the risks borne by projects to meet business need and deliver value to project sponsors.

Adept at personal communication and simplification of complex ideas, he has developed and delivered project training to numerous project teams in the fields of information management, manufacturing, production operations, and software development. Working around the world in locations in the Americas, Europe, and Asia, John has provided workshops and project consultation to functional teams in Malaysia, Belgium, Puerto Rico, and Canada.

As consultant and instructor, John's experience touches many aspects of project management, having developed and taught workshops on "Project Management," "Project Start-Up," "Capturing Requirements," "Risk Management," "Voice of the Customer," "Kano Analysis," project "Peer Reviews," and the "PMP® Exam Preparation." With James R. Sumara, he co-developed a unique technique for earned value measurement in time-constrained projects, a breakthrough methodology for projects needing earned value at a low cost of implementation.

Free value-added materials available from
the Download Resource Center at www.jrosspub.com

At J. Ross Publishing we are committed to providing today's professional with practical, hands-on tools that enhance the learning experience and give readers an opportunity to apply what they have learned. That is why we offer free ancillary materials available for download on this book and all participating Web Added Value™ publications. These online resources may include interactive versions of material that appears in the book or supplemental templates, worksheets, models, plans, case studies, proposals, spreadsheets and assessment tools, among other things. Whenever you see the WAV™ symbol in any of our publications, it means bonus materials accompany the book and are available from the Web Added Value Download Resource Center at www.jrosspub.com.

Downloads available for *Quantitative Methods in Project Management* consist of a glossary of terms and statistical and quantitative risk analysis charts, models, and examples for budgeting, cost analysis, and the project balance sheet.

PROJECT VALUE: THE SOURCE OF ALL QUANTITATIVE MEASURES

Project value is a consequence of
successful application of resources to an agreed scope,
taking measured risks to balance expectations with capability.

John C. Goodpasture

SUCCESSFUL PROJECTS

Successful projects return value to the business. Successful projects are relatively easy to identify; we usually know them when we see them. They are the projects that improve processes or product, reduce costs and operational inefficiencies, make contributions to the technical and functional competence of the organization, or add capacity and capability to serve customers and markets with greater satisfaction. They are projects that make good on the promises of the project charter, deliver the intended scope, and deliver that scope within a time frame commensurate with business objectives. The value cycle of successful projects is presented in Figure 1-1.

Mindful of the fact that projects, all projects, are one-time temporary endeavors[1] burdened with uncertainties, and not blessed with the error-reducing opportunities of repetitive ongoing operations, the project manager faces many

1

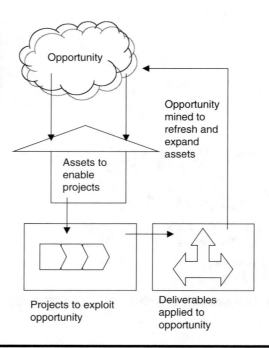

Figure 1-1   The Project Cycle of Value.

risks arising from internal stresses and external uncontrollables. The project manager's mission is then to *accomplish the assigned scope with the available resources, taking measured risks to do so.*

More often than not, successful projects "make the numbers." In the project's value equation, the resource commitment is to be more than paid back by the project benefits. That said, it might be the case that the numbers to make are spread over the life cycle of the project from concept through implementation, deployment, operations, and retirement. Figure 1-2 illustrates the life phases of a project.

The numbers may not be all financial; indeed, quantitative measures of resource consumption, customer satisfaction scores, market share, supplier value, and other business measures may be every bit as influential in judging project success. What would be your judgment of New Coke® or the Edsel automobile or the Apple Newton®? Very likely, the concept and development project efforts were sufficiently successful by conventional measures to warrant production, but over the product life cycle these were not very successful projects, largely due to customer dissatisfaction with feature and function, and perhaps inadequate product differentiation with competitors.

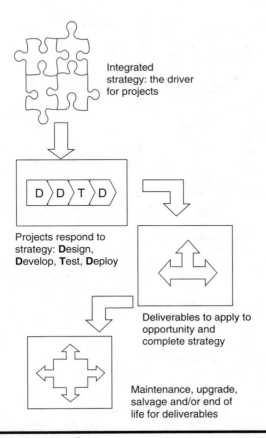

Integrated
strategy: the driver
for projects

Projects respond to
strategy: **D**esign,
Develop, **T**est, **D**eploy

Deliverables to apply to
opportunity and
complete strategy

Maintenance, upgrade,
salvage and/or end of
life for deliverables

Figure 1-2   The Project Life Cycle.

Valuable projects are "instruments of strategy."[2] Project value is made trace-able to opportunity by means of flow down from opportunity to goals deployed through strategic plans, as illustrated in Figure 1-3. We see in Figure 1-3 that opportunity is at the head of project value. Opportunity is the untapped market value that must be processed into business results. Tapping into opportunity provides the fuel to achieve goals. Goals are a state of being, quantitative and measurable, a destination to be achieved with strategy. Strategy is actionable steps toward the goal state. Strategy is a plan. To implement a planning step, a project may be needed. Therein lies project value: a means to an end to execute strategy and achieve goals. Once completed, a concept of operations employing the deliverables becomes day-to-day organizational activity.

Really valuable projects enhance core competencies; indeed, for many companies, project management and the ability to execute projects as envi-

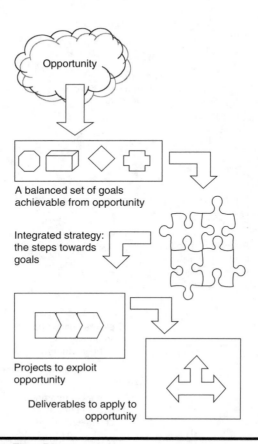

A balanced set of goals
achievable from opportunity

Integrated strategy:
the steps towards
goals

Projects to exploit
opportunity

Deliverables to apply to
opportunity

Figure 1-3   Value Flow Down.

sioned is a core competency. As defined by Gary Hamel and C.K. Parahalad in their 1990 *Harvard Business Review* article, "The Core Competence of the Corporation,"[3] and subsequently expanded in their 1994 book, *Competing for the Future,*[4] core competencies are integrated bundles of skills, often cross-departmental, that provide business with "gateways to future opportunities." To be a core competency in Hamel and Parahalad's view, an integrated skill set must meet three tests. First, it must be employed to make a material contribution to customer value in the products and services offered by the business. Certainly, the skill set required to pull off mission-enabling projects would meet this test. Second, a core competency must be competitively unique and add to the differentiation in the market between the firm and its competitors and substitutes. For example, within the defense industry, program management of complicated cost-reimbursable contracts is considered a core competency. The ability to manage huge complexity in a semi-regulated environment — with all of the unique accounting and contracting processes, procedures, and rules that are associated with the defense industrial community — separates defense firms from their commercial counterparts. Even within the defense community, integrated program management skills set apart firms into opportunity spaces by their ability to manage scope. Finally, a core competency enables extensions of the business into new products and services. If not for this, many companies might remain the best buggy whip manufacturers of all time.

BUSINESS VALUE IS THE MOTIVATOR FOR PROJECTS

The fact is, the "business of business is to increase shareholder wealth." This sentiment paraphrases the thinking of many executives going back all the way to Adam Smith in the 18th century. In his well-known book, *The Wealth of Nations,* published in 1776, business leader Smith wrote: *"Every individual endeavors to employ his capital so that its produce may be of greatest value. He generally neither intends to promote the public interest, nor knows how much he is promoting it. He intends only his own security, his own gain."* By all current measures, Mr. Smith was very self-centered and not community oriented. Nevertheless, it is as true today as it was more than two centuries ago that many businesses put financial performance at the top of the value chain.

Insofar as projects return more in financial resources than they absorb, we could then conclude that those projects are valuable to the business. It only remains to set up the mechanisms to make effective financial measures. We will take up financial measures in later chapters when we discuss capital budgeting and cost management. We will examine the concepts of sorting projects on the basis of their risk-adjusted returns calculated as either their net present value or their economic value add. Coupling scope with financial returns leads us to the concept of earned value. Earned value is indispensable for evaluating the true value of a project to the business.

Over time, several models have evolved to describe other sources of business value that are effective tools for project managers. Project managers are often called on to contribute to the selection of projects, to interpret the voice of the customer when setting scope, to evaluate the discretionary investments in upgrades and enhancements throughout the life cycle, and to assist with the rollout and deployment of the project deliverables to the end users and customers. Familiarity with the sources of value to executives, suppliers, users, and customers only enhances the value of project management per se. These value models convey understanding of the hot buttons of those constituents.

The Balanced Scorecard

One model in current and widespread use is the balanced scorecard. The balanced scorecard is an idea invented by Robert S. Kaplan and David P. Norton. Writing first in the *Harvard Business Review* in an article entitled "The Balanced Scorecard — Measures That Drive Performance,"[5] Kaplan and Norton described four scoring areas for business value. One, of course, is financial performance. Financial performance is often a history of performance over the reporting period. Though historical data provide a basis to calculate trends, in effect indexes for forecasting future results, by and large the focus of financial performance is on what was accomplished and the plans for the period ahead. Almost all projects and all project managers must respond to financial performance.

Three other balanced scorecard scoring areas also fit well into the business of chartering, scoping, and selecting projects. These scoring areas are the customer perspective of how well we are seen by those that depend on us for products and services, and exercise free will to spend their money with our business or not; the internal business perspective, often referred to as the operational effectiveness perspective; and the innovation and learning perspective that addresses not only how our business is modernizing its products and services but also how the stakeholders in the business, primarily the employees, are developing themselves as well.

For each of these scoring areas, it is typical to set goals (a state to be achieved) and develop strategy (actionable steps to achieve goals). The scoring areas themselves represent the opportunity space. As we saw in Figure 1-3, goal setting and strategy development in specific opportunity areas lead naturally to the identification of projects as a means to strategy. Specific performance measures are established for each scoring area so that goal achievement is measurable and reportable.

Typically, project performance measures are benefits and key performance indicators (KPIs). KPIs need not be, and most are not, financial measures. In this book, we make the distinction between benefits, returns, and a KPI. Benefits will be used in the narrow sense of dollar flows that offset financial investment in projects. Returns, typically expressed in ratios of financial measures, such as return on investment, and benefits, typically measured in dollars, are sometimes used interchangeably though it is obvious that benefits and returns are calculated differently. KPIs, on the other hand, are measures of operational performance, such as production errors per million, key staff turnover rate, credit memos per dollar of revenue, customer wait time in call centers, and such.

The Treacy–Wiersema Model

Michael Treacy and Fred Wiersema described a model of business value in their study, "Customer Intimacy and Other Value Disciplines,"[6] published in the *Harvard Business Review*, and expanded further in their book, *The Discipline of Market Leaders.*[7] Closely aligned with the balanced scorecard, the Treacy–Wiersema model has three focus areas. The first is customer intimacy, in which the concept of relationship management as a business value is foremost. Customer intimacy is characterized by a harmonious alignment of business values in a chain that interconnects the customer and the business. Product, service, and support are more or less tailored to an individual customer. Many projects, especially in the evolving "e-business" of integrated business systems, are aimed squarely at customer intimacy. The objective of these e-business projects is to provide complementary cross-user functionality and shared workload across the channel, presumably doing the task at the most effective end of the channel at the least or most effective cost. A subtler objective is to raise barriers to exit of the relationship and thereby close out competitors. It is almost axiomatic that the cost of sales to retain and nurture an existing customer is far less than the cost of marketing, selling, and closing a new customer.

The second focus area of the Treacy–Wiersema model is product excellence or superiority. The objective is to be differentiated from competitors and create an "ah-hah!" demand. Obviously, such demand can usually command a price premium. There must be a dedication to innovation, upgrade, and new ideas. Risk taking, at least in product and service development and delivery, is the norm. Naturally, this is a target-rich area for project managers, and the performance measures are typically market share, customer satisfaction, revenues, and profits.

The third area is operational excellence. Internal processes, methods, and procedures are made as "frictionless" as possible. Repetition is exploited to reduce errors and minimize variance to the mean outcome. This area is taken quite broadly and would in most businesses encompass some of the innovation and learning goals from the balanced scorecard. A good example of operational excellence exists in the back-office billing and administration systems. As an example, health-care administrator companies strive to be operationally excellent, providing uniformly the same service to each and all customers.

Treacy and Wiersema make the point that it is difficult, if not out and out inconsistent, to excel in all three areas. Product excellence and operational efficiency may conflict culturally and financially. Customer intimacy may also conflict with operational efficiency. You would not expect customer intimacy from your health-care administrator; you want a frictionless, repeatable experience with a call center if you need help. Operational efficiency could be the mantra of the low-cost commodity provider, and many customers would be quite happy with that. Of course, for commodity providers there are few barriers to exit, and customers vote with their feet and their pocketbook.

The Kano Model

The Kano model is more narrowly focused than the former two models discussed. Named for Dr. Noriaki Kano and widely described in the literature,[8,9] the model is aimed at capturing the voice of the customer for requirements for products and service. Originally conceived in the 1970s as a quality tool for obtaining a good match of customer need and product feature and function, project managers can apply this tool not only for grading requirements but also for evaluating budget allocations and priorities, and for assessing qualitative risks. In this regard, Kano models are quite useful for project managers who must make dollar decisions about where discretionary funds can be best leveraged for business value.

Kano really only addresses two of the focus areas already described: customer perspective and product excellence. The Kano model pretty much ignores operational effectiveness, except as operational effectiveness is reflected in product or service quality that influences customer satisfaction. Of the three models, the Kano model is very tactical and applies readily to projects.

The Kano model is most often represented as a graph, with two axes as shown in Figure 1-4. The vertical axis is the customer satisfaction scale, reaching from very satisfied, to indifferent in the center, to very dissatisfied. Although a numeric scale is not often used, project managers seeking more quantification could apply a scale.*

The horizontal axis is product or service functionality or performance. To the right is desired or available functionality or performance, with stronger desire or need represented by a farther distance outward from the center. To the left is missing functionality or poor performance. Again, the same ideas of numeric scaling could be applied to this axis. In the center is a neutral area in which functionality is unevaluated, but also this is where the center of the customer satisfaction axis crosses.

Of course, the axes are laid out on a graph to cross at the center and provide an orthogonal space in four quadrants suitable for plotting. In this space, a set

---

* The scales applied to the Kano model need not be linear. Indeed, a logarithmic scale going from the center origin toward the outer reaches of satisfaction, both positive and negative, could be quite helpful if there is great range to be plotted. Or, the logarithmic scale could be applied to product functionality, left and right. Applying a scale to one or the other of the axes creates a "log-linear" plotting space. Of course, project managers familiar with logarithmic scales will know that a straight line plotted on a log scale will be a curve.

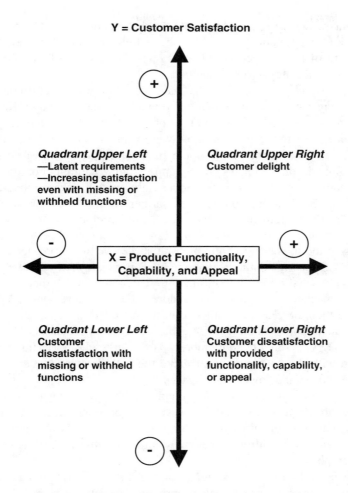

Y = Customer Satisfaction

Quadrant Upper Left
**—Latent requirements
—Increasing satisfaction
even with missing or
withheld functions**

Quadrant Upper Right
Customer delight

**X = Product Functionality,
Capability, and Appeal**

Quadrant Lower Left
**Customer
dissatisfaction with
missing or withheld
functions**

Quadrant Lower Right
**Customer dissatisfaction
with provided
functionality, capability,
or appeal**

*The Kano Chart is a grid that shows relationships
between customer satisfaction and product functionality.*

Figure 1-4   Kano Graph.

of curves is plotted. Let us consider the first quadrant in the upper left of the plotting space. We see this illustrated on the Kano graph. In this quadrant, customer satisfaction is increasing, but there is little expectation for functionality. In this space are latent, or unspoken, requirements — missing functionality but also unknown or unappreciated by the customer. In the upper left quadrant there is little or no impact on customer satisfaction. From the project management perspective, this space means that no investment need go into filling the missing functions since they have little impact. However, there is opportunity insofar as a function or feature might be "promoted" from the upper left quadrant to the upper right quadrant.

The upper right quadrant is the "ah-hah!" space where the customer recognizes increasing, available, or known functionality as real value add. Kano calls this the customer delight quadrant. In the upper right quadrant are functions and features that the customer did not know were wanted until the functions were revealed. This is the quadrant of "home runs" and new-to-the-world product risks. Spending is discretionary in the upper right quadrant. For the project manager, requirements plotted in the upper right quadrant carry above-average risk, increasingly so as the plot moves farther from the center origin. The impacts on cost management and schedule are more probable, making their risks rise to the top of the list of risks to be watched.

Moving to the lower half of the plotting space, we next consider the lower right quadrant shown on the Kano graph. This is an area of distress. The customer is not satisfied in spite of function, feature, or service that is provided. The project manager is compelled to address these requirements, dedicating resources to their fix. Resource allocation to this quadrant competes with the resources that might or should go into the upper right quadrant. The project manager, along with other team members, particularly whomever holds the best relationship with the customer, must make the call about resource contention between the upper and lower right spaces.

Finally we come to the lower left quadrant. This quadrant is the flip side of its cousin above. If functionality is missing or poorly provided, the customer is unhappy, perhaps very unhappy. This quadrant consumes resources for the needed fix, competing with the other two (upper and lower right) as shown on the Kano graph.

There is actually a fifth space, really only a line: the horizontal axis. Along this axis, function and feature may be provided, as on the right side, or not provided at all, as on the left side, but the customer cares not one way or the other. This is the line of total indifference on the part of the customer. In fact, we plot the first of our curves along this axis and label it the "I" curve for indifference.

What may lie along this axis? Actually, quite a lot usually goes here. Project managers put all the regulatory requirements, whether internal or external, on this axis. What about risk? Well, some of these requirements may carry quite a lot of risk but add nothing to customer satisfaction, at least as perceived by the customer. Certainly the project manager should take no more risk than necessary and challenge any new additions to the "I" requirements.

There are three other curves that are more interesting.* The first is the "L" curve, or the linear line that extends from the lower left to the upper right through the center. This is the "more is better" line. For features represented on this line, providing "more" simply increases customer satisfaction. A good example is computer memory: more is better, always! Correspondingly, a lack of memory will upset the customer, and the more missing the worse will be the effect. From the point of view of meeting the competition, it is almost mandatory to fund these requirements, at least to some degree, to stay in the race. Commensurate risks must be taken, or else product obsolescence will doom all future sales.

A third curve is the "M" curve, which stands for "must be there." The "M" curve is shown in Figure 1-5. Running along the horizontal axis on the right side, and dipping into the lower left quadrant, the "M" curve is appropriate where the presence of a function raises little reaction with the customer, but if the function is missing, then there is customer dissatisfaction. With requirements of this type, the project manager should take no risks and invest only that which is necessary to maintain the function without adding to it. Now, there is opportunity to "promote" from "M" to "I". Did Apple make this move when it dropped the floppy disk drive in its desktop computers?

Perhaps of most interest is the "A" curve, which stands for the "ah-hah!" reaction. It is the mirror image of the "M" curved flipped around so that it runs along the horizontal axis on the left side and then rises into the upper right quadrant. Requirements along the "A" line do not upset the customer if missing but engender a very favorable reaction if present. If acted on, "A"s are the requirements of greatest risk, perhaps new to the world. "A"s require the most attention in terms of funding, risk management, and performance measurement.

Table 1-1 provides a summary of a potential product analyzed with the Kano model. Here we see a list of requirements that are characterized by their funding need, risk potential, and fit to the Kano plot space.

---

* In the original Kano model, which grew out of work in the 1970s for the camera company Konica, there were in fact only three curves. The "I" curve along the axis was not included. Kano named his three curves a little differently than as presented here. Kano's names were: "excitement" for the curve this book calls the "ah-hah!" reaction, "performance" for "more is better," and "threshold" for "must have." Many references in the literature use the original names. Dr. Kano's research objective was to model "attractive quality" and distinguish that from "must-be" quality. "Must-be" quality was seen as a minimum or threshold to customer satisfaction. Below this threshold, customers would object; at the threshold, customers would not notice or would not make a competitive buying decision one way or the other.

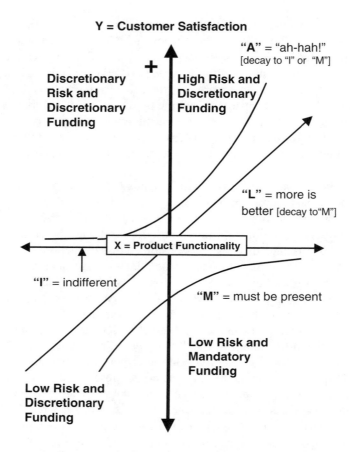

These curves illustrate the behavior of customer satisfaction as functions of product functionality.

Figure 1-5 Kano Curves.

A FRAMEWORK FOR VALUE, RISK, AND CAPABILITY: THE PROJECT BALANCE SHEET

Over a number of years of working with project teams and executive sponsors, this author has conceived and evolved the concept of the project balance sheet.[10,11] The project balance sheet is a conceptual and quantitative model suitable for relating business value with project capability and risk. To this point, we have discussed three well-known models of business value and customer expectation.

Table 1-1   Kano Example, Personal Computer

Requirement	Funding	Risk
Packaging and eye appeal	Discretionary investment targeted for high returns	Take all necessary risks to assure success
Faster CPU and larger memory	Constant refreshment required; reserve funds to meet needs	Take prudent risks to maintain market acceptance
FCC compliance	Mandatory funding to meet minimum requirements	Take no risks not essential to meeting compliance specification
Floppy disk drive	If market demands, fund lowest cost supplier	Take no risks; mature device
CD-RW drive	Initially, discretionary investment targeted for high returns	CD-RW decays to M quickly; minimize risk to balance rewards

Now it remains to couple these models to projects. Coupling to projects also provides a means to relate the numerical expressions of business value with the numerical measures of project capability and performance.

We begin with this premise: project sponsors and business executives who charter projects and invest in their success have an expectation of results, more often than not results that exceed the project investment, and for these investment gains, they are willing to accept some risk. These expected results support directly the goals and strategies that back up the value models we have discussed.

Project managers, on the other hand, accept the charter as their marching orders, developing a scope statement and an estimate of resources that corresponds. Now it often comes to pass that the project manager discovers that the available investment comes up short of the resources estimated, given that the full scope is embraced. Negotiations begin, but in the final analysis there usually remains a gap between capability and capacity on the project side and the value imperatives on the business side. What to do? The answer is: take a risk. How much risk? Only as much risk as is necessary to balance business needs and values on the one side with project abilities and needs on the other side. Who takes this risk? The project manager; the project manager is the ultimate risk manager.*

---

* The author is indebted to Lou Lavendol, Senior Systems Engineer at Harris Corporation, Melbourne, Florida, for his insightful discourse with the author regarding risk taking and business value in the context of proposing on defense industry programs. In those discussions in the early 1990s, the tension was between marketing (sales) that represented the voice of the customer and system engineering that represented the project. Often, there was a gap between marketing and engineering, a gap that could only be filled by someone taking a risk.

Financial Accounting

An understanding of balance sheet math is needed in order to proceed. For project managers not familiar with the balance sheet idea from the domain of financial accounting, here is a quick overview. First, the balance sheet is nothing more than a graphical or tabular way to show a numerical relationship: $y = a + b$. However, this relationship is not functional since all three of the variables are independent and, because of the equality sign, a relationship exists among the three that makes them interdependent as well. Thus, a change in one requires a change in another to maintain equality among the three. This equality is called "balance" in the accounting world, and the process by which *if one variable changes then another must change in a compensating way to maintain balance* is called "double entry accounting."

Second, accountants would understand the equation this way: assets ("y") = liabilities ("a") + equities ("b"). That is their "accounting equation." If assets increase, then so must either or both liabilities and equity increase in order to maintain balance. In fact, any change in the variables must be compensated by a change in one or two of the other two variables.

There is an important business concept to go along with the math: assets are property of the company put in the custody of the company managers to employ when they execute the business model. Assets are among the resources to be used by project managers to execute on projects. Assets are paid for by liabilities (loans from outsiders) and capital, also called equity. Equity is the property of the owners and liabilities are the properties of the creditors of the company. Thus, some stakeholders in the project arise naturally from the accounting equation: the financiers of the assets! As noted, these are the suppliers (accounts payable liabilities), creditors (long-term and short-term notes), and owners or stockholders (equity owners).

An asset cannot be acquired — that is, its asset dollar value increased — without considering how its acquisition cost is to be paid (increase in liability or capital, or sale of another asset). An asset cannot be sold — that is, its dollar value decreased — without accounting for the proceeds. Typical assets, liabilities, and equity accounts are shown in Table 1-2. A balance sheet for a small company is shown in Table 1-3.

Debits and Credits

Accountants have their own curious methods for referring to changes on each side of the balance sheet. Traditionally, assets are shown on the left and liabilities and capital are on the right. Dollar increases on the left side are called *debits*. Increases on the right side are called *credits*. Debits and credits are only

Table 1-2   Balance Sheet Example

Assets		Liabilities and Capital Employed	
Current Assets		**Current Liabilities**	
Cash on hand	$10,000	Vendor payables	$3,000
Receivables	$40,000	Short-term notes	$35,000
Finished inventory	$15,500		
Work in process	$5,500		
Long-Term Assets		**Long-Term Liabilities**	
Buildings	$550,000	Mortgages	$200,000
Software and equipment	$250,000		
Supplier loan	$35,000		
		Equities or Capital Employed	
		Capital paid in	$400,000
		Retained earnings	$170,000
		Stock ($1 par)	$98,000
Total Assets		**Total Liabilities and Equities**	
	$906,000		**$906,000**

Notes:
- *Cash on hand* is money in the bank.
- *Receivables* are monies owed to the business on invoices.
- *Finished inventory* is tangible product ready to sell.
- *Work in process* is incomplete inventory that could be made available to sell within one year.
- *Buildings, equipment, and software* are fixed assets that are less liquid than current assets. Software is usually considered an asset when the capitalized development, purchasing, or licensing cost exceeds certain predetermined thresholds.
- The *supplier loan* is money loaned to a supplier to finance its operations.

Notes:
- *Vendor payables* are invoices from vendors that must be paid by the business, in effect short-term loans to the business.
- *Short-term notes* are loans due in less than a year.
- *Mortgages* are long-term loans against the long-term assets.
- *Capital paid in* is cash paid into the business by the stockholders in excess of the par value of the stock.
- *Retained earnings* are cumulative earnings of the business, less any dividends to the stockholders.
- *Stock* is the paid-in par value, usually taken to be $1 per share, of the outstanding stock. In this case, there would be 98,000 shares in the hands of owners.

allowed to be positive numbers; that is, one does think of recording a negative debit. Debiting an asset always means increasing its dollar value. To reduce an asset's dollar value, it is credited. No particular connotation of good or bad should be assigned to the words debit and credit; they are simply synonyms for dollar increases left and right.

There may be a question at this point. If negative numbers are not used on the balance sheet, how do we keep track of things that have balances that go

Table 1-3   Balance Sheet Accounts

Assets	Liabilities and Capital Employed
Current Assets Cash in checking and savings accounts Monies owned by customers (receivables) Inventory that can be sold immediately	**Current Liabilities** Monies owed to suppliers Short-term bonds or other short-term debt

Long-Term Assets
Overdue receivables
Loans to suppliers
Investments in notes, real estate, other
  companies
Plant and equipment
Software (large value)
	Long-Term Liabilities
	Mortgages
	Long-term bonds
	Overdue payables
	
	Equity
	Cash paid in by investors for stock
	Retained earnings from operations and
	  investments

Notes: ■ *Current assets* are generally those assets that can be turned into cash within one year. Some companies may assign a shorter period. ■ *Long-term assets* are less liquid than current assets, but nevertheless have a cash value in the marketplace. ■ *The dollar value of all accounts on the left side must equal the dollar value of the accounts on the right side.*	Notes: ■ *Current liabilities* are generally those due and payable within one year. Some companies may assign a shorter period. ■ *Long-term liabilities* are less liquid than current liabilities, but nevertheless have a cash value in the marketplace. ■ *Equity* is the monies paid in by owners or monies earned from operations and investments. These funds finance the assets of the business, along with the liabilities.

up and down? Enter the "T" chart. We set up a "T" chart for a specific asset, like cash, defining both a right and left side on the cash "T" chart. (Refer to Figure 1-6 for an illustration.) We can then record all credits on the right side of the "T" chart and then net them with the starting balance and subsequent debits on the left side. Then, when it is time to compute a new balance sheet, we record the new net amount on the left side of the balance sheet for cash. "T" charts are not mini-balance sheets. They do not convey an equation. Their left and right sides do not need to balance. They are simply a recording mechanism, in chart form, for individual transactions, debits and credits.

However, if cash has been credited, we also need a second change, a debit, on the balance sheet to maintain the balance. If cash is to be credited, then a liability must be debited (decreased) or another asset is debited (increased). For example, we could use the cash to buy an asset and all would be in balance. Again refer to Figure 1-6 to see how this is done.

A listing of all the cash debits and credits during Period 1

Debits			Credits
Invoices (receivables) paid	$10,500	$1,525	Rents paid
Short-term note paid off	$25,000	$325	Purchased supplies
		$5,000	Short-term debt paid
Total debits	$35,500	$6,850	Total credits

Balance sheet entries for Period 1:
Assets
Debit cash $28,650
Credit note: –$25,000
Net assets change: $3,650

Debit payables: –$1,850
Debit short-term debt: –$5,000
Net liabilities change: –$6,850

Credit retained equity: $10,500
Net equity change: $10,500

Assets = Liabilities + Equity
$3,650 = –$6,850 + $10,500

Figure 1-6   "T" Chart for Cash.

Project managers in some companies are asked to review the monthly "trial balance." The trial balance is a listing of all the debits and credits recorded in a period. Naturally, they should balance. Of course, a debit or credit could have been made to a wrong account and the trial balance still balance. That is where the project manager can add value: by determining that all the project debits and credits have been applied to the proper accounts.

Here is an important point: balance sheets do not record flows, that is, a change in dollars over a period. They show only the balance in accounts on a specific date, like apples in a barrel. To see a flow, two balance sheets — one at period beginning and one at period ending — need to be compared.

How about your ATM or "debit" card that you carry around? Is it correctly named? Yes it is; let us see why. The money in your checking account is a short-term liability on the bank's balance sheet. It is money owned by outsiders (you) and thus it conforms to the definition of a liability. It finances or pays for an asset of equal amount, the bank's cash on hand. Everything is in balance. Suppose you want to take some of your money out of the bank. This will decrease the bank's liability to you. Recall that transactions to liabilities are credits (increases), so in order to decrease a liability we record a debit to the liability. To wit: a decrease of a liability is a debit to the liability; thus the "debit card." Now, of course, we still need the second transaction to the balance sheet to maintain the balance. If the liability is to be debited, then an asset must be credited (decreased), like the bank's cash on hand, or another liability is credited (increased), like a short-term note, to obtain the money to pay you.

Now that we understand a little bit about how accountants do their math, let us get back to project management.

The Project Balance Sheet

We now consider the insights about the business learned from the accounting balance sheet that will provide a quantitative framework for the project manager. First we direct our attention to the three elements that are necessary to form a balance sheet. To charter the project, business sponsors assign resources and state the required project returns needed for the business. Project returns are both functional and financial. Any one of the business value models we have discussed could be used to form the sponsor's view of the project. Sponsor-invested resources correspond roughly to the capital or equity investments on the accountant's balance sheet. As many companies are measured by the returns earned on the capital employed, so it is with projects. We will discuss in subsequent chapters that a project metric in wide use is the concept of economic value add (EVA). In effect, EVA demands positive returns on capital employed.

Second, the project manager is entrusted with resources owned by the business to carry out the project. These resources correspond roughly to the company-owned assets of the accountant's balance sheet. Like company managers who are often measured on their ability to create a return on the assets entrusted to them, so it is with project managers. Project managers are always judged on their ability to employ successfully the sponsor's resources to achieve the project objectives.

Software Project Example

	The Business	The Project	
Resources	$250K 10 FTEs Building A	Expected value: $275K 12 FTEs Building A	Resources
Scope	Deliver operational functionality to meet operational efficiency and customer satisfaction	Deliver operational functionality to meet operational efficiency and customer satisfaction	Scope
Business case	ROI = 12% IRR = 15% Operational 1 April	Pilot 1 April Operational 1 May	Schedule
KPIs	Customer satisfaction Operational efficiency	Cost: $25K 2 FTEs 1 month	Risk

The project manager must manage the risk values to balance *resource-scope-schedule* estimates with expectations.

Figure 1-7 The Project Balance Sheet.

Third, there is the gap between the investment made available and the resources required. On the accountant's balance sheet, this gap between investment and resources is filled with loans from outsiders: suppliers and creditors. On the project balance sheet, the gap is filled with risk! Risk is taken, or assumed, to fill the gap between expectations and capabilities, between sponsor investment and project estimates of resources. Figure 1-7 illustrates the tool we have been discussing.

We now have the elements for the "project equation," a direct analog to the accounting equation: "*Value delivered from resources invested = project capability and capacity plus risks taken.*"[12]

For project managers, their mission is now defined: *"The project manager's mission is to manage project capability and capacity to deliver expected value, taking measured risks to do so."*[12]*

Project Balance Sheet Details

The project balance sheet seeks to make a quantitative and qualitative connection between the business and the project. On the left side, the business side, is the sponsor's view of the project. The sponsor's view is conceptual and value oriented, nearly void of facts, or at least void of the facts as the project manager would understand them. Often the sponsor has no specific understanding of project management, of cost and schedule estimating for research and development, or of statistical analysis of risk, and does not seek to acquire an understanding. In system engineering parlance, the project sponsor sees the project as a "black box." However, the sponsor knows what the business requires and knows how much investment can be made toward the requirements.

The project manager has the facts about the project, even if they are only rough estimates. The project manager knows and understands the scope, even if the scope has "known unknowns" that require more investigation and definition.** We have already made the point that risk balances the facts with the concepts. However, a bridge is needed to couple unambiguously the sponsor's understanding and the project manager's understanding of the same project. That bridge between project manager and business manager is a common understanding of scope. Even with language and experience barriers, scope is the translator. The test for the project manager is then to ensure that there is good understanding of scope and then to convey the risks in business terms. This done, the project charter can be signed with expectation of good results to come.

Now what about debits and credits? Where do they come into the project balance sheet? Like the accounting equation, the project equation is not a functional equation of the form $y = f(x) + c$ that specifies y to be functionally dependent on x. Indeed, the left and right sides are pretty much independent, just like in the financial domain. By independent, we mean that the estimates of cost and schedule done by the project manager are based on the facts developed by the project team for the work specified in the work breakdown

---

* The author has paraphrased slightly the project equation and the project manager's mission from the text given in the reference (also the author's work).
** "Known unknowns" is a concept from risk management. The idea is simply that in framing the scope, there may be many unknowns, but the fact that there are undefined elements of scope is itself known.

structure (WBS). Those project team estimates are not, or should not be, dependent on the business value estimate developed by the project sponsor. However, once the charter is set, a change in one of the three elements (business value on the left side, risk or project capability on the right side) requires that another of the three elements must correspondingly change to maintain balance.

If, for instance, we continue to say debits are increases to the left and credits are increases to the right, then a debit of scope by the sponsor (that is, an increase in scope) must have a corresponding credit on the right or else balance is violated. By way of another example, if the situation were that the project manager had to credit the capability,* and no debit was available from the sponsor, then the required debit must go to risk in order to restore balance.

But is balance really all that important? Yes. The interpretation of imbalance is that there is not a meeting of the minds regarding the value demanded (left side) and the likelihood of successful delivery (right side). Consequently, the project may not be sustained, sponsor confidence in results may be challenged, and the project team may not be supported adequately during execution.

Integrating the Project Balance Sheet and Business Value Models

Now let us integrate the concepts discussed in this chapter to complete the framework on which we hang quantitative analysis to be discussed in the remainder of this book. The business models drive the left side of the project balance sheet. The model results, working through the value flow-down process, frame opportunity (new products, new markets and customers, operational and organizational needs) and quantify goals. Goals, deployed through strategy, lead to identified projects. It remains to select among the identified projects those that are affordable, most beneficial, or of highest priority to the business. We will discuss decision making in quantitative terms in Chapter 4. Suffice it to say there is a means to make these selections and charter the project. The generally accepted definition of the project charter is "*a document issued by senior management that formally authorizes the existence of a project...*"[13] More about the charter can be found in the literature, primarily *A Guide to the Project Management Body of Knowledge.*[14] With charter in hand, the project

---

* Recall that we are using the word "capability" to stand in for the set (scope, cost, time, and quality). To credit capability means that either cost or time has increased, scope has expanded without corresponding relief from the project sponsor, or there is a greater demand on quality. A greater demand on quality usually means tighter tolerances, less scrap and rework, fewer functional or performance errors in the production deliverable, or perhaps lesser life cycle investment forecast for service and maintenance after delivery.

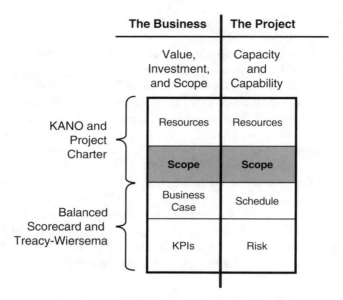

	The Business	The Project
	Value, Investment, and Scope	Capacity and Capability
KANO and Project Charter	Resources	Resources
	Scope	**Scope**
Balanced Scorecard and Treacy-Wiersema	Business Case	Schedule
	KPIs	Risk

Business models determine the value and investment side of the balance sheet to which the project must be matched, employing risk as the equalizer.

Figure 1-8 Business Models and Project Balance Sheet.

sponsor conveys the project requirements and investment allocation to the project manager. Doing so completes the chain from business executive to project sponsor, thence to project manager through the connectivity of the project charter and the left-to-right-side bridging effect of scope on the project balance sheet, as illustrated in Figure 1-8.

We now have a consistent and traceable path to and from the source of business value for numbers from the right side of the project balance sheet representing capability and risk. A traceable path is needed, after all, because projects draw their value only from the business.

On the right side of the balance sheet we have two elements: (1) project capability and capacity and (2) risk. A well-accepted method to express capability and capacity is with the so-called "iron triangle" of scope, time, and cost. Since there is interdependency among these three, it is traditionally to set the one of highest priority, optimize the second highest priority element, and the third becomes what is necessary to close the triangle. This author prefers the "project four-angle" of scope, schedule, resources, and quality as shown in

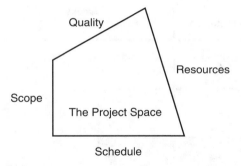

Quality

Resources

Scope

The Project Space

Schedule

The Project Space is bound by competing requirements that are managed, one against the other, to achieve a stable plan for the project.

Increasing or decreasing one requires compensation by another.

Strategy: fix the side of highest priority, optimize the next two, and the fourth will be derived from the remaining.

Figure 1-9   The Project Four-Angle.

Figure 1-9. The set-and-optimize process is about the same as in the iron triangle, except that two elements could be involved in the setting or optimizing.

We will see in Chapter 3 that the best quantification tool for scope is the WBS. Time and cost can be estimated for the scope on the WBS somewhat independently, but ultimately they are tied together through the concept of value. Earned value is the preferred numerical analysis tool, and that will be discussed in Chapter 6. There are numerous ways to evaluate quality. One we will address in Chapter 8 is Six Sigma.

Finally, there is risk. Risk in quantitative terms is expressed in the same units as the related item in the project capability and capacity. The risk component of the right side of the balance sheet holds the variance to the mean that must be managed in order not to endanger the business investment.

Figure 1-10 illustrates the points discussed.

SUMMARY OF IMPORTANT POINTS

Table 1-4 provides the highlights of this chapter.

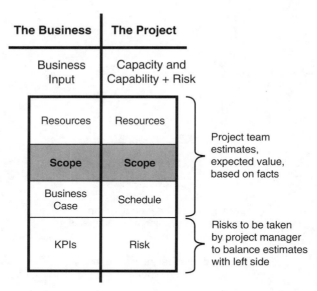

The project team works from a set of facts, developed during the estimating and planning phase of the project. These facts may or may not support the left side business view of the project.

Risk is estimated for the gap between left and right side and accepted by the project manager as a means to balance expectations with capacity.

Figure 1-10   Right Side Project Balance Sheet.

Table 1-4   Summary of Important Points

Point of Discussion	Summary of Ideas Presented
Successful projects	■ Successful projects return value to the business. ■ Successful projects improve processes or product, reduce costs and operational inefficiencies, make contributions to the technical and functional competence of the organization, or add capacity and capability to serve customers and markets with greater satisfaction. ■ They are projects that make good on the promises of the project charter and deliver the intended scope within a time frame commensurate with business objectives. ■ Valuable projects are "instruments of strategy." ■ Really valuable projects enhance core competencies or benefit directly from them.

Table 1-4 Summary of Important Points (continued)

Point of Discussion	Summary of Ideas Presented
Business value motivates projects	▪ Insofar as projects return more in financial resources than they absorb, then those projects are valuable to the business.
Balanced scorecard	▪ Four scoring areas seek to balance the goals and resource commitments of the business: financial, customer, internal operations, and innovation and learning.
Treacy–Wiersema model	▪ Business takes on a persona, seeking customer intimacy, operational effectiveness, or product superiority. ▪ It is difficult if not impossible to be all three; more likely the best success is found in optimizing one.
Kano model	▪ The Kano model is most useful in representing customer preferences compared to the product and service features offered by the business. ▪ The Kano model focuses on customers and products. ▪ The Kano model can be used by the project manager for resource allocation and risk assessment planning.
Accounting balance sheet	▪ Assets are property of the company put in the custody of the company managers to employ when they execute on the business model. ▪ Assets are among the resources to be used by project managers to execute on projects. ▪ Assets are paid for by liabilities (loans from outsiders) and capital. ▪ Capital is the property of the owners.
Project balance sheet	▪ The project equation: *Value delivered from resources invested = project capability and capacity plus risks taken.* ▪ The project manager's mission: "*...is to manage project capability and capacity to deliver expected value, taking measured risks to do so.*"

REFERENCES

1. *A Guide to the Project Management Body of Knowledge (PMBOK® Guide)* — 2000 Edition, Project Management Institute, Newtown Square, PA, p. 204.
2. Goodpasture, John C., *Managing Projects for Value,* Management Concepts, Vienna, VA, 2001.
3. Hamel, Gary and Parahalad, C.K., The core competence of the corporation, *Harvard Business Review*, pp. 79–90, May–June 1990.
4. Hamel, Gary and Parahalad, C.K., *Competing for the Future,* Harvard Business School Press, Boston, MA, 1994, chap. 9.
5. Kaplan, Robert S. and Norton, David P., The balanced scorecard — measures that drive performance, *Harvard Business Review*, pp. 71–79, January–February 1992.

6. Treacy, Michael and Wiersema, Fred, Customer intimacy and other value disciplines, *Harvard Business Review*, pp. 84–93, January–February 1993.
7. Treacy, Michael and Wiersema, Fred, *The Discipline of Market Leaders: Choose Your Customers, Narrow Your Focus, Dominate Your Market*, Perseus Books, Cambridge, MA, 1996.
8. Kano, Noriaki, Attractive quality and must-be quality, *Journal of the Japanese Society for Quality Control*, pp. 39–48, April 1984.
9. Shiba, Shoji, Graham, Alan, and Walden, David, *A New American TQM: Four Practical Revolutions in Management*, Productivity Press, Portland, OR, 1993, pp. 221–224.
10. Goodpasture, John C. and Hulett, David T., A balance sheet for projects: a guide to risk-based value, *PM Network*, May (Part 1) and June (Part 2) 2000.
11. Goodpasture, John C., *Managing Projects for Value*, Management Concepts, Vienna, VA, 2001, chap. 3.
12. Ibid., p. 46.
13. *A Guide to the Project Management Body of Knowledge (PMBOK® Guide)* — 2000 Edition, Project Management Institute, Newtown Square, PA, p. 204.
14. Ibid., p. 54.

2

INTRODUCTION TO PROBABILITY AND STATISTICS FOR PROJECTS

Lies, damned lies, and statistics!
"Nothing in progression can rest on its original plan."

Thomas Monson

THERE ARE NO FACTS ABOUT THE FUTURE

"There are no facts about the future!" This is a favorite saying of noted risk authority Dr. David T. Hulett that sums it up pretty well for project managers.* Uncertainty is present in every project, every project being a unique assembly of resources and scope. Every project has its ending some time hence. Time displaces project outcomes from the initial estimates; time displacement introduces the opportunity for something not to go according to plan. Perhaps such an opportunity would actually have an upside advantage to the project, or perhaps not. Successful project managers are those quick to grasp the need for

---

* The author has had a years-long association with Dr. Hulett, principal at Hulett Associates in Los Angeles, California. Among many accomplishments, Dr. Hulett led the project team that wrote the "Project Risk Management" chapter of the 2000 edition of *A Guide to the Project Management Body of Knowledge,* published by the Project Management Institute®.

the means to evaluate uncertainty. Risk management is the process, but probability and statistics provide the mathematical underpinning for the quantitative analysis of project risk. Probability and statistics for project managers are the subjects of this chapter.

PROBABILITY...WHAT DO WE MEAN BY IT?

Everyone is familiar with the coin toss — one side is heads, the other side is tails. Flip it often enough and there will be all but an imperceptible difference in the number of times heads comes up as compared to tails. How can we use the coin toss to run projects? Let us connect some "dots."

Coin Toss 101

As an experiment, toss a coin 100 times. Let heads represent one estimate of the duration of a project task, say writing a specification, of 10 days, and let tails represent an estimate of duration of 15 days for the same task. Both estimates seem reasonable. Let us flip a coin to choose. If the coin were "fair" (that is, not biased in favor of landing on one side or the other), we could reasonably "expect" that there would be 50 heads and 50 tails.

But what of the 101st toss? What will it be? Can we predict the outcome of toss 101 or know with any certainty whether the outcome of toss 101 will be heads or tails, 10 days duration or 15? No, actually, the accumulation of a history of 50 heads and 50 tails provides no information specifically about outcome of the 101st toss except that the range of possible performance is now predictable: toss 101 will be either discretely heads or tails, and the outcome of toss 101 is no more likely to come up heads than tails. So with no other information, and only two choices, it does not matter whether the project manager picks 10 or 15 days. Both are equally likely and within the predicted or forecast range of performance. However, what of the next 100 tosses? We can reasonably expect a repeat of results if no circumstances change.

The phenomenon of *random events* is an important concept to grasp for applications to projects: the *outcome of any single event*, whether it be a coin toss or a project, cannot be known with certainty, but the pattern of behavior of an event repeated many times is predictable.

However, projects rarely if ever repeat. Nonrepetitiveness is at the core of their uncertainty. So how is a body of mathematics based on repetition helpful to project managers? The answer lies in how project managers estimate outcomes and forecast project behavior. We will see the many disadvantages of a "single-point" estimate, sometimes called the deterministic estimate, and appreciate the helpfulness of forecasting a reasonable range of possibilities instead. In the coin toss, there is a range of possible outcomes, heads or tails. If we toss the coin many times, or *simulate* the tossing of many times, we can measure or observe the behavior of the outcomes. We can infer (that is, draw a conclusion from the facts presented) that the next specific toss will have similar behavior and the outcome will lie within the observed space. So it is with projects. From the nondeterministic probabilistic estimates of such elements as cost, schedule, or quality errors, we can simulate the project behavior, drawing an inference that a real project experience would likely lie within the observed behavior.

Calculating Probability

Most people would say that the probability of an outcome of heads or tails in a fair coin toss is 50%; some might say it is half, 0.5, or one chance in two. They all would be correct. There is no chance (that is, 0 probability) that neither heads nor tails will come up; there is 100% probability (that is, 1) that either heads or tails will come up.

What if the outcome was the value showing on a die from a pair of dice that was rolled or tossed? Again most people would say that the probability is 1/6 or one chance in six that a single number like a "5" would come up. If two dice were tossed, what is the chance that the sum of the showing faces will equal "7"? This is a little harder problem, but craps players know the answer. We reason this way: There are 36 combinations of faces that could come up with the repetitive roll of the die, like a "1" on both faces (1,1) or a "1" on one face and a "3" on the other (1,3). There are six combinations that total "7" (1,6; 6,1; 2,5; 5,2; 3,4; 4,3) out of a possible 36, so the chances of a "7" are 6/36 or 1/6.

The probability that no combination of any numbers will show up on a roll of the dice is 0; the probability that any combination of numbers will show up is 36/36, or 1. After all, there are 36 ways that any number could show up. Any specific combination like a (1,6) or a (5,3) will show up with probability of 1/36 since a specific combination can only show up one way. Finally, any specific sum of the dice will show up with probability between 1/36 and 6/36. Table 2-1 illustrates this opportunity space.

Relative Frequency Definitions

The exercise of flipping coins or rolling dice illustrates the "relative frequency" view of probability. Any specific result is an "outcome," like rolling the pair (1,6). The six pairs that total seven on the faces are collectively an "event." We see that the probability of the event "7" is 1/6, whereas the probability of the outcome (1,6) is 1/36. All the 36 possible outcomes are a "set," the event being

Table 2-1   Roll of the Dice

Combination Number	Face Value #1	Face Value #2	Sum of Face Values
1	1	1	2
2	2	1	3
3	3	1	4
4	4	1	5
5	5	1	6
6	6	1	7
7	1	2	3
8	2	2	4
9	3	2	5
10	4	2	6
11	5	2	7
12	6	2	8
13	1	3	4
14	2	3	5
15	3	3	6
16	4	3	7
17	5	3	8
18	6	3	9
....	....	....	....
36	6	6	12

Notes: The number "7" is the most frequent of the "Sum of Face Values," repeating once for each pattern of 6 values of the first die, for a total of 6 appearances in 36 combinations.
   Although not apparent from the abridged list of values, the number "5" appearing in the fourth-down position in the first pattern moves up one position each pattern repetition and thus has only 4 total appearances in 36 combinations.

a subset. "Population" is another word for "set." "Opportunity space" or sometimes "space" is used interchangeably with population, set, subset, and event. Context is required to clarify the usage.

The relative frequency interpretation of probability leads to the following equation as the general definition of probability:

$$p(A) = N(A)/N(M)$$

where $p(A)$ is probability of outcome (or event) A, $N(A)$ = number of times A occurs in the population, and $N(M)$ = number of members in the population.

AND and OR

Let's begin with OR. Using the relative frequency mathematics already developed, what is the probability of the event "5"? There are only four outcomes, so the event "5" probability is 4/36 or 1/9.

To make it more interesting, let's say that event "5" is the desired result of one of two study teams observing the same project problem in "dice rolling." One team we call study team 5; the other we call study team 7. We need to complete the study in the time to complete 36 rolls. Either team finishing first is okay since both are working on the same problem. The probability that study team 5 will finish its observations on time is 4/36. If any result other than "5" is obtained, more time will be needed.

Now let's expand the event to a "5" or a "7". Event "7" is our second study team, with on-time results if it observes a "7". Recall that there are six event "7" opportunities. There are ten outcomes between the two study teams that fill the bill, giving either a "5" or a "7" as the sum of the two faces. Then, by definition, the probability of the event "5 OR 7" is 10/36. The probability that one or the other team will finish on time is 10/36, which is less risky than depending solely on one team to finish on time. Note that 10/36 is the sum of the probabilities of event "7" plus event "5": 6/36 + 4/36 = 10/36.*

It is axiomatic in the mathematics of probability that if two events are mutually exclusive, then when one occurs the other will not:

$$p(A \text{ OR } B) = p(A) + p(B)$$

Now let's discuss AND. Consider the probability of the schedule event "rolling a 6 on one face AND rolling a 1 on the other face." The probability of rolling a "6" on one die is 1/6, as is the probability of rolling a "1" on the other. For the event to be true (that is, both a "6" and a "1" occur), both outcomes have to come up. Rolling the first die gives only a one-in-six chance of a "6"; there is another one-in-six chance that the second die will come up "1", altogether a one-in-six chance times a one-in-six chance, or 1/36. Of course 1/36 is very much less than 1/6. If the outcomes above were about our study teams finishing on time, one observing for a "6" on one die and the other observing for a "1" on the other die, then the probability of both finishing on time is the product of their individual probabilities. Requiring them both to finish on time increases the risk of a joint on-time finish event. We will study this "merge point" event is more detail in the chapter on schedules.

Another axiom we can write down is that if two events are independent, in no way dependent on each other, then:

$$p(A \text{ AND } B) = p(A * B) = p(A) * p(B)$$

---

* In the real world, events "5" and "7" could be the names given to two events in a "tree" or hierarchy of events requiring study. For example, events "5" and "7" could be error conditions that might occur. Rolling the dice is equivalent to simulating operational performance. Dr. David Hulett suggested the fault tree to the author.

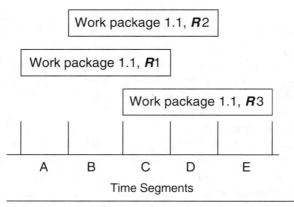

Project events consist of three activities from the WBS with need for the same resource, **R**.

The probability of success, that is availability of **R**i, is diminished by the probability of a need for **R** in two or more tasks at the same time.

The **R**1 resource, if provided in time-segment A, would not interfere with **R**2 and **R**3.

$p(\boldsymbol{R1} + \boldsymbol{R2} + \boldsymbol{R3}) = p(\boldsymbol{R1}) + p(\boldsymbol{R2}) + p(\boldsymbol{R3}) - p(\boldsymbol{R1} * \boldsymbol{R2}) - p(\boldsymbol{R1} * \boldsymbol{R3}) - p(\boldsymbol{R2} * \boldsymbol{R3}) - p(\boldsymbol{R1} * \boldsymbol{R2} * \boldsymbol{R3})$

If the work packages do not need the common resource, then we assume the work packages are otherwise independent of each other.

Figure 2-1   Overlapping Events.

AND and OR with Overlap or Collisions

We can now go one step further and consider the situation where events *A* and *B* are not mutually exclusive (that is, *A* and *B* might occur together sometimes or perhaps overlap in some way). Figure 2-1 illustrates the case. As an example, let's continue to observe pairs of dice, but the experiment will be to toss three die at once. All die remain independent, but the occurrence of the event "7" or "5" is no longer mutually exclusive. The event {3,4,1} might be rolled providing the opportunity for the (3,4) pair of the "7" event and the (4,1) pair of the "5" event. However, we are looking for p(*A*) or p(*B*) but not p(*A* * *B*); therefore, those tosses like event {3,4,1} where "*A* and *B*" occur cannot be counted, thereby reducing the opportunities for either *A* or *B*. Throwing out the occurrence of "*A* and *B*" reduces the chances for "*A* or *B*" alone to happen. From this reasoning comes a more general equation for OR:

$$p(A \text{ OR } B) = p(A) + p(B) - p(A * B)$$

Notice that if *A* and *B* are mutually exclusive, then $p(A * B) = 0$, which gives a result consistent with the earlier equation given for the OR situation.

Looking at the above equation, the savvy project manager recognizes that risk has increased for achieving a successful outcome of either *A* or *B* since the possibility of their joint occurrence, overlap, or collision of *A* and *B* takes away from the sum of $p(A) + p(B)$. Such a situation could come up in the case of two resources providing inputs to the project, but if they are provided together, then they are not useful. Such collisions or race conditions (a term from system engineering referring to probabilistic interference) are common in many technology projects.

Conditional Probabilities

When *A* and *B* are not independent, then one becomes a condition on the outcome of the other. For example, the question might be: What is the probability of *A* given the condition that *B* has occurred?*

Consider the situation where there are 12 marbles in a jar, 4 black and 8 white. Marbles are drawn from the jar one at a time, *without replacement*. The p(black marble on first draw) = 4/12. Then, a second draw is made. Conditions have changed because of the first draw. There are only 3 black marbles left and only 11 marbles in the jar. The p(black marble on the second draw given a black marble on the first draw) = 3/11, a slightly higher probability than 4/12 on the first draw. The probability of the second draw is conditioned on the results of the first draw.

The probability of a black marble on *each of the first two draws* is the AND of the probabilities of the first and second draw. We write the equation:

$$p(B \text{ and } A) = p(B) * p(A \mid B)$$

where *B* = event "black on the first draw," *A* = event "black on second draw, given black on first draw," and the notation "|" means "given." Filling in the numbers, we have:

$$p(B \text{ and } A) = (4/12) * (3/11) = 1/11$$

---

* *A* might be one approach in a project and *B* might be another approach. Such a situation comes up often in projects in the form of "if, then, else" conditional branching.

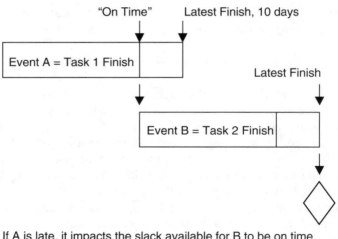

If A is late, it impacts the slack available for B to be on time (latest finish)

All probabilities are estimated by the project team

p(**B** on time, given **A** late as 10 days) = 0.4
p(**B** not on time, given **A** late as 10 days) = 0.6   } 1.0

p(**A** late as 10 days) = 0.45
p(**A** not late as 10 days) = 0.55   } 1.0

p(A late as 10 days and B on time) = 0.4 * 0.45 = 0.18

Figure 2-2   Conditions in Task Schedules.

Consider the project situation given in Figure 2-2. There we see two tasks, Task 1 and Task 2, with a finish-to-start precedence between them.* The project team estimates that the probability of Task 1 finishing at the latest finish of "on time + 10 days" is 0.45. Task 1 finishing is event *A*. The project team estimates that the probability of Task 2 finishing on time is 0.8 if Task 1 finishes on time, but diminishes to 0.4 if Task 1 finishes in "on time + 10 days." Task 2 finishing

---

* A finish-to-start precedence is a notation from precedence diagramming methodology. It denotes the situation that the finish of the first task is required before the start of the second (successor) task can ensue. It is often referred to as a "waterfall" relationship because, when drawn on paper, it gives the appearance of a cascade from one task to the other. More on critical path scheduling can be found in Chapter 6 of *A Guide to the Project Management Body of Knowledge.*[1]

is event B. If event A is late, it overlaps the slack available to B. We calculate the probability of "$A * B$" as follows:

$$p(A_{10} * B_0) = p(B_0 \,|\, A_{10}) * p(A_{10}) = 0.4 * 0.45 = 0.18$$

where A_{10} = event of Task 1 finishing "on time + 10 days" and B_0 = event of Task 2 finishing on time if Task 1 finishes "on time + 10 days." Conclusion: there is *less than one chance in five* that both events A_{10} and B_0 will happen. The project manager's risk management focus is on avoiding the outcome of B finishing late by managing Task 1 to less than "on time + 10 days."

There is a lot more to know about conditional probabilities because they are very useful to the project manager in decision making and planning. We will hold further discussion until Chapter 4, where conditional probabilities will be used in decision trees and tables.

The (1-p) Space

To this point, we have been using a number of conventions adopted for probability analysis:

- All quantitative probabilities lie in the range between the numbers 0 (absolute certainty that an outcome will not occur) and 1 (absolute certainty that an outcome will occur).
- The lower case "p" is the notation for probability; it stands for a number between 0 and 1 inclusively. Typically, "p" is expressed as a decimal.
- If "p" is the probability that project outcome A will happen, then "1-p" is the probability that project outcome A will not occur. We then have the following equation: p + (1-p) = 1 at all times. More rigorously, we write: $p(A) + [1-p(A)] = 1$, where the notation $p(A)$ means "probability that A will occur."
- "1-p" is the probability that something else, say project outcome B, will happen instead of A. After all, there cannot be a vacuum in the project for lack of outcome A. Sometimes outcome B is most vexing for project managers. B could well be a "known unknown." To wit: Known...A may not happen, but then unknown...what will happen, what is B?
- Sometimes it is said: B is in the (1-p) space of A, or the project manager might ask his or her team: "What is in the (1-p) space of A?"
- Project managers must always account for all the scope and be aware of all the outcomes. Thus: $p(A) + p(B) = 1$. A common mistake made by the project team is to not define or identify B, focusing exclusively on A.

Of course, there may be more possibilities than just **B** in the (1-p) space of **A**. Instead of just **B**, there might be **B**, **C**, **D**, **E**, and so forth. In that case, the project manager or risk analyst must be very careful to obey the following equation:

$$[1\text{-}p(A)] = p(B) + p(C) + p(D) + p(E) + \dots$$

The error that often occurs is that the right side sums up too large. That is, we have the condition:

$$p(A) + p(1\text{-}A) > 1$$

On the right side, there are either too many possibilities identified, their respective probabilities are too large, or on the left side, the probabilities of **A** are misjudged. It is left to the project team to recognize the error of the situation and take corrective measures.

Subjective Probability

What about statements like "there is a 20% chance of rain or snow today in the higher elevations"? A statement of this type does not express a relative frequency probability. We do not have an idea of the population (number of times it rains or snows in a time period), so there is no way to see the proportionality of the outcome to the total population. Statements of this type, quite commonly made, express a subjective notion of probability. We will see that statements of this type express a "confidence." We arrive at "confidence" by accumulating probabilities over a range. We discuss more about "confidence" later.

RANDOM VARIABLES AND THEIR FUNCTIONS IN PROJECTS

Random Variables

So far, we have discussed random events (tails coming up on a coin toss) and probability spaces (a coin toss can only be heads or tails because there is nothing else in the probability space), but we have not formally talked about the numerical value of an event. If the number of heads or tails is counted, then the *count* per se is a random variable, **CH** for heads and **CT** for tails.* *"Random variables" is the term we apply to numerical outcomes of events when the value cannot be known in advance of the event and where the value is a number within*

---

* Italicized bold capital letters will be used for random variables.

a range of numbers. When a random event is completed, like tossing a coin 100 times, then the random variables will have specific values obtained by counting, measuring, or observing. In the project world, task durations denoted *D* with values in hours, days, or weeks and cost figures denoted *C* with values in dollars, pesos, or euros are two among many random variables project managers will encounter.

If a variable is not a random variable, then it is a deterministic or single-point variable. A deterministic variable has no distribution of values but rather has one and only one value, and there is no uncertainty (risk) as to its measure.

As examples of random and deterministic variables, let us say that we measure cost with variable *C* and that *C* is a random variable with observed values of $8, $9, $10, $12, and $15. The range of values is therefore from $8 to $15. We do not know *C* with certainty, but we have an expectation that any value of *C* would be between $8 and $15. If *C* were deterministic and equal to $13.50, then $13.50 is the only value *C* can have. Thus, $13.50 is a risk-free measure of *C*.

If *C* were a random variable with values from $8 to $15, we would also be interested in the probability of *C* taking on a value of $8 or $12 or any of the other values. Thus we associate with *C* not only the range of values but also the probability that any particular value will occur.

Probability Functions

Random variables do not have deterministic values. In advance of a random outcome, like the uncertain duration or cost of a work package, the project team can only estimate the probable values, but the team will not know for sure what value is taken until the outcome occurs. Of course, we do not know for sure that the event will happen at all. The event itself can only be predicted probabilistically.

In the coin toss, the probability of any specific value of *H* or *T* happens to be the same: $H = 1$ or 0 on any specific toss, 1 if heads, else 0, and similarly for *T*.

$$p(H = T = 50 \text{ in toss of } 100) = 0.5$$

But equal values may not be the case for all random variables in all situations.

$$p(D = 7 \text{ in one roll of two die}) = 1/6 = 0.167$$

$$p(D = 5 \text{ in one roll of two die}) = 1/9 = 0.111$$

where *D* = value of the sum of the two faces of the die on a single roll.

The probability function* is the mathematical relationship between a random variable's value and the probability of obtaining that value. In effect, the probability function creates a functional relationship between a probability and an event:

$$f(X \mid \text{value}) = p(X = \text{some condition or value})$$

$f(X \mid a) = p(X = a)$, where the "$\mid$" is the symbol used to mean "evaluated at" or "given a value of" the number "a". Example: $f(H \mid \text{true}) = 0.5$ from the coin toss.

Discrete Random Variables

So far, our examples of random variables have been discrete random variables. H or T could only take on discrete values on any specific toss: 1 or 0. On any given toss, we have no way of knowing what value H or T will take, but we can estimate or calculate what the probable outcomes are, and we can say for certain, because the random variables are discrete, that they will not take on in-between values. For sure, H cannot take on a value of 0.75 on any specific toss; only values of 1 (true) or 0 (false) are allowed. Sometimes knowing what values cannot happen is as important as knowing what values will happen.

Random variables are quite useful in projects when counting things that have an atomic size. People, for instance, are discrete. There is no such thing as one-half a person. Many physical and tangible objects in projects fit this description. Sometimes actions by others are discrete random variables in projects. We may not know at the outset of a project if a regulation will be passed or a contract option exercised, but we can calculate the probability that an action will occur, yes or no.

Many times there is no limit to the number of values that random variables can take on in the allowed range. There is no limit to how close together one value can be to the next; values can be as arbitrarily close together as required. The only requirement is that for any and all values of the discrete random variable, the sum of all their probabilities of occurrences equals 1:

$$\Sigma \text{ all } f_i(X \mid a_i) = 1, \text{ for } i = 1 \text{ to "n"}$$

---

* The probability function is often called the "probability density function." This name helps distinguish it from the cumulative probability function and also fits with the idea that the probability function really is a density, giving probability per value.

where $f_i(X)$ is one of "n" probability functional values for the random variable, there being one functional value for each of the "n" values that X can take on in the probability space, and "a_i" is the ith probable value of X.

In the coin toss experiment, "n" = 2 and "a" could have one of two values: 1 or 0. In the dice roll, "n" = 36; the values are shown in Table 2-1.

Continuous Random Variables

As the number of values of X increases in a given range of values, the spacing between them becomes smaller, so small in the limit that one cannot distinguish between one unique value and another. So also do the value's individual probabilities become arbitrarily small in order not to violate the rule about all probabilities adding up to 1. Such a random variable is called a continuous random variable because there is literally no space between one value and another; one value flows continuously to the next. Curiously, the probability of a specific value is arbitrarily near but not equal to 0. However, over a small range, say from X_1 to $X_1 + dX$, the probability of X being in this range is not necessarily small.*

As the number of elements in the probability function becomes arbitrarily large, the Σ morphs smoothly to the integral $\int$: $\int_{a-b}$ all $f(X)$ dX means integrate over all continuous values of X from values of a_{lower} to b_{upper}

$$\int_{a-b} \text{ all } f(X) \ dX = 1$$

There are any number of continuous random variables in projects, or random variables that are so nearly continuous as to be reasonably thought of as continuous. The actual cost range of a work breakdown structure work package, discrete perhaps to the penny but for most practical applications continuous, is one example. Schedule duration range is another if measured to arbitrarily small units of time. Lifetime ranges of tools, facilities, and components are generally thought of as continuous.

Cumulative Probability Functions

It is useful in many project situations to think of the accumulating probability of an event happening. For instance, it might be useful to convey to the project sponsor that "...there is a 0.6 probability that the schedule will be 10 weeks

---

* "dX" is a notation used to mean a small, but not zero, value. Readers familiar with introductory integral calculus will recognize this convention.

or shorter." Since the maximum cumulative probability is 1, at some point the project manager can declare "...there is certainty, with probability 1, that the schedule will be shorter than x weeks."

We already have the function that will give us this information; we need only apply it. If we sum up the probability functions of X over a continuous range of values, a_i, then we have what we want: Σ all $f_i(X \mid a_i) = 1$, for i = "m" to "n" accumulates the probabilities of values between the limits of "m" and "n".

Table 2-2 provides an example of how a cumulative probability function works for a discrete random variable.

Table 2-2   Cumulative Discrete Probability Function

A	B	C
Outcome of Random Variable D_i for an Activity Duration	Probability Density of Outcome D_i	Cumulative Probability of Outcome D_i
3 days	0.1	0.1
5 days	0.3	0.4
7 days	0.4	0.8
10 days	0.15	0.95
20 days	0.05	1.0

D_i is an outcome of an event described by the random variable D for task duration.

The probability of a single-valued outcome is given in column B; the accumulating probability that the duration will be equal to or less than the outcome in column A is given in column C.

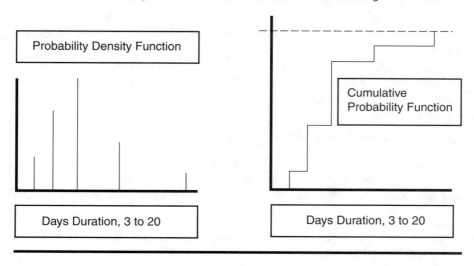

Probability Density Function

Days Duration, 3 to 20

Cumulative Probability Function

Days Duration, 3 to 20

Of course, for a continuous random variable, it is pretty much the same. We integrate from one limit of value to another to find the probability of the value of *X hitting in the range* between the limits of integration. For our purposes, *integration is nothing more than summation with arbitrarily small separation between values.*

PROBABILITY DISTRIBUTIONS FOR PROJECT MANAGERS

If we plot the probability (density) function (PDF) on a graph with vertical axis as probability and horizontal axis as value of X, then that plot is called a "distribution." The PDF is aptly named because the PDF shows the distribution of value according to the probability that that value will occur, as illustrated in Figure 2-3.* Although the exact numerical values may change from one plot to the next, the general patterns of various plots are recognizable and have well-defined attributes. To these patterns we give names: Normal distribution, BETA distribution, Triangular distribution, Uniform distribution, and many others. The attributes also have names, such as mean, variance, standard distribution, etc. These attributes are also known as statistics.

Uniform Distribution

The discrete Uniform distribution is illustrated in Figure 2-4. The toss of the coin and the roll of the single die are discrete Uniform distributions. The principal attribute is that each value of the random variable has the same probability. In engineering, it is often useful to have a random number generator to simulate seemingly totally random events, each event being assigned a unique number. It is very much desired that the random numbers generated come from a discrete Uniform distribution so that no number, thus no event, is more likely than another.

If the random variable is continuous, or the values of the discrete random variable are so close together so as to be approximately continuous, then, like all continuous distributions, the vertical axis is scaled such that the "area under the curve" equals 1. Why so? This is just a graphical way of saying that if all probabilities for all values are integrated, then the total will come to 1.

$$\text{Recall: } \int_{a\text{-}b} \text{all } f(X) \ \mathrm{d}X = 1$$

---

* The probability function is also known as the "distribution function" or "probability distribution function."

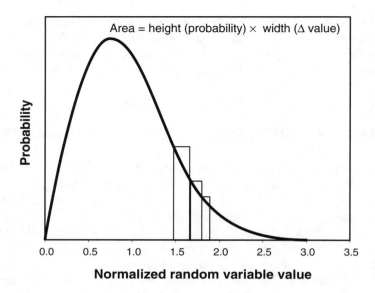

Normalized random variable value

The total area under a probability distribution curve must be equal to 1.0. Therefore, the probability axis is scaled to achieve the requirement of **area = 1.0**.

Finding the area is mathematically a matter of integrating the function that describes the curve, or summing a piece-wise set of rectangles that are arbitrarily small in width so that the area outside the curve is minimized.

Figure 2-3   Probability Distribution.

where dX represents an increment on the horizontal axis and $f(X)$ represents a value on the vertical axis. Vertical * horizontal = area. Thus, mathematical integration is an area calculation.

Triangular Distribution

The Triangular distribution is applied to continuous random variables. The Triangular distribution is usually shown with a skew to one side or the other. The Triangular distribution portrays the situation that not all outcomes are equally likely as was the case in the Uniform distribution. The Triangular distribution has finite tails that meet the horizontal value axis at some specific value.

These four distributions apply to a myriad of situations in projects. Normal distributions apply to the sum of schedule durations and work package costs. Uniform distributions apply to many risk factors that are just as likely to go one way as another.

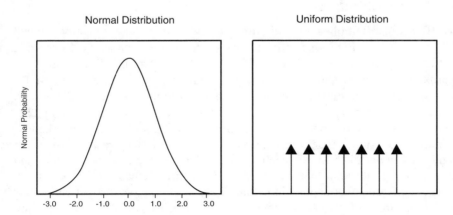

The BETA and Triangular distributions apply to individual events, costs, durations, resource commitments, and wherever there are unequal optimistic and pessimistic possibilities.

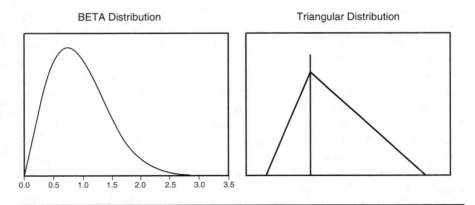

Figure 2-4   Common Distributions in Projects.

There is little in nature that has a Triangular distribution. However, it is a good graphical and mathematical approximation to many events that occur in projects. Project management, like engineering, relies heavily on approximation for day-to-day practice. For instance, the approximate behavior of both cost work packages and schedule task durations can be modeled quite well with the

Triangular distribution. The skew shows the imbalance in pessimism or optimism in the event.

The BETA Distribution

The BETA distribution is a distribution with two parameters, typically denoted "a" and "b" in its PDF, that influence its shape quite dramatically. Depending on the values of "a" and "b", the BETA distribution can be all the way from approximately Uniform to approximately Normal.* However, forms of the BETA distribution that are most useful to projects are asymmetrical curves that look something like rounded-off triangles. Indeed, it is not incorrect to think that the Triangular distribution approximates the BETA distribution. But for the rounded-off appearance of the BETA distribution, it appears in many respects the same as the Triangular distribution, each having a skew to one side or the other and each having finite tails that come down to specific values on the horizontal value axis. Events that happen in nature rarely, if ever, have distinct endpoints. Mother Nature tends to smooth things out. Nevertheless, the BETA distribution approximates many natural events quite well.

The Normal Distribution

The Normal distribution is a well-known shape, sometimes referred to as the "bell curve" for its obvious similarity to a bell. In some texts, it will be referred to as the Gaussian distribution after the 19th century mathematician Carl Friedrich Gauss.** The Normal distribution is very important generally in the study of probability and statistics and useful to the project manager for its rather accurate portrayal of many natural events and for its relationship to something called the "Central Limit Theorem," which we will address shortly.

Let's return to the coin toss experiment. The values of H and T are uniformly distributed: H or T can each be either value 1 or value 0 with equal probability = 0.5. But consider this: the *count* of the number of times T comes up heads in 100 tosses is itself a random variable. Let CT stand for this random variable. CT has a distribution, as do all random variables. CT's distribution is Normal, with the value of 50 counts of T at the center. At the tails of the Normal distribution are the counts of T that are not likely to occur if the coin is fair.

---

* If the sum of "a" and "b" is a large number, then the BETA will be more narrow and peaked than a Normal; the ratio of a/b controls the asymmetry of the BETA.
** Carl Friedrich Gauss (1777–1855) in 1801 published his major mathematical work, *Disquisitiones Arithmeticae*. Gauss was a theorist, an observer, astronomer, mathematician, and physicist.

Theoretically, the Normal distribution's tails come asymptotically close to the horizontal axis but never touch it. Thus the integration of the PDF must extend to "infinite" values along the horizontal axis in order to fully define the area under the curve that equals 1. As a practical matter, project managers and engineers get along with a good deal less than infinity along the horizontal axis. For most applications, the horizontal axis that defines about 99% of the area does very nicely. In the "Six Sigma" method, as we will discuss, a good deal more of the horizontal axis is used, but still not infinity.

Other Distributions

There are many other distributions that are useful in operations, sales, engineering, etc. They are amply described in the literature,[2] and a brief listing is given in Table 2-3.

KEY STATISTICS USED IN PROJECTS

Strictly speaking, statistics are data. The data need not be a result of analysis. Statistics are any collection of data. We often hear, "What are the statistics on that event?" In other words, what are the numbers that are meaningful for understanding? Perhaps the most useful definition of statistics is that statistics is the "methods and techniques whereby collections of data are analyzed to obtain understanding and knowledge."[3] *Statistical methods are by and large methods of approximation and estimation.* As such, statistical methods fit very well with project management since the methods of project management are often approximate and based only on estimates.

Informational data, of course, are quite useful to project managers and to members of the project management team for estimating and forecasting, measuring progress, assessing value earned, quantifying risk, and calculating other numerical phenomena of importance to the project. Statistical methods provide some of the tools for reducing such data to meaningful information which the team uses to make decisions.

Expected Value and Average

The best-known statistic familiar to everyone is "average" (more properly, arithmetic average), which is arithmetically equal to a specific case of expected value. *Expected value, E, is the most important statistic for project managers.* The idea of expected value is as follows: In the face of uncertainty about a random variable that has values over a range, *"expected value"[4] is the "best"*

Table 2-3   Other Distributions

Distribution	General Application
Poisson	• The Poisson distribution is used for counting the random arrival or occurrence of an event in a given time, area, distance, etc. For example, the random clicks of a Geiger counter or the random arrival of customers to a store or website is generally Poisson distributed. • The Poisson distribution has a parameter, λ, for arrival rate. As λ becomes large, the Poisson distribution is approximately Normal with $\mu = \lambda$.
Binomial	• The Binomial distribution applies to events that have two outcomes, like the coin toss, where the outcomes are generally referred to as success or failure, true or false. If X is the number of successes, n, in a series of repeated trials, then X will have a Binomial distribution. • As n becomes large, the Binomial distribution is approximately Normal. • The number of heads in a coin toss is Binomial for small n, becoming all but Normal for large n.
Rayleigh	• The Rayleigh distribution is an asymmetrical distribution of all positive outcomes. It approximates outcomes that tend to cluster around a most likely value, but nonetheless have a finite probability of great pessimism. • The Rayleigh has a single parameter, "b", that is the most likely value of the outcome.
Student's t	• The Student's t, or sometimes just t-distribution, is used in estimating confidence intervals when the variance of the population is unknown and the sample size is small. • The Student's t is closely related to the Normal distribution, being derived from it. • The Student's t has a parameter ν, for "degrees of freedom." For large values of ν, the Student's t is all but Normal.
Chi-square	• The distribution of random variables of the form χ^2 is often the Chi-square, named after the Greek letter chi χ. • The Chi-square distribution is always positive and highly asymmetrical, appearing like a decaying exponential when a parameter, n, for degrees of freedom, is small. • The Chi-square finds application in hypothesis testing and in determining the distribution of the sample variance.

single number to represent a range of estimated value of that random variable. "Best" means expected value is an unbiased maximum likelihood estimator for the population mean.* We will discuss unbiased maximum likelihood estimators more in subsequent paragraphs. Reducing a range of value to a single number comes into play constantly. When presenting a budget estimate to

---

* "Best" may not be sufficiently conservative for some organizations, depending on risk attitude. Many project managers forecast with a more pessimistic estimate than the expected value.

project sponsors, more often than not, only one number will be acceptable, not a range. The same is true for schedule, resource hours, and a host of other estimated variables.

Mathematically, to obtain expected value we add up all the values that a random variable can take on, weighting or multiplying each by the probability that that value will occur. Sound familiar? Except for "weighting each value by the probability," the process is identical to calculating the arithmetic average. But wait: in the case of the arithmetic average, there actually are weights on each value, but every weight is 1/n. Calculating expected value, E:

$$E(X) = [(p_1 * X_1) + (p_2 * X_2) + (p_3 * X_3) + (p_4 * X_4) + \ldots]$$

$$E(X) = \Sigma\ (p_i * X_i) \text{ for all values of "i"}$$

where p_i is the probability of specific value X_i occurring. If $p_i = 1/n$, where "n" is the number of values in the summation, then E(X) is mathematically equal to the calculation of *arithmetic average.*

Consider this example: a work package manager estimates a task might take 2 weeks to complete with a 0.5 probability, optimistically 1.5 weeks with a 0.3 probability, but pessimistically it could take 5 weeks with a 0.2 probability. What is the expected value of the task duration?

$$E(\text{task duration } D) = 0.3 * 1.5w + 0.5 * 2 + 0.2 * 5w$$

$$E(\text{task duration } D) = 2.45w$$

Check yourself on the "p"s:

$$p_1 + p_2 + p_3 = 0.3 + 0.5 + 0.2 = 1$$

There are a couple of key things of which to take note. E(X) is not a random variable. As such, E(X) will have a deterministic value. E(X) does not have a distribution. E(X) can be manipulated mathematically like any other deterministic variable; E(X) can be added, subtracted, multiplied, and divided.*

Transforming a space of random variables into a deterministic number is the source of power and influence of the expected value. This concept is very

---

* *Caution*: Strictly speaking, arithmetic operations on the expected value depend on whether or not only linear equations of probability were involved, like summations of cost or schedule durations. For example, nonlinear effects arise in schedules due to parallel and merging paths. In such cases, arithmetic operations are only approximate, and statistical simulations are best.

important to the project manager. Very often, the expected value is the number that the project manager carries to the project balance sheet as the estimate for a particular item. The range of values of the distributions that go into the expected value calculation constitutes both an opportunity (optimistic end of the range) and a threat (pessimistic end of the range) to the success of the project. The project manager carries the risk element to the risk portion of the project balance sheet.

If X is a continuous random variable, then the sum of all values of X morphs into integration as we saw before. We know that p_i is the shorthand for the probability function $f(X \mid X_i)$, so the expected value equation morphs to:

$$E(X) = \int X * f(X \mid X_i)\ dX,\ \text{integrated over all values of "}X\text{"}$$

Fortunately, as a practical matter, project managers do not really need to deal with integrals and integral calculus. The equations are shown for their contribution to background. Most of the integrals have approximate formulas amenable to solution with arithmetic or tables of values that can be used instead.

Mean or "μ"

Expected value is also called the "mean" of the distribution.* A common notation for mean is the Greek letter "μ". Strictly speaking, "μ" is the notation for the population mean when all values in the population range are known. If all the values in a population are not known, or cannot be measured, then the expected value of those values that are known becomes an estimate of the true population mean, μ. As such, the expected value calculated from only a sample of the population may be somewhat in error of μ. We will discuss more about this problem later.

Variance and Standard Deviation

Variance and standard deviation are measures of the spread of values around the expected value. As a practical matter for project practitioners, the larger the spread, the less meaningful is the expected value per se.

Variance and standard deviation are related functionally:

$$SD = \text{sqrt(VAR)} = \sqrt{VAR}$$

---

* You may also hear the term "moment" or "method of moments." Expected value is a "moment of X"; in fact, it is the "first moment of X." $E(X^n)$ is called the "nth moment of X." An in-depth treatment of moments requires more calculus than is within the scope of this book.

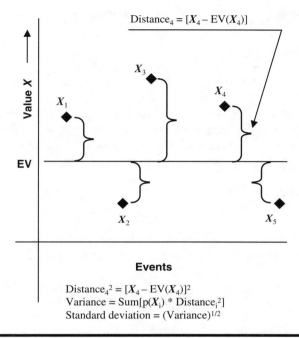

Figure 2-5   Variance and Standard Deviation.

where VAR (variance) is always a positive number and so, therefore, is SD (standard deviation). Commonly used notation is $\sigma = SD$, $\sigma^2 = VAR$.

Variance is a measure of distance or spread of a probable outcome from the expected value of the outcome. Whether the distance is "negative" or "positive" in some arbitrary coordinate system is not important for judging the significance of the distance. Thus we first calculate distance from the expected value as follows:

$$\text{Distance}^2 = [X_i - E(X)]^2$$

The meaning of the distance equation is as follows: the displacement or distance of a specific value of X, say for example a value of "X_i", from the expected value is calculated as the square of the displacement of X_i from $E(X)$. Figure 2-5 illustrates the idea. Now we must also account for the probability of X taking on the value of "X_i".

$$\text{Probabilistic distance} = p(X_i) * [X_i - E(X)]^2$$

Now, to obtain variance, we simply add up all the probabilistic distances:

$$\text{VAR}(X) = \sigma^2(X) = \Sigma\ p(X) * [X_i - E(X)]^2 \text{ for all "i"}$$

which simplifies to:

$$\text{VAR}(X) = \sigma^2(X) = E(X^2) - [E(X)]^2$$

To find the standard deviation, σ, we take the square root of the variance.

Let's return to the example of task duration used in the expected value discussion to see about variance. The durations and the probability of each duration are specified. Plugging those figures into the variance equation:

$$\sigma^2(\text{task duration } \boldsymbol{D}) = 0.3 * (1.5 - 2.45)^2 + 0.5 * (2 - 2.45)^2$$
$$+ 0.2 * (5 - 2.45)^2$$

where 2.45 weeks is the expected value of the task duration from prior calculation, σ^2(task duration $\boldsymbol{D}$) = 1.67 weeks-squared, and σ(task duration $\boldsymbol{D}$) = 1.29 weeks.*

It is obvious that variance may not have physical meaning, whereas standard deviation usually does have some physical meaning.**

Mode

The mode of a random outcome is the most probable or most likely outcome of any single occurrence of an event. If you look at the distribution of outcome values versus their probabilities, the mode is the value at the peak of the distribution curve. Outcomes tend to cluster around the mode. Many confuse the concept of mode, the most likely outcome of any single event, with expected value, which is the best estimator of outcome considering all possible values and their probabilities. Of course, if the distribution of values is symmetrical about the mode, then the expected value and the mode will be identical.

Median

The median is the value that is half the distance between the absolute value of the most pessimistic value and the most optimistic value.

$$\text{Median} = 1/2 * |\ (\text{optimistic value} - \text{pessimistic value})\ |$$

---

* "σ" is the lower case "s" in the Greek alphabet. It is pronounced "sigma."

** An exception to the idea that variance has no physical meaning comes from engineering. The variance of voltage is measured in power: VAR(voltage) = watts.

THE ARITHMETIC OF OPERATIONS ON STATISTICS AND RANDOM VARIABLES

When it comes to arithmetic, random variables are not much different than deterministic variables. We can add, subtract, multiply, and divide random variables. For instance, we can define a random variable $Z = X + Y$, or $W = X^2$. We can transform a random variable into a deterministic variable by calculating its expected value. However, many functional and logical operations on random variables depend on whether or not the variables are mutually exclusive or independent. As examples, the functional operation of expected value does not depend on independence, but the functional operation of variance does.

Similarly, there are operations on statistics that both inherit their properties from deterministic variables and acquire certain properties from the nature of randomness. For instance, the variance of a sum is the sum of variances if the random variables are independent, but the standard deviation of the sum is not the sum of the standard deviations.

Table 2-4 provides a summary of the most important operations for project managers.

PROBABILITY DISTRIBUTION STATISTICS

Most often we do not know every value and its probability. Thus we cannot apply the equations we have discussed to calculate statistics directly. However, if we know the probability distribution of values, or can estimate what the probability function might be, then we can apply the statistics that have been derived for those distributions. And, appropriately so for project management, we can do quite nicely using arithmetic approximations for the statistics rather than constantly referring to a table of values. Of course, electronic spreadsheets have much better approximations, if not exact values, so spreadsheets are a useful and quick tool for statistical analysis.

Three-Point Estimate Approximations

Quite useful results for project statistics are obtainable by developing three-point estimates that can be used in equations to calculate expected value, variance, and standard deviation. The three points commonly used are:

- **Most pessimistic** value that yet has some small probability of happening.
- **Most optimistic** value that also has some small probability of happening.
- **Most likely value** for any single instance of the project. The most likely value is the mode of the distribution.

Table 2-4   Operations on Random Variables and Statistics

Item	All Arithmetic Operations	All Functional Operations with Random Variables as Arguments	Limiting Conditions
Random variables	Yes	Yes	
Probability density functions	Yes	Yes	
Cumulative probability density functions	Yes	Yes	If a random variable is dependent upon another, the functional expression is usually affected.
Expected value, or mean, or sample average, or arithmetic average	Yes	Yes	
Variance	Yes	Yes	If the random variables are not independent, then a covariance must be computed.
Standard deviation	Cannot add or subtract	Yes	To add or subtract standard deviations, first compute the sum of the variances and then take the square root.
Median	No	No	Median is calculated on the population or sample population of the combined random variables.
Mode or most likely	No	No	Most likely is taken from the population statistics of the combined random variables.
Optimistic and pessimistic random variables	Yes	Yes	None

It is not uncommon that the optimistic and most likely values are much closer to each other than is the pessimistic value. Many things can go wrong that are drivers on the pessimistic estimate; usually, there are fewer things that could go right. Table 2-5 provides the equations for the calculation of approximate values of statistics for the most common distributions.

Table 2-5 Statistics for Common Distributions

Statistic	Normal*	BETA**	Triangular	Uniform***
Expected value or mean	$O + [(P - O)/2]$	$(P + 4 * ML + O)/6$	$(P + ML + O)/3$	$O + [(P - O)/2]$
Variance, σ^2	$(P - O)^2/36$	$(P - O)^2/36$	$[(O - P)^2 + (ML - O) * (ML - P)]/18$	$(P^3 - O^3)/ [3 * (P - O)] - (P - O)^2/4$
Standard deviation, σ	$(P - O)/6$	$(O - P)/6$	Sqrt(VAR)	Sqrt(VAR)
Mode or most likely	$O + [(P - O)/2]$	By observation or estimation, the peak of the curve	By observation or estimation, the peak of the curve	Not applicable

Note: O optimistic value, P = pessimistic value, ML = most likely value.

* Formulas are approximations only to more complex functions.

** BETA formulas apply to the curve used in PERT calculations. PERT is discussed in Chapter 7. In general, a BETA distribution has four parameters, two of which are fixed to ensure the area under the curve integrates to 1, and two, α and β, determine the shape of the curve. Normally, fixing or estimating α and β then provides the means to calculate mean and variance. However, for the BETA used in PERT, the mean and variance formulas have been worked out such that α and β become the calculated parameters.

Since in most project situations the exact shape of the BETA curve does not need to be known, the calculation for α and β is not usually performed. If α and β are equal, then the BETA curve is symmetrical.

If the range of values of the BETA distributed random variable is normalized to a range of 0 to 1, then for means less than 0.5 the BETA curve will be skewed to the right; the curve will be symmetrical for mean = 0.5 and skewed left if the mean is greater than 0.5.

*** In general, variance is calculated as $Var(X) = E(X^2) - [E(X)]^2$. This formula is used to derive the variance of the Triangular and Uniform distributions.

The variance for the Uniform reduces to $(P - O)^2/12$ if the optimistic value is 0; similarly, the standard deviation reduces to $(P - O)/3.45$.

It is useful to compare the more common distributions under the conditions of identical estimates. Figure 2-6 provides the illustration. Rules of thumb can be inferred from this illustration:

■ As between the Normal, BETA, and Triangular distributions for the same estimates of optimism and pessimism (and the same mode for the BETA and Triangular), the expected value becomes more pessimistic moving from BETA to Triangular to Normal distribution.

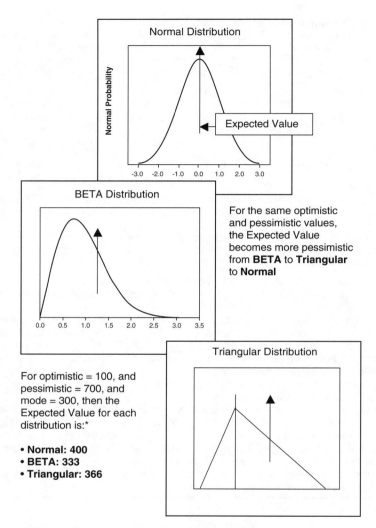

For the same optimistic and pessimistic values, the Expected Value becomes more pessimistic from **BETA** to **Triangular** to **Normal**

For optimistic = 100, and pessimistic = 700, and mode = 300, then the Expected Value for each distribution is:*

• **Normal: 400**
• **BETA: 333**
• **Triangular: 366**

*Mode for BETA and Triangular = 300 in this example; all calculations are based on the equations in Table 2-5.

Figure 2-6   Statistical Comparison of Distributions.

■   The variance and standard deviation of the Normal and BETA distributions are about the same when the pessimistic and optimistic values are taken at the 3σ point. However, since the BETA distribution is not symmetrical, the significance of the standard deviation as a measure of spread around the mean is not as great as in the case of the symmetrical Normal distribution.

In addition to the estimates given above, there are a couple of exact statistics about the Normal distribution that are handy to keep in mind:

- 68.3% of the values of a Normal distribution fall within $\pm 1\sigma$ of the mean value.
- 95.4% of the values of a Normal distribution fall within $\pm 2\sigma$ of the mean value, and this figure goes up to 99.7% for $\pm 3\sigma$ of the mean value.
- A process quality interpretation of 99.7% is that there are three errors per thousand events. If software coding were the object of the error measurement, then "three errors per thousand lines of code" probably would not be acceptable. At $\pm 6\sigma$, the error rate is so small, 99.9998%, it is more easily spoken of in terms of "two errors per million events," about 1,000 times better than "3σ".*

THE CENTRAL LIMIT THEOREM AND LAW OF LARGE NUMBERS

Two very important concepts for the project practitioner are the Law of Large Numbers and the Central Limit Theorem because they integrate much of what we have discussed and provide very useful and easily applied heuristics for managing the quantitative aspects of projects. Let's take them one at a time.

The Law of Large Numbers and Sample Average

The Law of Large Numbers deals with estimating expected value from a large number of observations of values of events from the same population. The Law of Large Numbers will be very valuable in the process of rolling wave planning, which we will address in the chapter on scheduling.

To proceed we need to define what is meant by the "sample average":

$$\alpha(x) = (1/n) * (X_1 + X_2 + X_3 + X_4 + X_5 + X_6 + ...)$$

---

* The Six Sigma literature commonly speaks of 3.4 errors per million events, not 2.0 errors per million. The difference arises from the fact that in the original program developed at Motorola, the mean of the distribution was allowed to "wander" $\pm 1.5\sigma$ from the expected mean of the distribution. This "wandering" increases the error rate from 2.0 to 3.4 errors per million events. An older shorthand way of referring to this error rate is "five nines and an eight" or perhaps "about six nines."

where $\alpha(x)$ is the "arithmetic average of a sample of observations of random variable X," using the lower case alpha from the Greek alphabet. $\alpha(x)$ is a random variable with a distribution of possible values; $\alpha(x)$ will probably be a different value for each set of X_is that are observed.

We call $\alpha(x)$ a "sample average" because we cannot be sure that the X_i that we observe is the complete population; some outcomes may not be in the sample. Perhaps there are other values that we do not have the opportunity to observe. Thus, the X_i in the $\alpha(x)$ is but a sample of the total population. $\alpha(x)$ is not the expected value of X since the probability weighting for each X_i is not in the calculation; that is, $\alpha(x)$ is an arithmetic average, and a random variable, whereas $E(X)$ is a probability weighted average and a deterministic nonrandom variable.

Now here is where the Law of Large Numbers comes in. It can be proved, using a couple of functions (specifically Chebyshev's Inequality and Markov's Inequality*), that as the number of observations in the sample gets very large, then:

$$\alpha(x) \approx E(X) = \mu$$

This means that the sample average is approximately equal to the expected value or mean of the distribution of the population of X. Since X_i are observations from the same distribution for the population X, $E(X_i) = E(X)$. That is, all values of X share the same population parameters or expected value and standard deviation.

Maximum Likelihood and Unbiased Estimators

Hopefully, you can see that the Law of Large Numbers simplifies matters greatly when it comes to estimating an expected value or the mean of a distribution. Without knowledge of the distribution, or knowledge of the probabilities of the individual observations, we can nevertheless approximate the expected value and estimate the mean by calculating the average of a "large" sample from the population. *In fact, we call the sample average the "maximum likelihood" estimator of the mean of the population.* If it turns out that the expected value of the estimator is in fact equal to the parameter being estimated,

---

* Chebyshev's Inequality: probability that the absolute distance of sample value X_i from the population mean is greater than some distance, y, varies by $1/y^2$: $p(|X_i - \mu| \geq y) \leq \sigma^2/y^2$. Markov's Inequality applies to positive values of y, so the absolute distance is not a factor. It says that the probability of an observation being greater than y, regardless of the distance to the mean, is proportional to $1/y$: $p(X \geq y) \leq E(X) * (1/y)$.

then the estimator is said to be *"unbiased." The sample average is an unbiased estimator of* μ *since the expected value of the sample average is also* μ:

$$E[\alpha(x)] = E(X) = \mu$$

The practical effect of being unbiased is that as more and more observations are added to the sample, the expected value of the estimator becomes ever increasingly identical with the parameter being estimated. If there were a bias, the expected value might "wander off" with additional observations.*

Working the problem the other way, if the project manager knows expected value from a calculation using distributions and three-point estimates, then the project manager can deduce that a sample might contain the X_i. In fact, using Chebyshev's Inequality we find that the probability of an X_i straying very far from the mean, μ, goes down by the square of the distance from the mean. The probability that the absolute distance of sample value X_i from the population mean is greater than some distance, y, varies by $1/y^2$:

$$p(|X_i - \mu| \geq y) \leq \sigma^2/y^2$$

Sample Variance and Root-Mean-Square Deviation

There is one other consequence of the Law of Large Numbers that is very important in both risk management and rolling wave planning: the variance of the sample average is 1/n smaller than the variance of the population variance:

$$\sigma^2[\alpha(x)] = (1/n) * \sigma^2(X)$$

$$\sigma^2[\alpha(x)] = (1/n) * [X - \alpha(x)]^2$$

Notice that even though the expected value of the sample average is approximately the same as the expected value of the population, the variance of the sample average is improved by 1/n, and of course the standard deviation of the sample average is improved by $\sqrt{(1/n)}$. The standard deviation of the sample variance is often called the *root-mean-square (RMS) deviation* because of the

---

* Unlike the sample average, the sample variance, $(1/n) \Sigma [X_i - \alpha(x)]^2$, is not an unbiased estimator of the population variance because it can be shown that its expected value is not the variance of the population. To unbias the sample variance, it must be multiplied by the factor [n/(n-1)]. As "n" gets large, you can see that this factor approaches 1. Thus, for large "n", the bias in the sample variance vanishes and it becomes a practical estimator of the population variance.

fact that the standard deviation is the square root of the mean of the "squared distance."

In effect, the sample average is less risky than the general population represented by the random variable X, *and therefore* $\alpha(x)$ *is less risky than a single outcome,* X_i, *of the general population.*

For all practical purposes, we have just made the case for diversification of risk: a portfolio is less risky than any single element, whether it is a financial stock portfolio, a project portfolio, or a work breakdown structure (WBS) of tasks.

Central Limit Theorem

Every bit as important as the Law of Large Numbers is to sampling or diversification, the Central Limit Theorem helps to simplify matters regarding probability distributions to the point of heuristics in many cases. Here is what it is all about. Regardless of the distribution of the random variables in a sum or sample — for instance, $(X_1 + X_2 + X_3 + X_4 + X_5 + X_6 + ...)$ with BETA or Triangular distributions — as long as their distributions are all the same, the distribution of the sum will be Normal with a mean "n times" the mean of the unknown population distribution!

$$\Sigma \ (X_1 + X_2 + X_3 + X_4 + X_5 + X_6 + ...) = S$$

S will have a Normal distribution regardless of the distribution of X:

$$E(X_1 + X_2 + X_3 + X_4 + X_5 + X_6 + ...) = E(S) = n * E(X_i) = n * \mu$$

$$\text{For } n = \Sigma \ i$$

"Distribution of the sum will be Normal" means that the distribution of the sample average, as an example, is Normal with mean $= \mu$, regardless of the distribution of the X_i. We do not have to have any knowledge whatsoever about the population distribution to say that a "large" sample average of the population is Normal. What luck! *Now we can add up costs or schedule durations, or a host of other things in the project, and have full confidence that their sum or their average is Normal regardless of how the cost packages or schedule tasks are distributed.*

As a practical matter, even if a few of the distributions in a sum are not all the same, as they might not be in the sum of cost packages in a WBS, the distribution of the sum is so close to Normal that it really does not matter too much that it is not exactly Normal.

Once we are working with the Normal distribution, then all the other rules of thumb and tables of numbers associated with the Normal distribution come into play. We can estimate standard deviation from the observed or simulated pessimistic and optimistic values without calculating sample variance, we can work with confidence limits and intervals conveniently, and we can relate matters to others who have a working knowledge of the "bell curve."

CONFIDENCE INTERVALS AND LIMITS FOR PROJECTS

The whole point of studying statistics in the context of projects is to make it easier to forecast outcomes and put plans in place to affect those outcomes if they are not acceptable or reinforce outcomes if they present a good opportunity for the project. It often comes down to "confidence" rather than a specific number. Confidence in a statistical sense means "with what probability will the outcome be within a range of values?" Estimating confidence stretches the project-forecasting problem from estimating the probability of a specific value for an outcome to the problem of forecasting an outcome within certain limits of value.

Mathematically, we shift our focus from the PDF to the cumulative probability function. Summing up or integrating the probability distribution over a range of values produces the cumulative probability function. The cumulative probability equals the sum (or integral) of the probability distribution over all possible outcomes.

The "S" Curve

Recall that the cumulative probability accumulates from 0 to 1 regardless of the actual distribution being summed or integrated. We can easily equate the accumulating value as accumulating from 0 to 100%. For example, if we accumulate all the values in a Normal distribution between $\pm 1\sigma$ of the mean, we will find 68.3% of the total value of the cumulative total. We can say with 68.3% "confidence" that an outcome from a Normal distribution will fall in the range of $\pm 1\sigma$ of the mean; the corollary is that with 31.7% confidence, an outcome will lie outside this range, either more pessimistic or more optimistic.

Integrating the Normal curve produces an "S" curve. In general, integrating the BETA and Triangular curves will also produce a curve of roughly an "S" shape.* Figure 2-7 shows the "S" curve.

---

* For a normal curve, the slope changes such that the curvature goes from concave to convex at exactly $\pm 1\sigma$ from the mean. This curvature change will show up as an inflection on the cumulative probability curve.

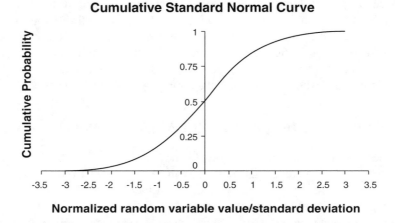

Figure 2-7   Confidence Curve for the Normal Distribution.

Confidence Tables

A common way to calculate confidence limits is with a table of cumulative values for a "standard" Normal distribution. A standard Normal distribution has a mean of 0 and a standard deviation of 1. Most statistics books or books of numerical values will have a table of standard Normal figures. It is important to work with either a "two-tailed" table or double your answers from a "one-tail" table. The "tail" refers to the curve going in both directions from the mean in the center.

A portion of a two-tailed standard Normal table is given in Table 2-6. Look in this table for the "y" value. This is the displacement from the mean along the horizontal axis. Look at y = 1, one standard deviation from the mean. You will see an entry in the cumulative column of 0.6826. This means that the "area under the curve" from ±1σ is 0.6826 of all the area. The confidence of a value falling around the mean, ±1σ, is 0.6826, commonly truncated to 68.3%.

COVARIANCE AND CORRELATION IN PROJECTS

It often arises in the course of executing projects that one or more random variables, or events, appear to bear on the same project problem. For instance, fixed costs that accumulate period by period and the overall project schedule duration are two random variables with obvious dependencies. Two statistical terms come into play when two or more variables are in the same project space: covariance and correlation.

Table 2-6   Standard Normal Probabilities

"y" Value	Probability	"y" Value	Probability
0.1	0.0796	1.6	0.8904
0.2	0.1586	1.7	0.9108
0.3	0.2358	1.8	0.9282
0.4	0.3108	1.9	0.9426
0.5	0.4514	**2.0**	**0.9544**
0.6	0.5160	2.1	0.9643
0.7	0.5762	2.2	0.9722
0.8	0.6318	2.3	0.9786
1.0	**0.6826**	2.4	0.9836
1.1	0.7286	2.5	0.9876
1.2	0.7698	2.6	0.9907
1.3	0.8064	2.7	0.9931
1.4	0.8384	2.8	0.9949
1.5	0.8664	2.9	0.9963
		3.0	**0.9974**

For $p(-y < X_i < y)$ where X_i is a standard normal random variable of mean 0 and standard deviation of 1.

For nonstandard Normal distributions, look up $y = a/\sigma$, where "a" is the value from a nonstandard distribution with mean = 0 and σ is the standard deviation of that nonstandard Normal distribution.

If the mean of the nonstandard Normal distribution is not equal to 0, then "a" is adjusted to "$a = b - \mu$," where "b" is the value from the nonstandard Normal distribution with mean μ: $y = (b - \mu)/\sigma$.

Covariance

Covariance is a measure of how much one random variable depends on another. Typically, we think in terms of "if X gets larger, does Y also get larger or does Y get smaller?" The covariance will be negative for the latter and positive for the former. The value of the covariance is not particularly meaningful since it will be large or small depending on whether X and Y are large or small. Covariance is defined simply as:

$$Cov(X,Y) = E(X * Y) - E(X) * E(Y)$$

If X and Y are independent, then $E(X * Y) = E(X) * E(Y)$, and $COV(X,Y) = 0$.

Table 2-7 provides a project situation of covariance involving the interaction of cost and schedule duration on a WBS work package. The example requires an estimate of cost given various schedule possibilities. Once these estimates

Table 2-7 Covariance and Correlation Example

Table 2-7-A Cost * Duration Calculations

Work Package Duration, D Value	Work Package Cost, $C	p($D * C$) of a Joint Outcome	Joint Outcome, $D * C$	E($D * C$)
2 months	$10	0.1	20	2
	$20	0.15	40	6
	$60	0.05	120	6
3 months	$10	0.2	30	6
	$20	0.3	60	18
	$60	0.08	180	14.4
4 months	$10	0.02	40	0.8
	$20	0.05	80	4
	$60	0.05	240	12
Totals:		1		69.2

Table 2-7-B Cost Calculations

Work Package Cost, $C	p(C) of a Cost Outcome, Given All Schedule Possibilities	E(C), $	σ^2 Variance
$10	0.32	$3.2	$62.7 = 0.32(10 - 24)^2$
$20	0.5	$10	$8 = 0.5(20 - 24)^2$
$60	0.18	$10.8	$233.2 = 0.18(60 - 24)^2$
	1	**$24.00**	$\sigma_c^2 = 304$
			$\sigma_c = \$17.44$

Table 2-7-C Duration Calculations

Work Package Duration, D Value	p(D) of a Schedule Outcome, Given All Cost Possibilities	E(D), months	σ^2 Variance and Standard Deviation
2 months	0.3	0.6	$0.2 = 0.3(2 - 2.82)^2$
3 months	0.58	1.74	$0.018 = 0.58(3 - 2.82)^2$
4 months	0.12	0.48	$0.17 = 0.12(4 - 2.82)^2$
	1	**2.82**	$\sigma_D^2 = 0.39$
			$\sigma_D = 0.62$ month

COV(D,C) = E(DC) − E(D) * E(C)

COV(D,C) = 69.2 − 2.82 * 24 = 1.52
Meaning: Because of the positive covariance, cost and schedule move in the same way; if one goes up, so does the other.

r(DC) = COV(D,C)/(σ_D * σ_c) = 1.52/(0.62 * $17.44) = 0.14
Meaning: Judging by a scale of −1 to +1, the "sensitivity" of cost to schedule is weak.

are made, then an analysis can be done of the expected value and variance of each random variable, the cost variable, and schedule duration variable. These calculations provide all that is needed to calculate the covariance.

If the covariance of two random variables is not 0, then the variance of the sum of X and Y becomes:

$$VAR(X + Y) = VAR(X) + VAR(Y) + 2 * COV(X,Y)$$

The *covariance of a sum* becomes a governing equation for the project management problem of shared resources, particularly people. If the random variable X describes the availability need for a resource and Y for another resource, then the total variance of the availability need of the combined resources is given by the equation above. If resources are not substitutes for one another, then the covariance will be positive in many cases, thereby broadening the availability need (that is, increasing the variance) and lengthening the schedule accordingly. This broadening phenomenon is the underlying principle behind the lengthening of schedules when they are "resource leveled."[5]

Correlation

Covariance does not directly measure the strength of the "sensitivity" of X on Y; judging the strength is the job of correlation. Sensitivity will tell us how much the cost changes if the schedule is extended a month or compressed a month. In other words, sensitivity is always a ratio, also called a density, as in this example: $cost change/month change. But if cost and time are random variables, what does the ratio of any single outcome among all the possible outcomes forecast for the future? Correlation is a statistical estimate of the effects of sensitivity, measured on a scale of −1 to +1.

The Greek letter rho, ρ, used on populations of data, and "r", used with samples of data, stand for the correlation between two random variables: $r(X,Y)$. The usual way of referring to "r" or "ρ" is as the "correlation coefficient." As such, their values can range from −1 to +1. "0" value means no correlation, whereas −1 means highly correlated but moving in opposite directions, and +1 means highly correlated moving in the same direction.

The correlation function is defined as the covariance normalized by the product of the standard deviations:

$$r(X,Y) = COV(X,Y)/(\sigma_X * \sigma_Y)$$

We can now rewrite the variance equation:

$$\text{VAR}(X + Y) = \text{VAR}(X) + \text{VAR}(Y) + 2 * \rho(\sigma X + \sigma Y)$$

Table 2-7 provides a project example of correlation.

SUMMARY OF IMPORTANT POINTS

Table 2-8 provides the highlights of this chapter.

Table 2-8   Summary of Important Points

Point of Discussion	Summary of Ideas Presented
No facts about the future	▪ Uncertainty is present in every project. ▪ Risk management is the process, but probability and statistics provide the mathematical underpinning for the quantitative analysis of project risk.
Probability and projects	▪ The *outcome of any single event,* whether it is a coin toss or a project, cannot be known with certainty, but the pattern of behavior of a random event can be forecast. ▪ Single-point deterministic estimates forego the opportunity to estimate and forecast the impact of opportunity and threat. ▪ The relative frequency use of probability, such as "one chance in ten," forecasts a specific outcome; the subjective use of probability, such as "there is a 20% chance of rain today," expresses a "confidence" of an event within a range. ▪ Project events that are not mutually exclusive, or impose conditions that obviate independence between them, generally reduce the probability that either event will happen as planned. ▪ All probabilities of a single event must fall in the space of "zero to one" such that the equation $p + (1\text{-}p) = 1$ holds at all times.
Random variables	▪ If the outcome of a specific event has a numerical value, then the outcome is a variable, and because its value is not known with certainty before the fact, and could take on more than one value from event to event, it is a random variable. ▪ Random variables can be discrete or continuous over a range. ▪ The *probability function, or probability distribution*, relates the functional mathematical relationship between a random variable's value and the probability of obtaining that value. Summing or integrating the probability function over the range gives the *cumulative probability function.* The cumulative probability function ranges over 0 to 1.
Probability distributions for projects	▪ There are four probability distributions commonly used in projects: Normal, BETA, Triangular, and Uniform. Other distributions are helpful in estimating statistical parameters relevant to projects, but are usually left to statisticians.

Table 2-8   Summary of Important Points (continued)

Point of Discussion	Summary of Ideas Presented
	■ BETA and Triangular are often employed at the work package level in the WBS. The Normal distribution is often employed in summary results.
Useful statistics for project managers	■ Statistics are data; data do not have to be analyzed to be statistics. ■ *Statistical methods are by and large methods of approximation and estimation.* ■ Expected value is the most important statistic for project managers. It is the single best estimator of the true mean of a random variable. ■ Other useful statistics include: arithmetic average, sample average, variance, standard deviation, mean, mode, and median.
Statistics of distributions	■ For the same range of value of a random variable, the expected value becomes more pessimistic moving from BETA to Triangular to Normal. ■ Approximations to all the major statistics are available in simple arithmetic form for the most used distributions in projects.
The Law of Large Numbers and the Central Limit Theorem	■ Regardless of the distribution of a random variable, the *sample average* of a number, n, of observations of the random variable's outcome will itself be a random variable of Normal distribution with mean equal to the mean of the population distribution and variance $1/n$ of the population variance. ■ The probability that an event outcome will have a value different from the mean grows less probable as $1/y^2$ where y is the distance from the mean.
Confidence limits	■ Confidence in a statistical sense means "with what probability the outcome will be within a range of values." ■ Estimating confidence stretches the project-forecasting problem from estimating the probability of a specific value for an outcome to the problem of forecasting an outcome within certain limits of value.
Covariance and correlation	■ Oftentimes, the outcome of one random variable is dependent on another. The degree of dependence is described by the correlation of one on the other. The covariance, equal to the correlation times a factor, adds to or subtracts from the sum of the variances of each of the random variables.

REFERENCES

1. *A Guide to the Project Management Body of Knowledge (PMBOK® Guide)* — 2000 Edition, Project Management Institute, Newtown Square, PA, chap. 6, p. 69.
2. Downing, Douglas and Clark, Jeffery, *Statistics the Easy Way,* Barrons Educational Series, Hauppauge, NY, 1997, pp. 90–155.

3. Balsley, Howard, *Introduction to Statistical Method,* Littlefield, Adams & Co., Totowa, NJ, 1964, pp. 3–4.

4. Schyuler, John R., *Decision Analysis in Projects*, Project Management Institute, Newtown Square, PA, 1996, chap. 1, p. 11.

5. *A Guide to the Project Management Body of Knowledge (PMBOK® Guide)* — 2000 Edition, Project Management Institute, Newtown Square, PA, chap. 6, p. 76.

ORGANIZING AND ESTIMATING THE WORK

There likely is no factor that would contribute more
to the success of any project than having
a good and complete definition of the project's scope of work.

Quentin Fleming and Joel Koppelman
Earned Value Project Management

In the normal course of project events, business leaders develop the need for a project after recognizing opportunity that can be transformed into business value. Such a project is defined on the business side of the project balance sheet. Although the business and the project team may have differences about resources and schedule, the common conveyance of ideas across the project balance sheet is scope. Understand the scope clearly and the project management team should be able to then estimate required resources, schedule, and quality. Defining scope and estimating the work are inextricably tightly coupled.

The Department of Defense, certainly a proponent of rigorous project management, sees the benefit of having a structured approach to organizing the project scope when it says that such a structure:[1]

- "Separates (an)…item into its component parts, making the relationships of the parts clear and the relationship of the tasks to be completed — to each other and to the end product — clear.

- Significantly affects planning and the assignment of management and technical responsibilities.
- Assists in tracking the status of…(project) efforts, resource allocations, cost estimates, expenditures, and cost and technical performance."
- Helps ensure that contractors are not unnecessarily constrained in meeting item requirements.

ORGANIZING THE SCOPE OF WORK

Organizing and defining the project scope of work seems a natural enough step and a *required prerequisite* to all analytical estimates concerning projects. Though constructing the logical relationships among the deliverables of the project scope appears straightforward, in point of fact developing the scope structure is often more vexing than first imagined because two purposes are to be served at the same time: (1) provide a capture vessel for all the scope of the project and (2) provide quantitative data for analysis and reporting to project managers and sponsors.

Work Definition and Scoping Process

The general process (input, methods, output) for scope or work definition and organization is given in Figure 3-1. *Inputs* to the process are assembled from all the ideas and prerequisite information from the business side of the project balance sheet that describe the desired outcomes of the project, including constraints, assumptions, and external dependencies. *Methods* are the steps employed in the scope definition process to organize this information, decompose the given material into a finer granularity of functional and technical scope, and relate various elements of the project deliverables to each other. The *outcome* of the work definition and scoping process is an "organization of the deliverables" of the project, often in hierarchical list or chart form, or in relational form that supports multiple views.

We should note that the "organization of the deliverables" is not an organization chart of the project in the sense of responsibility assignments, reporting, and administration among project members. The "organization" we speak of is the logical relationship among, and definition of, the deliverables for which the project manager makes quantitative estimates for resources needs, risks, and schedule requirements on the project side of the project balance sheet. *The name given to the organization of project deliverables is work breakdown structure (WBS).* Suffice to say: all the scope of the project is contained in the WBS.

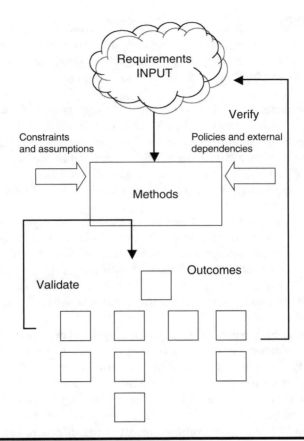

Figure 3-1 Work Definition and Scoping Process.

The process includes loops to validate and verify the completeness of the WBS. Validation refers to determining that everything on the WBS is there for a reason and is not inappropriate to the project scope. Validation also determines the proper hierarchical level for all deliverables and ensures hierarchical integrity. Verification is closely aligned with validation. Verification extends the concept back to the business owner or project sponsor to ensure that all scope has been accounted for and is on the WBS.

Multiple Views in Scope Organization

One purpose of the WBS organization is to serve the informational needs of those who will use the WBS in the course of managing and overseeing the project. Thus, the WBS should be organized to most effectively serve the management team. There are many possible ways to organize the information provided by the business, project team, project vendors, and others. Consider, for instance, these possibilities as illustrated in Figure 3-2:*

- **Deliverables view**: Because there are many points of view regarding project scope, more than one version of the WBS of the same project is possible as shown in Table 3-1. The preferred view is that of product or deliverables, focusing the WBS on the accomplishments of the project insofar as the sponsor or business is concerned. Unless otherwise noted, in this book the product or deliverable view will always be the view under discussion.

- **Organizational view**: Some project scopes are organized according to the departments that will deliver the work. Organizational project scope may be appropriate if there are facility, technology, or vendor boundaries that must be factored into the scope structure. For instance, in the semiconductor industry, there are usually quite significant boundaries between design, wafer fabrication, and end-device assembly and test.

- **Methodology view**: The methodology used to execute the project often influences scope, either temporally or in terms of scope content. Projects in different domains, for instance software development, building construction, and new consumer products, generally follow differing methodologies from planning to rollout and project completion, thereby generating many different deliverables along the way. These deliverables are often organized into methodology phases, or builds, on the WBS.

- **Phases view**: Scope phases that respond to the business needs or business capacity add a temporal dimension to the WBS organization. Ordinarily, *the WBS is blind to time*. In fact, a useful way to think of the WBS is that the WBS is the schedule collapsed to present time; in effect, the WBS is the "present value" of the schedule. Of course, the corollary is that the schedule is merely the WBS laid out on a calendar.

---

* There is no single "right way" for constructing a WBS of a given project, though there may be policies and standard practices in specific organizations or industries that govern the WBS applied therein. The only rule that must be honored is that all the project scope must appear on the WBS.

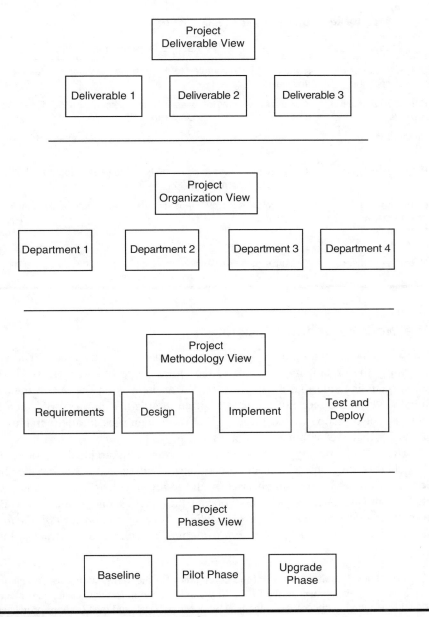

Figure 3-2 Project Views on the WBS.

Table 3-1   Views of the Project Scope

View	Scope Organization
Business owner or project sponsor	Organize by deliverables to the business required to make good on the business case
Business financial manager	Organize by types or uses of money, such as R&D funds, capital funds, expense funds, O&M funds
Project manager	Organize by methodological steps, such as design, develop, test and evaluation, training, and rollout
Project developer	Organize by phases such as the baseline phase, upgrade phase, pilot phase, production phase
Manufacturing, operations, and maintenance provider	Organize by life cycle steps, such as plan, implement, manufacture, rollout, maintain
Customer or user	Organize by deliverables to the user, such as the training and operational deliverables only available to the user

The Work Breakdown Structure

The WBS has been a fixture of project management for many years.* The WBS is simply the organizing structure of the entire scope of the project. There is one organizing rule that governs overall: if an item is on the WBS, then that item is within the scope of the project; if an item is not on the WBS, then that item is out of scope of the project. The WBS identifies the deliverables and activities that are within the scope of the project.

The WBS is most typically shown as an ordered hierarchical list, or equivalent chart or diagram, of project deliverables. By their nature, hierarchies have levels. A higher level is an abstract of all the levels below it and connected to it. For emphasis, let us term this concept the "completeness rule" for WBSs: to wit, *an element at a higher level is defined by all of, but only all of, the lower level elements that connect to it.* For example, "bicycle" is an abstract of lower

---

* A brief but informative history of the development of the WBS, starting as an adjunct to the earliest development of the PERT (Program Evaluation Review Technique) planning and scheduling methodology in the late 1950s in the Navy, and then finding formalization in the Department of Defense in 1968 as MIL-STD-881, subsequently updated to MIL-HDBK-881 in 1998, can be found in Gregory Haugan's book, *Effective Work Breakdown Structures.*[3]

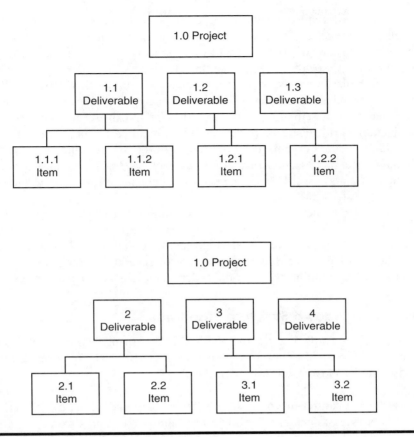

Figure 3-3 WBS Numbering Schemes.

level items such as frame, handlebar, seat, wheels, etc. all related to and connected to "bicycle," but on the other hand "bicycle" consists of *only* lower level items such as frame, handlebar, seat, wheels, etc. all related to and connected to "bicycle."

At the highest level of the WBS is simply "Project," an abstract of everything in the project. Typically, "Project" is called level 1. At the next level is the first identification of distinct deliverables, and subsequent levels reveal even more detail. The next level is called level 2. Of course alpha characters could also be used, or alpha and numeric characters could be combined to distinctly identify levels and elements of the WBS. A couple of schemes are given in Figure 3-3.

Deliverables are typically tangible, measurable, or otherwise recognizable results of project activity. In short, *deliverables are the project "nouns."* The project nouns are what are left when the project is complete and the team has gone on to other things. Of course, materiel items that make up an item, like nuts and bolts, are typically not identified as deliverables themselves. Following this line of thinking, project activities (for example, design, construction, coding, painting, assembling, and so forth) are transitory and not themselves deliverables. However, the project activities required to obtain the deliverables are identified and organized by the scoping process. Activities are the actions of the project process; *activities are the project "verbs."* The syntax of the WBS is then straightforward: associate with the "nouns" the necessary "verbs" required to satisfy the project scope.

Apart from showing major phases or rolling waves, the WBS is blind to time.* In fact, a useful way to think of the WBS is that it is the deliverables on the schedule all viewed in present time. It follows that all nouns and verbs on the WBS must be found in the project schedule, arranged in the same hierarchy, but with all the time-dependent durations and dependencies shown.

Work Breakdown Structure Standards

There are standards that describe the WBS.** Perhaps the most well known is the Department of Defense handbook, "MIL-HDBK-881."[2] As defined therein (with emphasis from the original), the WBS is:

- "A **product-oriented family tree** composed of hardware, software, services, data, and facilities. The family tree results from…efforts during the acquisition of a…materiel item.
- A WBS displays and defines the product, or products, to be developed and/or produced. It **relates the elements** of work to be accomplished to each other and to the end product.
- A WBS can be expressed down to any level of interest. However (if)…items identified are high cost or high risk…(then)…is it important to take the work breakdown structure to a lower level of definition."

---

* Rolling waves is a planning concept that we discuss more in subsequent chapters. In short, the idea is to plan near-term activities in detail, and defer detailed planning of far-future activities until their time frame is more near term.

** The WBS is covered extensively in publications of the Department of Defense (MIL-HDBK-881) and the National Aeronautics and Space Administration (Work Breakdown Structure Guide, Program/Project Management Series, 1994) as well as *A Guide to the Project Management Body of Knowledge,*[4] among others.

Table 3-2   WBS Do's and Don'ts

Scope Organization

Do not include elements that are not products. A signal processor, for example, is clearly a product, as are mock-ups and Computer Software Configuration Items (CSCIs). On the other hand, things like design engineering, requirements analysis, test engineering, aluminum stock, and direct costs are not products. Design engineering, test engineering, and requirements analysis are all engineering functional efforts; aluminum is a material resource; and direct cost is an accounting classification. Thus, none of these elements are appropriate WBS elements.

Program phases (e.g., design, development, production, and types of funds, or research, development, test, and evaluation) **are inappropriate as elements in a WBS.**

Rework, retesting, and refurbishing are not separate elements in a WBS. They should be treated as part of the appropriate WBS element affected.

Nonrecurring and recurring classifications are not WBS elements. The reporting requirements of the CCDR will segregate each element into its recurring and nonrecurring parts.

Cost-saving efforts such as total quality management initiatives, should-cost estimates, and warranty are not part of the WBS. These efforts should be included in the cost of the item they affect, not captured separately.

Do not use the structure of the program office or the contractor's organization as the basis of a WBS.

Do not treat costs for meetings, travel, computer support, etc. as separate WBS elements. They are to be included with the WBS elements with which they are associated.

Use actual system names and nomenclature. Generic terms are inappropriate in a WBS. The WBS elements should clearly indicate the character of the product to avoid semantic confusion. For example, if the Level 1 system is Fire Control, then the Level 2 item (prime mission product) is Fire Control Radar.

Treat tooling as a functional cost, not a WBS element. Tooling (e.g., special test equipment and factory support equipment like assembly tools, dies, jigs, fixtures, master forms, and handling equipment) should be included in the cost of the equipment being produced. If the tooling cannot be assigned to an identified subsystem or component, it should be included in the cost of integration, assembly, test, and checkout.

Include software costs in the cost of the equipment. For example, when a software development facility is created to support the development of software, the effort associated with this element is considered part of the CSCI it supports or, if more than one CSCI is involved, the software effort should be included under integration, assembly, test, and checkout. Software developed to reside on specific equipment must be identified as a subset of that equipment.

Do's and don'ts are excerpted from MIL-HDBK-881.

As a standard, MIL-HDBK-881 makes definitive statements about certain "do's and don'ts" that make the WBS more useful to managers. Table 3-2 summarizes the advice from MIL-HDBK-881.

Adding Organizational Breakdown Structure and Resource Assignment Matrix to the Work Breakdown Structure

In fact, the WBS is not one entity, but actually three:

- The WBS itself is the hierarchical structure of deliverables (nouns), and when applying the WBS in the context of contractor-subcontractor, the prime WBS is often referred to as the project or program WBS (PWBS) and the subcontractor's WBS is referred to as the contract or contractor WBS (CWBS).
- A structure similar to the WBS can be made for the organizations that participate in the project. Such a structure is called the organizational breakdown structure (OBS).
- The OBS and the WBS are cross-referenced with the resource assignment matrix (RAM).

Figure 3-4 shows the three component parts working together.

The RAM is where the analytical aspects of the WBS come into play. At each node of the RAM where there is an intersection of the OBS and WBS, the resource commitment of the organizations is allocated to the WBS. From the RAM, the resources can be added vertically into the WBS hierarchy and horizontally into the OBS hierarchy. Such an addition is shown in Figure 3-5. Note that the following equation holds:

$$\Sigma \text{ (All WBS resources)} = \Sigma \text{ (All OBS resources)} = \text{Project resources}$$

Budgeting with the Work Breakdown Structure

From Figure 3-5, we see that OBS department budgets and WBS project budgets intersect. Eventually, these budgeted items must find their way to the chart of accounts of the business. Let us introduce additional nomenclature to go with the chart of accounts:

- The WBS itself is often numbered hierarchically for each work element identified. The WBS numbering scheme is sometimes called the "code of accounts."[5]
- At the lowest level of the WBS where cost is assigned, the WBS element is called a "work package." The project manager assigns responsibility to someone on the project team for the work package.
- Work packages need not all be at the same level on the WBS. However, to make the WBS uniform in level for data collection and reporting,

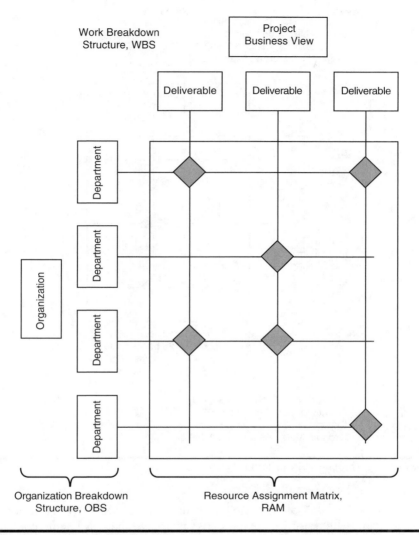

Figure 3-4 WBS Components.

"pull downs" of "dummy" levels are employed. As an example, let us say that "bicycle" is decomposed down to level 3 with work packages 1.1.1 (stationary parts) and 1.1.2 (moving parts). Let us say that there is also a "wagon" on the WBS, and that "wagon" ends at level 4 with work package 1.2.1.1 (wheels) and 1.2.1.2 (axles). To create uniform metric reporting at the fourth level of the WBS we would create a "level

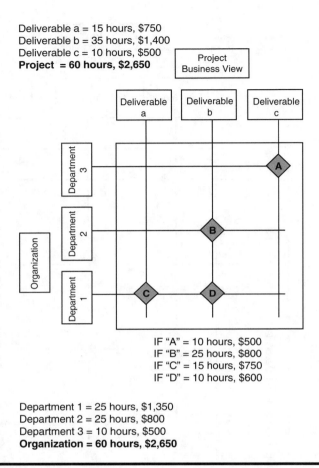

Deliverable a = 15 hours, $750
Deliverable b = 35 hours, $1,400
Deliverable c = 10 hours, $500
Project = 60 hours, $2,650

Project Business View

Deliverable a
Deliverable b
Deliverable c

Organization

Department 3
Department 2
Department 1

IF "A" = 10 hours, $500
IF "B" = 25 hours, $800
IF "C" = 15 hours, $750
IF "D" = 10 hours, $600

Department 1 = 25 hours, $1,350
Department 2 = 25 hours, $800
Department 3 = 10 hours, $500
Organization = 60 hours, $2,650

Figure 3-5   Adding Up the RAM.

4 pull down" of "bicycle" with dummy elements 1.1.1.1 (stationary parts) and 1.1.2.1 (moving parts) that have the exact same content as their third-level parents. Similarly, there would be a fourth-level pull down for "wagon" for element 1.2.2. Our example WBS is illustrated in Figure 3-6.

■ Cost accounts are roll ups of work packages and any in-between levels of the WBS. The project manager assigns responsibility for performance of a cost account to someone on the team, and, by extension, that person is responsible for the work packages that roll into the cost account.

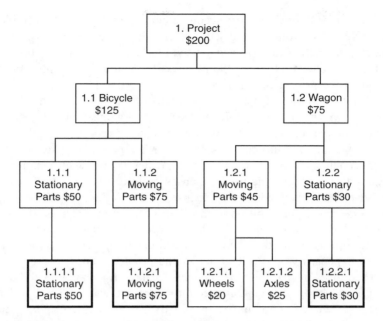

Fourth-level pull downs for "bicycle" and "wagon"
provide a consistent reporting level for project metrics.

Figure 3-6   Bicycle and Wagon.

Cost Accounts and Work Packages

Returning to Figure 3-5, we see that there are four work packages: A, B, C, and D. What, then, are the cost accounts? Typically, cost accounts are either one or more work packages rolled up vertically (project view) or horizontally (organizational view). Depending on the project management approach regarding "matrix management" and project responsibilities, either roll up could be possible.* So, there are either three cost accounts corresponding to "depart-

* See *A Guide to the Project Management Body of Knowledge*[5] for a discussion of project management organizing ideas and matrix management. For a strongly "projectized" approach, the cost accounts will be in the project view, summed vertically, with "project" managers assigned. For an organizational approach to the project, the cost accounts will be in the organizational view, summed horizontally, with an "organizational" manager assigned.

ments 1, 2, and 3" or three cost accounts corresponding to "deliverables a, b, and c." We know from prior discussion that the total project expense is not dependent on whether the cost accounts are rolled up vertically or horizontally. Therefore, the choice is left to the business to decide how responsibility is to be assigned for project performance.

Now, let us consider the chart of accounts of the business. The chart might well be shown as in Figure 3-7. We see that Organization has expense and Project has expense. We would not want to count expenses in both categories since that would be counting the same expense twice. If both were fed to the chart of accounts, an accounting process known as "expense elimination" would be required to reconcile the total expenses reported. To avoid the accounting overhead to eliminate redundant expenses, the solution, of course, is not to connect one or the other roll up to the chart of accounts. That is, if the project is going to have an account on the chart of accounts, then the project expenses would not roll up under department and organization; instead, project-specific, or direct, expenses would roll up under the project itself.

We see also on the chart of accounts a place for capital accounts. From Chapter 1, we know that capital accounts represent asset values that have not yet been "expensed" into the business expense accounts. Capital purchases made on behalf of projects are usually not recorded as project expenditures at the time the purchases are made. Rather, the practice is to depreciate the capital expenditure over time and assign to the project only the depreciation expense as depreciation is recorded as an expense in the chart of accounts. As capital is depreciated from the capital accounts, depreciation becomes expense in the expense accounts, flowing downward through the WBS to the RAM where depreciation expense is assigned to a work package.

In the foregoing discussion we established an important idea: *the WBS is an extension of the chart of accounts.* Just as a WBS element can describe a small scope of work, so also can a WBS element account for a small element of cost or resource consumption (hours, facilities usage, etc.).

Of course, not only is the budget distributed among the work packages on the RAM, but so also are the actual performance figures gathered and measured during project execution. Thus, work package actuals can be added across the OBS and up the WBS hierarchy all the way to the level 1 of the WBS or Organization of the OBS. The variance to budget is also additive across and up the WBS. In subsequent chapters, we will discuss earned value as a performance measurement and forecasting methodology. Within the earned value methodology is a concept of performance indexes, said indexes computed as ratios of important performance metrics. Indexes per se are not additive across and up the WBS. Indexes must be recomputed from summary data at each summarization level of the WBS or the OBS.

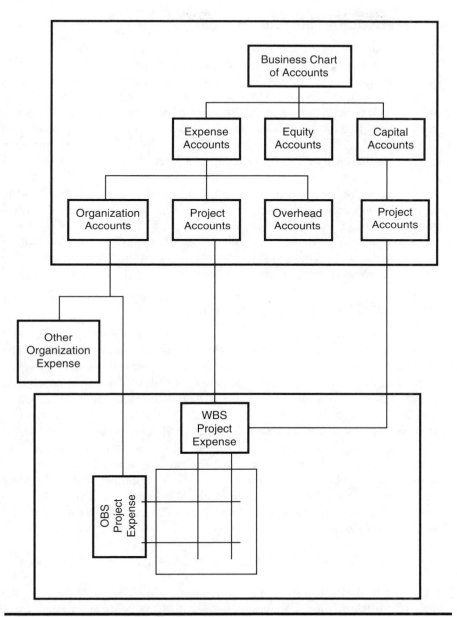

Figure 3-7   Chart of Accounts and the WBS.

Work Breakdown Structure Dictionary

We add to our discussion of the WBS with a word about the WBS dictionary. It is common practice to define the scope content, in effect the statement of work, for each element of the WBS in a WBS dictionary. We see that this is an obvious prerequisite to estimating any specific element of the WBS. Typically, the WBS dictionary is not unlike any written dictionary. A dictionary entry is a narrative of some form that is explanatory of the work that needs to be done and the expected deliverable of the work package. For all practical purposes, the dictionary narrative is a scope statement for the "mini-project" we call the work package.

The total scope assigned to a cost account manager is then defined as the sum of the scope of each of the related work packages defined in the WBS dictionary. Though cost, facility requirements, skills, hours, and vendor items are not traditionally contained or defined in the dictionary, the total resources available to the cost account manager for the scope in the WBS dictionary are those resources assigned to each of the constituent work packages.

Work Breakdown Structure Baseline

For quantitative estimating purposes, we need a target to shoot at. It is better that the target be a static target, not moving during the time of estimation. The scope captured on the WBS at the time estimating begins is the project "baseline scope." Baselines are "fixed" until they are changed. Changing the baseline is a whole subject unto itself. Suffice to say that once resources are assigned to a baseline, and then that baseline is changed, the task of the project manager and project administrator is to map from the RAM in the baseline to the RAM of the changed baseline. A common practice is to consider all resource consumption from initial baseline to the point of rebaseline to be "sunk cost," or actuals to date (ATD), not requiring mapping. Expenditures going forward are either mapped from the initial baseline, or the WBS of the subsequent baseline is re-estimated as "estimate to complete" (ETC). Total project cost at completion then becomes:

Cost at completion = ATD of WBS Baseline-1 + ETC of WBS Baseline-2

The practical effect of rebaselining is to reset variances and budgets on the WBS. The WBS dictionary may also be modified for the new baseline. Considering the need for cost and performance history, and the connection to the chart of accounts, there are a couple of approaches that can be taken. To preserve history, particularly valuable for future and subsequent estimations, WBS Baseline-1 may be given a different project account number on the chart of accounts from that assigned to the WBS Baseline-2. The cost history of WBS Baseline-1 and the WBS Baseline-1 dictionary can then be saved for future reference.

A second and less desirable approach from the viewpoint of preserving history is to make a lump sum entry into the chart of accounts for the ATD of WBS Baseline-1. Then WBS Baseline-2 is connected to the chart of accounts in substitution for WBS Baseline-1 and work begins anew.

ESTIMATING METHODS FOR PROJECTS

There is no single method that applies to all projects. Estimating is very domain specific. Construction, software, pharmaceuticals, packaging, and services, just to name a few of perhaps hundreds if not thousands of domains, have unique and specific estimating methodologies. Our intent is to discuss general principles that apply universally. Project managers are in the best position to adapt generalities to the specific project instance.

Estimating Concepts

The objectives of performing an estimate are twofold: to arrive at an expected value for the item being estimated and to be able to convey a figure of merit for that estimate. In this book we will focus on estimating deliverables on a WBS. The figure of merit we will use is the confidence interval that is calculable from the statistical data of the underlying distribution of the expected value of the estimate.

Most estimating fits into one of four models as illustrated in Figure 3-8:

- **Top-down** value judgments from the business side of the project balance sheet conveyed to the project team
- **Similar-to** judgments from either side of the project balance sheet, but most often from the business side
- **Bottom-up** facts-driven estimates of actual work effort from the project side of the project balance sheet conveyed to the project sponsor
- **Parametric** calculations from a cost-history model, developed by the project team, and conveyed to the project sponsor

Naturally, it is rare that a project would depend only on one estimating technique; therefore, it is not unusual that any specific project team will use all the estimating methods available to it that fit the project context. However, let us consider them one by one.

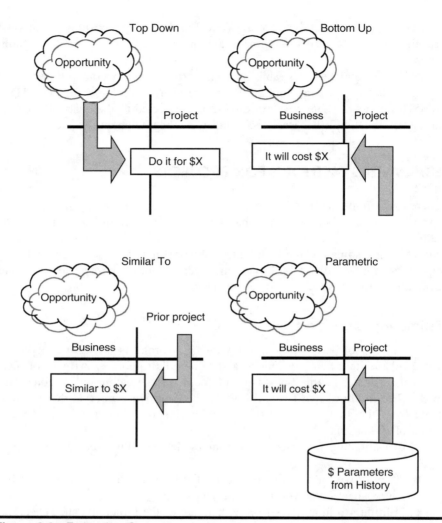

Figure 3-8 Estimating Concepts.

Top-Down Estimates

Top-down estimates could be made by anyone associated with the project, but most often top-down estimates come from the business and reflect a value judgment based on experience, marketing information, benchmarking data, consulting information, and other extra-project information. Top-down estimates rarely have concrete and verifiable facts of the type needed by the project team to validate the estimate with the scope laid out on the WBS.

Table 3-3   Top-Down Estimates

Step	Description
Receive estimates from the business	Estimates from the business reflect a judgment on the investment available given the intended scope and value to the business.
Interview business leaders to determine the intended scope	Scope is the common understanding between the business and the project. Interviews provide the opportunity to exchange information vital to project success.
Verify assumptions and validate sources, if any	The business judgment on investment and value is based on certain assumptions of the business managers and may also include collateral information that is useful to the project manager.
Develop WBS from scope	WBS must contain all the scope, but only the scope required by the business sponsors.
Allocate top-down resources to WBS	Allocation is a means of distributing the investment made possible by the business to the elements of scope on the WBS.
Cost account managers identify risks and gaps	Cost account managers have responsibility for elements of the WBS. They must assess the risk of performance based on the allocation of investment to the WBS made by the project manager.
Negotiate to minimize risks and gaps	Once the risks are quantified and understood, a confidence estimate can be made of the probability of meeting the project scope for the available investment. Negotiations with the business sponsors narrow the gap between investment and expected cost.
Top-down estimate to the business side of project balance sheet	The business makes the judgment on how much investment to make. This investment goes on the business side of the project balance sheet.
Expected value estimate and risks to project side of balance sheet	Once the allocation is made to the WBS, there is opportunity for the project manager to develop the risks to performance, the expected value, and the confidence of meeting the sponsor's objectives.

Working with top-down estimates requires the steps shown in Table 3-3. *Project risks are greatest in this estimating methodology,* and *overall cost estimates are usually lowest.* In its purest form, top-down estimating foregoes the quantitative information that could be developed by the project team regarding the project cost. Usually, if there is an independent input to cost developed by the project team, the purpose of such an independent input from the project side is to provide comparative data with the top-down estimate. Such a comparison serves to establish the range or magnitude of the risks of being able to execute the project for the top-down budget. Because risks are greatest in top-down estimating, the risks developed in response to top-down budgets require careful identification, minimization planning, and estimation before the project begins. Risks are quantified and made visible on the project side of the project balance sheet.

A common application of the top-down methodology is in competitive bidding to win a project opportunity as a contractor to the project sponsor. In this scenario, the top-down estimate usually comes from a marketing or sales assessment of what the market will bear, what the competition is bidding, and in effect *"what it will take to win."* If the top-down estimate is the figure offered to the customer as the price, then the project manager is left with the task of estimating the risk of performance and developing the risk management plan to contain performance cost within the offered price:

Top-down offer to do business = Independently estimated cost of performance offered + Risk to close gap with top-down offer

From the steps in Table 3-3, we see that the project manager must allocate the top-down budget to the WBS. Doing so involves the following quantitative steps:

- Develop the WBS from the scope statement, disregarding cost.
- By judgment, experience, prototyping, or other means, determine or identify the deliverable of least likely cost, or the deliverable that represents the smallest "standard unit of work." Give that deliverable a numerical cost weight of 1 and call it the "baseline" deliverable, B. This procedure normalizes all costs in the WBS to the cost of the least costly deliverable.
- Estimate the normalized cost of all other deliverables, D, as multiples, M, of the baseline deliverable: $D_i = M_i * B$, where M is a random variable with unknown distribution and "i" has values from 1 to n. "n" is the number of deliverables in the WBS.
- Sum all deliverable weights and divide the sum into the available funds to determine an absolute baseline cost of the least costly deliverable.

($Top-down budget)$/(\Sigma M_i)$ = Allocated cost of baseline task B

- A "sanity check" on the cost of B is now needed. Independently estimate the cost of B to determine an offset, plus or minus, between the allocated cost and the independent estimate. This offset, O, is a bias to be applied to each deliverable in the WBS. The total bias in the WBS is given by:

Total cost bias in WBS = n * O

- Complete the allocation of all top-down budgets to the deliverables in the WBS according to their weights.
- It is helpful at this point to simplify the disparate deliverables on the WBS to an average deliverable and its statistics. We know from the Central Limit Theorem that the average deliverable will be Normal distributed, so the attributes of the Normal distribution will be helpful to the project manager:

Average deliverable cost $= \alpha_d = (1/n) * \sum[D_i + (M_i * O)]$

σ^2 of average deliverable $= (1/n) * \sum[(D_i + O) - \alpha_d]^2$, and

σ of average deliverable $= \sqrt{(1/n) * \sum[(D_i + O) - \alpha_d]^2}$

It is easier to calculate these figures than it probably appears from looking at the formulas. Table 3-4 provides a numerical example. In this example, a $30,000 top-down budget is applied to a WBS of seven deliverables. An offset is estimated at 23% of the allocated cost. Immediately, it appears that there may be a $6,900 risk to manage (23% of $30,000). However, we see from the calculations employing the Normal distribution that the confidence of hitting the top-down budget is only 24%, and with the $6,900 risk included, the confidence increases to only 50%. At 68% confidence, the level needed for many firms to do fixed price bidding, the risk increases significantly. Clearly if the risk is to be reduced, then the scope will have to be downsized or the budget increased, or more time given to estimating the offsets in order for this project to go forward.

Once the risks are calculated, all the computed figures can be moved to the right side of the project balance sheet. Let us recap what we have so far. On the business side of the project balance sheet, we have the top-down budget from the project sponsors. This is a value judgment about the amount of investment that can be afforded for the deliverables desired. On the right side of the balance sheet, the project manager has the following variables:

- The estimated "fixed" bias between the cost to perform and the available budget. In the example, the bias is $6,900.
- The average WBS for this project and the statistical standard deviation of the average WBS. In this example, the average WBS is $36,900 (equal to the budget + bias) and the standard deviation is $9,616.
- And, of course, the available budget, $30,000.

Table 3-4   Top-Down Allocation to WBS

WBS Element	Weight, M_i	Allocated Budget, D_i	Allocated Budget + $(M_i * O)$	Distance^2 $(d - average\ d)^2$
a	b	c	d	e
1				
1.1.1	8	$10,435	$12,835	57,204,324
1.1.2	5	$6,522	$8,022	7,564,208
1.1.3	**1**	**$1,304**	**$1,604**	13,447,481
1.2.1	2	$2,609	$3,209	4,254,867
1.2.2	2.5	$3,260	$4,010	1,591,202
1.3.1	1.5	$1,957	$2,407	8,207,691
1.3.2	3	$3,913	$4,813	210,117
Totals:	**23**	**$30,000**	**$36,900**	92,479,890

Given: Top-down budget = $30,000
Evaluated least costly baseline deliverable, B = $1,304.35
Estimated independent cost of B = $1,604.35
Calculated baseline offset, O, = $300 = $1,604.35 − $1,304.35
n = 7
ΣM_i = 23
$\Sigma D_i = \Sigma(M_i * B)$ = $30,000

Average deliverable, **average d**, with offset = $36,900/7 = $5,271
Variance, σ^2 = 92,479,890/7 = 13,211,413
Standard deviation, σ = $3,635

Confidence calculations:
Total standard deviation of WBS = $\sqrt{7} * \sigma^2 = \sqrt{92,479,890}$ = $9,616
24% confidence: WBS total ≤ $30,000*
50% confidence: WBS total ≤ $36,900
68% confidence: WBS total ≤ $36,900 + $9,616 = $46,516

* From lookup on single-tail standard Normal table for probability of outcome = ($36,900 − $30,000)/$9,616 = 0.71σ below the mean value. Assumes summation of WBS is approximately Normal with mean = $36,900 and σ = $9,616.

As was done in the example, confidences are calculated and the overall confidence of the project is negotiated with the project sponsor until the project risks are within the risk tolerance of the business.

Similar-To Estimates

"Similar-to" estimates have many of the features of the top-down estimate except that there is a model or previous project with similar characteristics and a cost history to guide estimating. However, the starting point is the same. The business declares the new project "similar to" another completed project and provides the budget to the new project team based on the cost history of the completed project. Of course, some adjustments are often needed to correct for the escalation of labor and material costs from an earlier time frame to the present, and there may be a need to adjust for scope difference. In most cases, the "similar-to" estimate is very much like a top-down estimate except that there is usually cost history at the WBS deliverable level available to the project manager that can be used by the project estimating team to narrow the offsets. In this manner, the offsets are not uniformly proportional as they were in the top-down model, but rather they are adjusted for each deliverable to the extent that relevant cost history is available.

The quantitative methods applied to the WBS are not really any different from those we employed in the top-down case except for the individual treatment of the offsets. Table 3-5 provides an example. We assume cost history can improve the offset estimates (or provide the business with a more realistic figure to start with). If so, the confidence in budget developed by the business as a "similar to" is generally much higher.

Bottom-Up Estimating

So far we have seen that the project side of the balance sheet is usually a higher estimate than the figure given by the business. Although there is no business rule or project management practice that makes this so in every case, it does happen more often than not. That trend toward a higher project estimate continues in bottom-up estimating.

Bottom-up estimating, in its purest form, is an independent estimate by the project management team of the activities in the WBS. The estimating team may actually be several teams working in parallel on the same estimating problem. Such an arrangement is called the Delphi method. The Delphi method is an approach to bottom-up estimating whereby independent teams evaluate the same data, each team comes to an estimate, and then the project manager synthesizes a final estimate from the inputs from all teams.

The starting point for the estimating team(s) is the scope statement provided by the business. A budget from the business is provided as information and guidance. Parametric data developed from cost history are assumed to be unavailable. In practice, parametric data in some form are usually available, but we will discuss parametric data next.

Best practice in bottom-up estimating employs the "n-point" estimate rather than a single deterministic number. The number of points is commonly taken to be three: most likely, most pessimistic, and most optimistic (thus the expres-

Table 3-5   Similar-To Estimates

WBS Element	Allocated Budget from Cost History, D_i	Offset	Allocated Budget + (M_i * O)	Distance^2 (d – *average d*)^2
a	b	c	d	e
1				
1.1.1	$10,435	$200	$10,635	39,813,357
1.1.2	$6,522	–$100	$6,422	4,396,315
1.1.3	**$1,304**	$300	$1,604	7,401,948
1.2.1	$2,608	$50	$2,658	2,778,889
1.2.2	$3,261	–$75	$3,186	1,297,618
1.3.1	$1,957	$100	$2,057	5,145,994
1.3.2	$3,913	–$200	$3,713	374,491
Totals:	**$30,000**	**$275**	**$30,275**	61,208,612

Given: Top-down budget = $30,000

Evaluated least costly baseline deliverable, B = $1,304

n = 7

ΣM_i = 23

$\Sigma D_i = \Sigma(M_i * B)$ = $30,000

Average deliverable, ***average d***, with offset = $30,275/7 = $4,325
Variance, σ^2 = (1/7) * (61,208,612) = 8,744,087
Standard deviation, σ = $2,957

Confidence calculations:
Total standard deviation of WBS = $\sqrt{61,208,612}$ = $7,823
46% confidence: WBS total ≤ $30,000*
50% confidence: WBS total ≤ $30,275
68% confidence: WBS total ≤ $30,275 + $7,823 = $38,098

* From lookup on single-tail standard Normal table for probability of outcome = ($30,275 – $30,000)/$2,957 = 0.09σ below the mean value. Assumes summation of WBS is approximately Normal with mean = $30,275 and σ = $2,957.

sion "three-point estimates"). A distribution must be selected to go with the three-point estimate. The Normal, BETA, and Triangular are the distributions of choice by project managers. The BETA and Triangular are used for individual activities and deliverables; the Normal is a consequence of the interaction of many BETA or Triangular distributions in the same WBS. However, if there are deliverables with symmetrical optimistic and pessimistic values, then the Normal is used in those cases.

Table 3-6 provides a numerical example of bottom-up estimating using the BETA distribution. Recall that the Triangular distribution will give more pessimistic statistics than the BETA. Although individual deliverables are esti-

Table 3-6   Bottom-Up Estimates

WBS Element	Most Likely Estimate	Most Pessimistic Offset	Most Optimistic Offset	BETA Expected Value	BETA Variance
1					
1.1.1	$11,000	$3,000	−$1,000	$11,333	444,444
1.1.2	$6,800	$4,000	−$700	$7,350	613,611
1.1.3	$1,500	$800	−$300	$1,583	33,611
1.2.1	$3,000	$2,000	−$500	$3,250	173,611
1.2.2	$3,100	$1,800	−$750	$3,275	180,625
1.3.1	$1,800	$800	−$300	$1,883	33,611
1.3.2	$3,700	$1,900	−$600	$3,917	173,611
Totals:				**$32,591**	**1,653,124**

Business desires project outcome = $30,000

Average deliverable from BETA = $32,591/7 = $4,656
Variance, σ^2 = 1,653,124/7 = 236,161
Standard deviation, σ = $486

Confidence calculations:
Total standard deviation of WBS = $\sqrt{1,653,124}$ = $1,286
50% confidence: WBS total ≤ $32,591*
68% confidence: WBS total ≤ $32,591 + $1,286 = $33,877

* Assumes approximately Normal distribution of WBS summation with mean = $32,594 and
  σ = $1,286.

mated with somewhat wide swings in optimistic and pessimistic range, overall the confidence of hitting a lower number with greater certainty is higher.

Parametric Estimating

Parametric estimating is also called model estimating. Parametric estimating depends on cost history and an estimate of similarity between that project history available to the model and the project being estimated. Parametric estimating is employed widely in many industries, and industry-specific models are well published and supported by the experiences of many practitioners.* The software industry is a case in point with several models in wide use. So also

---

* A current listing of some of the prominent sources of information about parametric estimating can be found in "Appendix E, Listing of WEB Sites for Professional Societies, Educational Institutions, and Supplementary Information," of the Joint Industry/Government "Parametric Estimating Handbook," Second Edition, 1999, sponsored by the Department of Defense. Among the listings found in Appendix E are those for the American Society of Professional Estimators, International Society of Parametric Analysis, and the Society of Cost Estimating and Analysis.

do the general industry that builds hardware, as well as the construction industry, environmental industry, pharmaceuticals, and many others have many good
models in place. The general characteristics of some of these models are given
in Table 3-7.

Table 3-7   Parametric Estimating Models

Estimating Application	Model Identification	Key Model Parameters and Calibration Factors	Model Outcome
Construction	PACES 2001	Covers new construction, renovation, and alteration	Specific cost estimates (not averages) of specified construction according to model
		Covers buildings, site work, area work	
		Regression model based on cost history in military construction	
		Input parameters (abridged list): size, building type, foundation type, exterior closure type, roofing type, number of floors, functional and utility space requirements	Project costs

Life cycle costs |
		Media/waste type: cleanup facilities and methods	
Environmental	RACER	Handles natural attenuation, free product removal, passive water treatment, minor field installation, O&M, and phytoremediation	Programming and budgetary estimates for remedial environmental projects
		Technical enhancements to over 20 technologies	
		Ability to use either system costs or user-defined costs	
		Professional labor template that creates task percentage template	
Hardware	Price H®	Key parameters: weight, size, and manufacturing complexity	Cost estimates

Other parameter reports |
| | | Input parameters: quantities of equipment to be developed, design inventory in existence, operating environment and hardware specifications, production schedules, manufacturing processes, labor attributes, financial accounting attributes | |

Table 3-7 Parametric Estimating Models (continued)

Estimating Application	Model Identification	Key Model Parameters and Calibration Factors	Model Outcome
	SEER H®	WBS oriented	Production cost estimates, schedules, and risks associated with hardware development and acquisition
		Six knowledge bases support the WBS elements: application, platform, optional description, acquisition category, standards, class	
		Cost estimates are produced for development and production cost activities (18) and labor categories (14), as well as "other" categories (4)	
	NAFCOM (NASA Air Force Cost Model)	WBS oriented	Estimates design, development, test, and evaluation (DDT&E) flight unit, production, and total (DDT&E + production) costs
		Subsystem oriented within the WBS	
	Available to qualified government contractors and agencies	Labor rate inputs, overhead, and G&A costs Integration point inputs Test hardware and quantity Production rates Complexity factors Test throughput factors	
		Integrates with some commercial estimating models	
Software	COCOMO 81 (waterfall methodology)	Development environment: detached, embedded, organic	Effort and duration in staff hours or months
		Model complexity: basic, intermediate, detailed	
		Parameters used to calibrate outcome (abridged list): estimated delivered source lines of code, product attributes, computer attributes, personnel attributes, project attributes (with breakdown of attributes, about 63 parameters altogether)	Other parametric reports
	COCOMO II (object oriented)	Development stages: applications composition, early design, post architecture (modified COCOMO 81)	Effort and duration in staff hours or months

Table 3-7   Parametric Estimating Models (continued)

Estimating Application	Model Identification	Key Model Parameters and Calibration Factors	Model Outcome
		Parameters used to calibrate outcome (abridged list): estimated source lines of code, function points, COCOMO 81 parameters (with some modification), productivity rating (Stage 1)	Other parametric reports
	Price S	Nine categories for attributes: project magnitude, program application, productivity factor, design inventory, utilization, customer specification and reliability, development environment, difficulty, and development process	Effort and duration in staff hours or months Other parametric reports
	SEER-SEM	Three categories for attributes: size, knowledge base, input Input is further subdivided into 15 parameter types very similar to the other models discussed	Effort and duration in staff hours or months Other parametric reports

Most parametric models are "regression models." We will discuss regression analysis in Chapter 8. Regression models require data sets from past performance in order that a regression formula can be derived. The regression formula is used to predict or forecast future performance. Thus, to employ parametric models they first must be calibrated with cost history. Calibration requires some standardization of the definition of deliverable items and item attributes. A checklist specific to the model or to the technology or process being modeled is a good device for obtaining consistent and complete history records. For instance, to use a software model, the definition of a line of code is needed, and the attributes of complexity or difficulty require definitions. In publications, the page size and composition require definition, as well as the type of original material that is to be received and published. Typically, more than ten projects are needed to obtain good calibration, but the requirements of cost history are model specific.

Once a calibrated model is in hand, to obtain estimates of deliverable costs the model is fed with parameter data of the project being estimated. Model parameters are also set or adjusted to account for similarity or dissimilarity between the project being estimated and the project history. Parameter data could be the estimated number of lines of software code to be written and their appropriate attributes, such as degree of difficulty or complexity. Usually, a methodology is incorporated into the model. That is to say, if the methodology for developing software involves requirements development, prototyping, code and unit test, and system tests, then the model takes this methodology into account. Some models also allow for specification of risk factors as well as the severity of those risks.

Outcomes of the model are applied directly to the deliverables on the WBS. At this point, outcomes are no different than bottom-up estimates. Ordinarily, these outcomes are expected values since the model will have taken into account the risk factors and methodology to arrive at a statistically useful result. The model may or may not provide other statistical information, such as the variance, standard deviation, or information about any distributions employed. If only the expected value is provided, then the project manager must decide whether to use some independent evaluation to develop statistics that can be used to develop confidence intervals. The model outcome may also specify or identify dependencies accounted for in the result; as we saw in the discussion of covariance, dependencies change the risk factors.

Table 3-8 provides a numerical example of parametric estimating practices in the WBS.

Estimating "Completion" versus "Level of Effort"

In almost every project there are some WBS elements for which the tasks and activities of a deliverable cannot be scoped with certainty. Estimates for cost accounts of this type are called "level of effort." Level of effort describes a concept of indefinite scope and application of "best effort" by the provider. How then to contain the risk of the estimate? We call on three-point estimates, a sober look at the most pessimistic possibilities, and the use of statistical estimates to get a handle on the range of outcomes.

Completion estimates are definitive in scope, though perhaps uncertain in total cost or schedule. After all, even with a specific scope there are risks. Nevertheless, completion estimates have a specific inclusion of tasks, a most likely estimate of resource requirement, and an expectation of a specific and measurable deliverable at the end. In the examples presented in this chapter, the underlying concept is completion.

Let us consider a couple of examples where level of effort is appropriate. Project management itself is usually assigned to a WBS cost account just for management tasks. Although there are tangible outcomes of project management, like plans, schedules, and budgets, the fact is that the only real evidence of successful completion of the cost account is successful completion of the project. Work packages and cost accounts of this type

Table 3-8   Parametric Estimating

WBS Element	Deliverable	Units	Quantity	Parametric Cost	Model Expected Value	Model Standard Deviation, σ	Calculated Variance, σ^2
1							
1.1.1	Software code	Lines of code	5,000	$25	$125,000	$25,000	625,000,000
1.1.2	Software test plans	Pages	500	$400	$200,000	$10,000	100,000,000
1.1.3	Software requirements	Numbered items	800	$100	$80,000	$12,000	144,000,000
1.2.1	Tested module	Unit tests	2,000	$100	$200,000	$30,000	900,000,000
1.2.2	Integrated module	Integration points	1,800	$50	$90,000	$3,500	12,250,000
1.3.1	Training manuals	Pages	800	$400	$320,000	$4,000	16,000,000
1.3.2	Training delivery	Students	900	$500	$450,000	$5,000	25,000,000
Totals:					$1,465,000		1,822,250,000

Average deliverable from model = $1,465,000/7 = $209,286
Variance, σ^2 = 1,822,250,000/7 = 260,321,429
Standard deviation, $\sigma = \sqrt{260,321,429}$ = $16,134

Confidence calculations:
Standard deviation of total expected value = $\sqrt{(1,822,250,000)}$ = $42,687
50% confidence: WBS total ≤ $1,465,000*
68% confidence: WBS total ≤ $1,465,000 + $42,687 = $1,507,687

* Assumes approximately Normal distribution of WBS summation with mean = $1,465,000 and σ = $42,687.

are usually estimated from parametric models and "similar-to" estimates, but the total scope is indefinite.

Research and development efforts for "new to the world" discoveries are an obvious case for level of effort, particularly where the root problem is vague or unknown or where the final outcome is itself an "ah-hah!" and not specifically known in advance. In projects of this type, it is appropriate to base funding on an allocation of total resources available to the business, set somewhat short-term milestones for intermediate results, and base the WBS on level of effort tasks. If prior experience can be used to establish parameters to guide the estimating, then that is all to the advantage of the project sponsor and the project manager.

SUMMARY OF IMPORTANT POINTS

Table 3-9 provides the highlights of this chapter.

Table 3-9 Summary of Important Points

Point of Discussion	Summary of Ideas Presented
Work definition and scoping	▪ Organizing and defining the project scope of work is a *required prerequisite* to all analytical estimates concerning projects. ▪ The WBS serves two purposes: (1) organizing the work and (2) providing data on the project deliverables. ▪ The WBS is not a project organization chart or a project schedule. ▪ The WBS may support more than one view of the project: sponsor's view, developer's view, operations and maintenance view. ▪ Most often, the WBS is a hierarchical structure of the project deliverables.
The OBS and RAM	▪ The people who work on projects may be assigned exclusively to the project or participate in the project and a "home" organization. The "home" organization breakdown structure is called the OBS. ▪ The OBS maps to the WBS by means of the RAM.
Work packages and cost accounts	▪ The work package is the lowest level of work identified with cost on the WBS. ▪ The cost account is a summation of subordinate work packages.
Chart of accounts	▪ The chart of accounts is a WBS of the business organized by financial accounts like expense accounts, capital accounts, and equity accounts. ▪ The WBS is typically an extension of the chart of accounts structure, touching expense and capital accounts most often.
WBS dictionary	▪ The WBS dictionary of a set of definitions of the work packages and cost accounts on the WBS.

Table 3-9   Summary of Important Points (continued)

Point of Discussion	Summary of Ideas Presented
WBS baseline	▪ The WBS baseline is the scope and cost decided on at the outset of the contract. The baseline is managed as a fixed set of numbers until changed through a change management process.
Project estimates	▪ The objectives of performing an estimate are twofold: to arrive at an expected value for the item being estimated and to be able to convey a figure of merit for that estimate.
Top-down estimates	▪ Top-down value judgments from the business side of the project balance sheet conveyed to the project team.
Similar-to estimates	▪ Similar-to judgments from either side of the project balance sheet, but most often from the other business side.
Bottom-up estimates	▪ Bottom-up facts-driven estimates of actual work effort from the project side of the project balance sheet conveyed to the project sponsor.
Parametric estimates	▪ Parametric calculations from a cost-history model, developed by the project team, and conveyed to the project sponsor.
Confidence intervals in estimates	▪ Every estimate should include some assessment of the risk of completing the project for the estimated figures. ▪ The Normal distribution is invoked by means of the Central Limit Theorem to describe the project outcome distribution probabilities. ▪ Cumulative probabilities from statistical distributions provide the data to assess the confidence of meeting the project outcome. ▪ Confidence intervals can be estimated for any WBS regardless of the estimating methodology.
Completion and level of effort estimates	▪ Level of effort is appropriate where the scope is indefinite. ▪ Completion should be used whenever it is possible to make the scope definitive.

REFERENCES

1. Editor, MIL-HDBK-881, OUSD(A&T)API/PM, U.S. Department of Defense, Washington, D.C., 1998, paragraph 1.4.2.
2. Ibid, paragraph 1.6.3.
3. Haugan, Gregory T., *Effective Work Breakdown Structures*, Management Concepts, Vienna, VA, 2001, chap. 1, pp. 7–13.
4. *A Guide to the Project Management Body of Knowledge (PMBOK® Guide)* — 2000 Edition, Project Management Institute, Newtown Square, PA, chap. 5.
5. Ibid., chap. 2.

4

MAKING QUANTITATIVE DECISIONS

Decision analysis...is the discipline for helping decision makers choose wisely under conditions of uncertainty.

John Schuyler
Risk and Decision Analysis in Projects, 2001

In this chapter we will discuss making project decisions using quantitative methods. We will focus on the so-called decision tree and its companion, the decision table. Quantitative decisions, whether in trees or tables, often employ an interesting extension of statistical methods called Bayes' Theorem. We will take a look at Bayes' Theorem and see how it can help with making decisions conditioned on other decisions and events.

A PROJECT POLICY FOR DECISIONS

Quantitative decision making is most useful when there is a rational policy for obtaining the outcomes. Rationality, used in this sense, means that the decision is a consequence of all the inputs having been applied systematically to a decision-making methodology. Given the inputs and the methodology, the decision outcomes are predictable. If only it were so easy in real projects!

Decision Policy Elements

Consider what many would say are necessary policy elements in order that quantitative decisions can be made.*

Let's start with an obvious one. If we are trying to choose between one project or another, the first element of decision policy is that we would give priority to those projects that are traceable to goals through strategy. If such is the case, we are assured that the deliverables, applied according to the concept of operations, will yield benefits to the business.

Second, all things otherwise being equal, we would decide in favor of that initiative that brings the most financial gain to the business. Now, if the project or initiative is in the public sector, this principle might not be second. Indeed, this principle may not even be a part of the decision policy. But for profit-making businesses, the financial benefit is always available as a tiebreaker.

Third, as among financial benefits, we would decide in favor of those benefits that are measurable consequences of project outcomes. If cause and effect can be established, then we say we have a consequential benefit. Project managers call such benefits "hard benefits." For example, a project targeted as improving operational efficiency has hard benefits if the cost input of the organization is reduced as a result of project activity. However, if the benefit of the project is "avoided increased costs" in the future, then the benefits are said to be "soft." Between two projects with benefits as described above, the former would have precedence over the latter.

Sometimes financial benefits are not specifically estimated. Project managers say that there is no ROI (return on investment) for the project. Such can be the case for projects in the public sector, but so can it also be the case for research projects. Corporate "internal research and development (IR&D)" projects are done many times because we must explore and innovate. The invention of nylon is said to be more of an accident than anything planned. Was going to the moon in the Apollo program decided on the basis of an ROI? No, but there were benefits set for Apollo and its companion Mercury and Gemini programs. As a matter of policy, projects that advance the mission or respond directly to the commitments of senior managers are often selected first.

Policy should dictate that a quantitative statistical estimate of risk be made. Each risk has a downside and an upside. Every manager and every organization has a risk tolerance. Tolerance usually controls the downside. If the downside is unaffordable, the decision may be that the project cannot go forward. So the

---

* These principles of decision policies are a summarization of the author's experience in many project situations over many years. The material is an expansion of that given in the author's book, *Managing Projects for Value.*[2]

policy statement is that for projects of equal quantitative risk estimates, the project that is most risk averse is to be selected over projects of greater risk; if the downside risk exceeds a threshold, then the project cannot be selected, even if it is the least risky of all alternatives.

Finally, the policy should always state that projects must be lawful, ethical, and consistent with all regulatory controls and organizational policies. Of course, the latter two are subject to waivers and set-asides by senior authority.

Table 4-1 summarizes the rational decision-making discussion.

Table 4-1   Decision Policy Elements

Policy Element	Policy Justification
Project alternatives traceable to business goals and strategies	Project choices are most supported and more likely to result in recognizable business results when the choices have clear links to the business goals and strategies. Such linkage is all the more important when the project's resources are challenged for reassignment elsewhere, or when project risks call into question the wisdom of proceeding to invest in the project's progress.
Financial advantage is a tie breaker	Almost all projects have some functional benefit to the business. The only common denominator universally recognized and understood by all business managers is the dollar value returned to the business for having done the project. In the face of essentially equal functional benefit to the business, the tie breaker is always the financial advantage brought to the business by the project. The project with greatest advantage is selected.
Hard benefits trump soft benefits	Hard benefits are measurable and tangible and have clear cause–effect relationships to the project; hard benefits are most often measured in dollars and are therefore most easily understood and evaluated by business leaders. Soft benefits have uncertain cause–effect and the benefits to the business are largely functional. Soft benefits are often difficult to reduce to dollars. The "before and after" principle can be invoked to obtain dollars, but the cause–effect ambiguity discounts the dollars calculated in such a method.
Mission trumps financial when directed by senior authority	Sometimes "we have to do it" and the dollars are much less important. Technically speaking, such a decision is not "rational" based on the definition used in this book, but the decision is most certainly rational considered in a larger context often not involving the project manager or sponsor.
The least risky project trumps a more risky project	All else being equal, a project of lesser risk is always chosen over one with more risk.
All alternatives are legal, ethical, and in compliance with regulation and policy	Project choices should reflect the standards of conduct of the organization. American business usually adopts a standard that prohibits behavior that would jeopardize the business and obviate any benefits returned from the project.

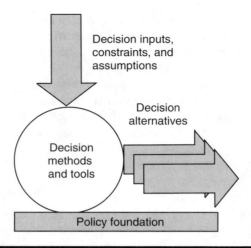

Figure 4-1   Context for Decisions.

A Context for Quantitative Decisions

Figure 4-1 illustrates the space containing policy, method, inputs, and outcomes. Policy we have discussed. Specific methods will be discussed in subsequent sections, but methods are the tools and processes we apply to input to generate outcomes. Processes can invoke or be constrained by policy, such as applying the hurdle rate for internal rate of return (IRR) and being held to the number of years that go into the calculation. Such policies may be project specific or project portfolio specific, with different figures for each. We will discuss IRR and other financial measures in another chapter.

Inputs are all the descriptions, data, assumptions, constraints, and experience that can be assembled about a prospective project, event, or alternative that is to be decided. Project managers should have wide latitude to bring any and all relevant material to the decision process. Policy will control the application of input to method, so there is no need to otherwise constrain the assembling of input. The first bit of input needed is a description of the scope of the thing being decided: Is it a choice among projects; a choice among implementation alternatives; a choice of tools, staff, or resources to be applied in a project; or just what? Decisions, by their very nature, are choices among competing alternatives, so a full and complete scope statement of each choice is required. The second component of input is all the attributes of the alternatives. Attributes could include cost, availability, time to develop or deliver, size, weight, color, or any number of other modifiers that distinguish one alternative from another. Third, of course, if there are any constraints (whether physical, logical, mathematical, regulatory, or other), then whatever constraints apply should be scoped and given a full measure of attributes as well.

Once all the inputs, assumptions, experience, and constraints are assembled and organized into separable choices, then a decision methodology can be applied. The fact is that many project managers have trouble organizing the choices and fail to resolve the "if, and, or but" problems of presenting alternatives. However, assembling the choices is the place to stop if the team cannot decide what the alternatives are. If the choices are ambiguous, there is no point in expending the energy to make a decision.

The Utility Concept in Decision Making

When the project manager begins to apply the decision policy to the project situation, the risk attitudes of the decision makers need to be taken into account. If the decision maker is risk neutral, then the decisions will be based on the risk-adjusted estimates without regard to the affordability of the downside or the strategy to exploit the opportunities of the upside. However, decisions are rarely risk neutral if the amount at stake is material to the well being of the organization. In situations where the decision making takes into account the absolute affordability of an opportunity, we call decision making of this type "risk averse." A quantitative view of this concept is embodied in the idea of "utility." Utility simply means that the decision maker's view of risk is either discounted or amplified compared to the risk-neutral view. Figure 4-2 shows this concept. The principal application to projects is evaluating the downside risks attendant to one or more alternatives that are up for a decision. Regardless of the advantageous expected value of a particular opportunity, if its downside is a "bet the company" risk, then the decision may well go against the opportunity.

THE DECISION TREE

The decision tree is a tool to be applied in a decision methodology. In effect, the decision tree, and its cousin the decision table, sums up all the expected values of each of the alternatives being decided and presents those expected values to the decision maker. At the root of the tree is the decision itself. Extending out from the root is the branch structure representing various paths from the root (decision) to the choices. For those familiar with the "fishbone" diagram from the Total Quality Management toolkit, the decision tree will look very familiar. Along the pathways or branches of the decision tree are quantitative values that are summed along the way at summing nodes. Normally, the project manager makes the decision by following the organization's decision

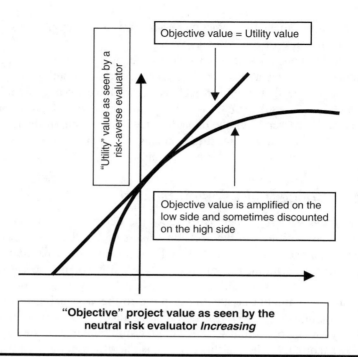

Figure 4-2   Utility Function.

policy in favor of the most advantageous quantitative value. In some cases, deciding most advantageously means picking the larger value, but sometimes the most advantageous value is the smaller one.

The Basic Tree for Projects

Figure 4-3 shows the basic layout. It is customary, as described by John Schuyler in his book, *Risk and Decision Analysis in Projects, Second Edition,*[1] to show the tree laying on its side with the root to the left. Such an orientation facilitates adding to the tree by adding paper to the right. We use a somewhat standard notation: the square is the decision node; the decision node is labeled with the statement of the decision needed. Circles are summing nodes for quantitative values of alternatives or of different probabilistic outcomes. Diamonds are the starting point for random variables, and the triangle is the starting point for deterministic variables.

In Figure 4-3, the decision maker is trying to decide between alternative "A" and alternative "B". There are several components to each decision as

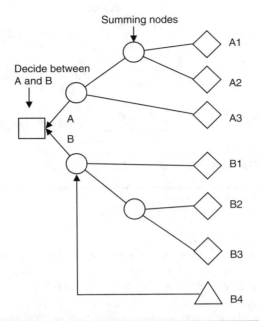

Figure 4-3   Decision Tree.

illustrated on the far right of the figure. Summing nodes combine the disparate inputs until there is a value for "A" and a value for "B". An example of a decision of this character is well known to project managers: "make or buy a particular deliverable."

Since our objective is to arrive at the decision node with a quantitative value for "A" and "B" so that the project manager can pick according to best advantage to the project, we apply values in the following way:

- Fixed deterministic values, whether positive or negative, are usually shown on the connectors between summing nodes or as inputs to a summing node. We will show them as inputs to the summing node.
- Random variable values are assigned a value and a probability, one such value–probability pair on each connector into the summing node. The summing node then sums the expected value (value * probability) for all its inputs. Naturally, the probabilities of all random variables leading to a summing node must sum to 1. Thus, the project manager must be cognizant of the 1-p space as the inputs are arrayed on the decision tree.

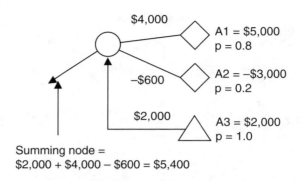

Summing node =
$2,000 + $4,000 − $600 = $5,400

Figure 4-4   Summing Node Detail.

Figure 4-4 shows a simple example of how the summing node works. Alternative "A" is a risky proposition: it has an upside of $5,000 with 0.8 probability, but it has a downside potential of −$3,000 with a 0.2 probability. "A" also requires a fixed procurement of $2,000 in order to complete the scope of "A". The expected value of the risky components of "A" is $3,400. Combined with the $2,000 fixed expenditure, "A" has an expected value of $5,400 at this node. The most pessimistic outcome of "A" at this node is −$1,000: $2,000 − $3,000; the most optimistic figure is $7,000: $2,000 + $5,000. These figures provide the range of threat and opportunity that make up the risk characteristics of "A".

Now, let's add in the possibility of event "A_4". The situation is shown in Figure 4-5. If the project team estimates the probability of occurrence of "A_4" as 0.4, then the probability of the events on the other leg coming into the final summing node becomes equal to the "1-p" of "A_4", or 0.6. Adding risk-weighted values, we come to a final conclusion that the expected value of "A" is $4,840.

The most pessimistic outcome of "A" at this node remains −$1,000 since if "$A_2$" should occur, "$A_1$" and "$A_4$" will not; the most optimistic figure remains $7,000 since if "$A_1$" occurs, then the other two will not. If "A_4" should occur, then "A_1" and "A_2" will not. However, "A_3" is deterministic; "A_3" always occurs. So the optimistic value with "A_4" is $6,000: $2,000 + $4,000. Obviously, $6,000 is less than the outcome with "A_1".

If the analysis of "B" done in similar manner to that of "A" should result in "B" having a value less than $4,840, the decision would be to pick "A". Of course, the risk tolerance of the business must be accommodated. At the decision node there will be an expected value for "A" and another of "B". The project manager can follow the tree branches and determine the most pessimis-

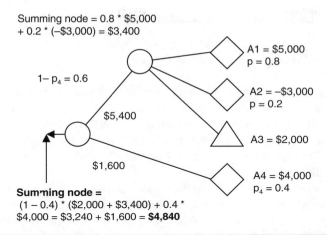

Summing node = 0.8 * $5,000
+ 0.2 * (–$3,000) = $3,400

$1– p_4 = 0.6$

A1 = $5,000
p = 0.8

A2 = –$3,000
p = 0.2

$5,400

A3 = $2,000

$1,600

A4 = $4,000
$p_4 = 0.4$

Summing node =
(1 – 0.4) * ($2,000 + $3,400) + 0.4 *
$4,000 = $3,240 + $1,600 = **$4,840**

Figure 4-5   Summing Node A.

tic outcomes. If the most pessimistic outcomes fit within the risk tolerance of the business, then the outcome, "A" or "B", is decided on the basis of best advantage to the project and to the business. If the most pessimistic outcomes are not within the risk tolerance of the business, and if there is not a satisfactory plan for mitigating the risks to a tolerable level, then the choice of project defaults to the decision policy element of picking on the basis of the risk to the business. Risk managing the most pessimistic outcome is a subject unto itself and beyond the scope of this book.

By now you may have picked up on a couple of key points about decision trees. First, all the A_is and B_is must be identified in order to have a fair and complete input set to the methodology. The responsibility for assembling estimates for the A_is and B_is rests with the project manager and the project team. Second, there is a need to estimate the probability of an occurrence for each discrete input. Again, the project team is left with the task of coming up with these probabilities. The estimating task may not be straightforward. Delphi techniques* applied to bottom-up estimates or other estimating approaches may be required. Last, the judgment regarding risk tolerance is subjective. The concept of tolerance itself is subjective, and then the ability of the project team to adequately mitigate the risk is a judgment as well.

---

* The Delphi technique refers to an approach to bottom-up estimating whereby independent teams evaluate the same data, each team comes to an estimate, and then the project manager synthesizes a final estimate from the inputs of all teams.

A Project Example with Decision Tree

Let's see how a specific project example might work with the decision tree methodology learned so far. Here is the scenario:

- You are the project manager making a make or buy decision on a particular item on the work breakdown structure (WBS). Alternative "A" is "make the item" and alternative "B" is "buy the item."
- There are risks in both alternatives. The primary risk is that if the outcome of either "A" or "B" is late, the delay will cost the project $10,000 per day.
- If you decide to make the item, alternative "A", then there is a fixed materials and labor charge of $125,000. If you decide to buy the item, alternative "B", there is a fixed purchase cost of $200,000. Putting risks aside, "A" seems to be the more attractive by a wide margin.
- Although manufacturing costs are fixed, your team estimates there is a 60% chance the "make" activity will be 20 days late. Your judgment is that you simply do not have a lot of control over in-house resources that do not report to you. However, your team's estimate is that there is only a 20% chance the "buy" activity will be late 20 days, and the purchase price is fixed.

What is your decision? Figure 4-6 shows the decision tree for this project scenario. The decision node is the decision you are seeking: "make or buy." The tree branches lead back through each of the two alternatives. Inputs to the decision-making process are both quantitative and qualitative or judgmental. You know the manufacturing cost, the alternative procurement cost, and the cost of a day's delay in the project. You make judgments about the performance expectations of your in-house manufacturing department and about the performance of an alternative vendor. Perhaps there is a project history you can access of former "similar-to" projects that provide the data for the judgments.

As the mathematics show, there is only a $5,000 difference between these two alternatives when all the risk adjustments are factored into the calculation. In fact, the decision favors a "buy" based on the decision policy element to take the alternative of most advantage to the project, just the opposite from the initial conclusion made before risk was taken into account.

How about the downside considerations? If you make the item and the 20-day delay materializes, you are out $325,000. If you buy the item and the 20-day delay happens, you are out $400,000. Since you budget for expected value, either $245,000 or $240,000, the most pessimistic figures provide the information about how much unbudgeted downside risk you are managing:

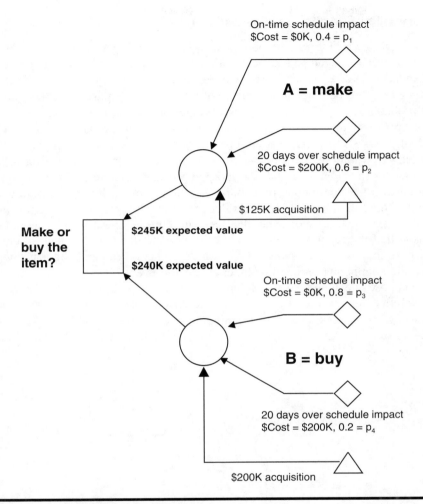

On-time schedule impact
$Cost = $0K, 0.4 = p_1

A = make

20 days over schedule impact
$Cost = $200K, 0.6 = p_2

$125K acquisition

Make or buy the item?

$245K expected value

$240K expected value

On-time schedule impact
$Cost = $0K, 0.8 = p_3

B = buy

20 days over schedule impact
$Cost = $200K, 0.2 = p_4

$200K acquisition

Figure 4-6 Project Decision Example.

Downside risk (buy) $\leq$ \$240,000 − (\$200,000 + \$200,000) = −\$160,000

or

Downside risk (make) $\leq$ \$245,000 − (\$125,000 + \$200,000) = −\$80,000

You, or your project sponsor, must also decide if the unbudgeted risk is affordable if all risk mitigations fail and the 20-day delay occurs.

Probability Functions in Decision Trees

You might be asking: What about delays other than 20 days, or why 20 days? The project manager and project team may be able to estimate much finer segments than 20 days. There really is no limit to how many individual discrete estimates could be made and summed at a node. It is required that the sum of all probabilities equal 1. So as more discrete estimates are made, say for 1, 2, 5, 10, or other days of delay, the individual probabilities must be made individually less so that the total summation of the "p"s equaling 1 is honored.

Now you may recognize this discussion as similar to the discussion in the chapter on statistics regarding the morphing of the discrete probability distribution into the continuous probability function. Obviously, the values at the input of the summing node are the values from the discrete probability function of the random variable or event that feeds into the summing node. There is no reason that the random variable could not be continuous rather than discrete. There is no reason that the discrete probability function cannot be replaced with a single continuous probability function for the event.

Suppose the inputs to the summing nodes are replaced with continuous probability functions for a continuous random variable. Figure 4-7 shows such a case. Now comes the task of summing these continuous functions. We know we can sum the expected values, and if they are independent random variables,

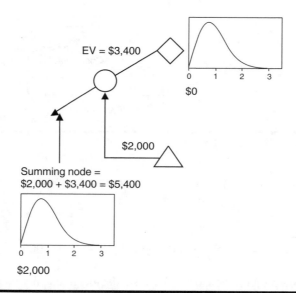

Figure 4-7   Decision Tree with Continuous Distribution.

we know we can sum the variances with simple arithmetic. However, to sum the distribution functions to arrive at a distribution function at the decision square is another matter. The mathematics for such a summing task is complex. The best approach is to use a Monte Carlo simulation in the decision tree. For such a simulation you will need software tools, but they are available.

DECISION TABLES

Let's see how the example just discussed would look in a decision table. Tables are alternatives to diagrams and often work better than diagrams because they are much easier to work with if the number of summing nodes is more than a couple. Table 4-2 shows the decision we have just worked on in tabular format. Tables, like their diagram counterpart, handle discrete inputs very well, and because tables can easily be computed on spreadsheets or from databases, tables are excellent tools for decision analysis. Maintenance of information is much easier on a spreadsheet or in a database compared to a graphical depiction. We are all familiar with the calculation power of spreadsheets: a single number entry can be recalculated automatically throughout the entire spreadsheet. It is harder to do that with a graphic, which requires less common tools than spreadsheets if a graphic of even small complexity is to be maintained.

For the remaining examples in this book, we will rely more on decision tables. We will use decision trees only when the tree form more easily conveys the concepts we are discussing.

DECISIONS WITH CONDITIONS

It would be nice if, but it is rare that, project managers can make decisions without consideration for other activities or constraints going on in the project.

Table 4-2   Project Decision Example

Alternative ID	Description	Probability of Schedule Delay	Face Value of Delay, *D*, @ $10,000 per Day	Expected Value of Delay	Acquisition Cost	Expected Value of Alternative
A	MAKE	0.6 Yes 0.4 No	$200,000 Yes $0 No	$120,000	$125,000	$245,000
B	BUY	0.2 Yes 0.8 No	$200,000 Yes $0 No	$40,000	$200,000	$240,000

Other activities that bear on the decision complicate matters somewhat on the decision tree. Such activities "condition" the decision. Generally, conditions are of two types: independent conditions that establish prerequisites but do not in and of themselves affect performance thereafter, and dependent conditions that do affect performance. An example of an independent condition is that of a sponsor deciding whether or not to exercise a scope option, and then a make–buy decision by the project team that is conditioned only on the sponsor's decision to buy or not.

On the other hand, dependent conditions affect performance or value. That is to say, the performance in a project work package is conditioned on the first decision made. Using the foregoing example, if the sponsor's decision in some way affected the expected value of the maker or provider decision, then the project decision is dependent on the sponsor's decision.

Decisions with Independent Conditions

Let us first discuss the project situation of a decision to be made conditioned on the prior or prerequisite activity of some other work package or some other external event. However, let us say that the alternatives we are deciding between per se are not affected by the prerequisite; just our ability to make decisions about the alternatives is affected.

For illustrating decision making in the context of independent conditions, we will continue with the decision scenario we have been developing in this chapter. The matter before the project team for decision is whether or not to make or buy an item on the WBS. Now, let us impose a condition that is independent of the performance of the in-house manufacturing or of the performance of the vendor if selected:

- The make or buy decision is conditioned on whether or not the project sponsor exercises an option to have the item included in the project deliverables. That is to say, the WBS item in question is optional with the sponsor. It is up to the sponsor to say whether or not it is to be delivered.
- The sponsor's decision is a random variable, S, with values 1 or 0. $S = 1$ means the item will be included in the project deliverables; $S = 0$ means it will not be included. Once this prerequisite is satisfied, then the project team can make the decision about make or buy.
- The performance, D, of the subsequent make or buy is independent of the sponsor's decision unless the sponsor decides not to exercise the option for the item. In that case, there would be no subsequent make or buy.

■ Our account manager dealing with the sponsor estimates that there is a 75% chance the sponsor will decide in favor of exercising the option for the item. Probability of $S = 1$ is 0.75. In the "1-p" space there is a 25% chance the sponsor will not exercise the option for the item: probability of $S = 0$ is 0.25.

Under these new circumstances, what is the decision of the project team, what is the expected value of the item, and what are the downside considerations? We proceed as follows: We must add columns to the decision table to take into account the preconditioning of the sponsor's decision, S, about adding the item to the project deliverables. We then recalculate the outcomes taking special care to account for all events in the "1-p" spaces. Table 4-3 illustrates the results.

Following the mathematics through the table row by row, you can see that the probability of the decision by the sponsor weights the probability of a subsequent delay and weights the acquisition cost. By this we mean that there could only be performance if the sponsor decides favorably to go forward and include the item in the project deliverables. Overall, the probability of delay is the probability that the sponsor makes the decision favorably times the probability of delay given that the decision is favorable. Certainly if the sponsor decides unfavorably, $S = 0$, so that there is to be no item in the project deliverables, and there is no chance for a delay.

Summing the buy and the make from Table 4-3:

Expected value (buy) = $0 + \$180,000 = \$180,000$

Expected value (make) = $0 + \$183,750 = \$183,750$

Under the conditions of the scenario in Tables 4-2 and 4-3, we see that the decision is not changed: it is still "buy." We further see that the expected value of the final decision, \$180,000, has a higher unbudgeted downside risk compared to the decision tree without conditions:

Downside risk (make) $\leq \$183,750 - (\$125,000 \text{ acquisition} + \$200,000 \text{ delay})$
$\leq -\$141,250$

Upside (make) = \$125,000, the acquisition cost without delay

Downside risk (buy) $\leq \$180,000 - (\$200,000 \text{ acquisition} + \$200,000 \text{ delay})$
$\leq -\$220,000$

Upside (buy) = \$200,000, the acquisition cost without delay

Table 4-3   Decision with Independent Conditions

Alternative ID	Description	Probability Sponsor Exercises Option	Sponsor's Decision Value, S	Probability of 20-Day Schedule Overrun	Face Value of Delay, D, @ $10,000 per Day	EV of Delay, D (p of Option * p of Overrun * $Face Value * Sponsor's Decision Value)	EV of Acquisition Cost (p of Option * $Face Value * D)	Expected Value of Alternative
A	MAKE	0.75 Yes	1	0.6 Yes	$200,000 Yes	$90,000 = 0.75 * 0.6 * $200,000	$93,750	$183,750
		0.75 Yes	1	0.4 No	$0 No			
A	MAKE	0.25 No	0	0.6 Yes	$200,000 Yes	$0	$0	$0
		0.25 No	0	0.4 No	$0 No			
B	BUY	0.75 Yes	1	0.2 Yes	$200,000 Yes	$30,000 = 0.75 * 0.2 * $200,000	$150,000	$180,000
		0.75 Yes	1	0.8 No	$0 No			
B	BUY	0.25 No	0	0.2 Yes	$200,000 Yes	$0	$0	$0
		0.25 No	0	0.8 No	$0 No			

The decision tree or table provides the project manager with the expected value of the decision-making process. As we know from previous discussion, expected value is the best single-number representation of a range of uncertainty. Any single instance of the project could fall anywhere in the range. Understanding the range is the purpose of the upside and downside analysis.

Furthermore, the acquisition cost of either alternative ($125,000 for "make" or $200,000 for "buy") has been transformed from deterministic to random by the dependency acquired from the effect of the sponsor's decision. In other words, the sponsor's decision to acquire the item is the random variable, S, with discrete density function $S_0 = 0$, p = 0.25 and $S_1 = 1$, p = 0.75 becomes the density of the acquisition cost, AC:

$AC_0 = 0$, p = 0.25, do not acquire the item

$AC_1 = 1 *$ make or buy cost, p = 0.75, acquire the item

Therefore, for decision-making purposes the decision maker would look first to the expected values, weighing first the most advantageous expected value. Then the decision maker would look to the risks and opportunities, downside and upside, and weigh those values in terms of possible effects on the business. The decision policy elements for both risk consideration and expected value are considered jointly in the decision process.

Figure 4-8 shows the "make" part of the scenario we have been discussing. It is evident that decision tree charts grow unwieldy in the face of conditions. Thus, the project team should understand and use tables to simplify matters, especially since tables lend themselves to setup, computation, and maintenance in spreadsheets.

Bayes' Theorem

Another degree of complication is introduced when the conditions of performance leading to a decision are interdependent. In this scenario, the probability structure becomes more difficult to manage without a good understanding of dependent probabilities. Thus, we introduce "Bayes' Theorem," named after the English mathematician Thomas Bayes who published his theory, *Essay Towards Solving a Problem in the Doctrine of Chances,* in 1764. Although Bayes' Theorem can be presented in a couple of forms, it is conveniently shown as follows for project management purposes:

$$p(A \mid B) = p(A \text{ and } B)/p(B)$$

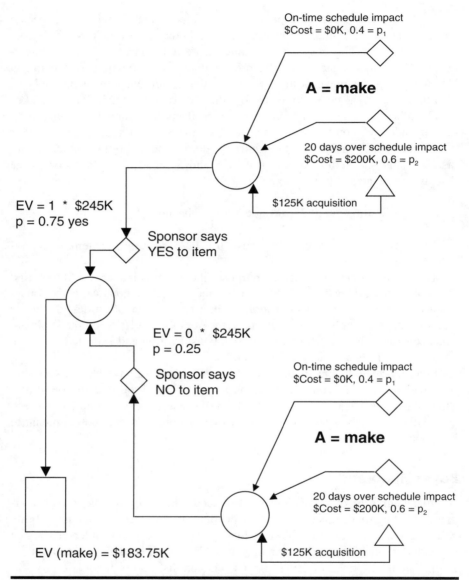

On-time schedule impact
$Cost = $0K, 0.4 = p_1

A = make

20 days over schedule impact
$Cost = $200K, 0.6 = p_2

$125K acquisition

EV = 1 * $245K
p = 0.75 yes

Sponsor says
YES to item

EV = 0 * $245K
p = 0.25

Sponsor says
NO to item

On-time schedule impact
$Cost = $0K, 0.4 = p_1

A = make

20 days over schedule impact
$Cost = $200K, 0.6 = p_2

$125K acquisition

EV (make) = $183.75K

Figure 4-8 Decision Tree with Independent Conditions.

in which $p(A \mid B)$ is read as "probability of A given B." Rearranging terms, Bayes' Theorem is also in the following two forms: $p(A \text{ and } B) = p(A \mid B) * p(B)$ and $p(B) = p(A \text{ and } B)/p(A \mid B)$.

If A and B are independent, then:

$$p(A \mid B) = p(A) * p(B)/p(B) = p(A)$$

because

$$p(A \text{ and } B) = p(A) * p(B)$$

Let's try Bayes' Theorem in natural language with the project examples we have studied so far:

- "The probability of a 20-day delay, D, given a "make" decision, $M = 1$, is 0.6." In equation form: $p(D \mid M_1) = 0.6$. If we were interested in solving for $p(M_1)$, we would have to estimate $p(D \text{ and } M_1)$.
- "The probability of a 20-day delay, D, given a sponsor's decision, S, to include the item in the project deliverables" is $p(D)$ since D and S are independent.
- "The probability of a 'make' decision, M, given a sponsor's decision, $S = 1$, to include the item in the project deliverables" is $1.33 * p(M_1 \text{ and } S_1)$. We have no other information about $p(M_1 \mid S_1)$ unless we independently measure or estimate $p(M_1 \text{ and } S_1)$.

Decision Trees with Dependent Conditions

With Bayes' Theorem in hand, we can proceed to project decisions that are interdependent. Let's continue with our project for which there is an item on the WBS that may or may not be included by the sponsor's decision in the final project scope and for which there is a make or buy decision for satisfying the acquisition to be made by the project team. However, let's change the situation and recognize that a late decision by the sponsor affects the subsequent performance of either make or buy:

- Let SD be the random variable that represents a sponsor's decision that may or may not be delayed beyond a point that the delay affects subsequent make or buy performance or value. In this example, we will say that our confidence in an on-time sponsor's decision is 70%, 0.7. In that event, using our "1-p" analysis, we have $p(SD \text{ late}) = 0.3$, 30%.
- If SD is on time, then the situation reverts to a case of independent conditions.

The problem at hand is to determine what is p(Make or Buy performance given SD late). In other words, we need to solve for:

Table 4-4   Dependent Scenarios

Project Situation: MAKE

MAKE 1:
p[MAKE late (or on time) given *SD* late] = p[MAKE late (or on time) AND *SD* late]/p(*SD* late)

MAKE 2:
p[MAKE late (or on time) given *SD* on time] = p[MAKE late (or on time)]

Project Situation: BUY

BUY 1:
p[BUY late (or on time) given *SD* late] = p[BUY late (or on time) AND *SD* late]/p(*SD* late)

BUY 2:
p[BUY late (or on time) given *SD* on time] = p[BUY late (or on time)]

$$p(\text{Make performance given } SD \text{ late}) = p(\text{Make performance and } SD \text{ late}/p(SD \text{ late})$$

and

$$p(\text{Buy performance given } SD \text{ late}) = p(\text{Buy performance and } SD \text{ late})/p(SD \text{ late})$$

where performance can be on time or late.

Table 4-4 arrays the scenarios that fall out of the situation in this project. Looking at this table carefully, you will see that there are actually six probabilities since "late or on time" is a shorthand notation for two distinctly different probabilities.

Now we come to a vexing problem: to make progress we must estimate the joint probabilities of "make late (or on time) and late *SD*" and "buy late (or on time) and late *SD*." We have already said that we have pretty high confidence that *SD* will be on time, so looking at a joint probability involving "*SD* late" will be a pretty small space. We do know one thing that is very useful: all the joint probabilities involving "*SD* late" have to fit in the space of 30% confidence that *SD* will be late:

$$p(\text{Make late and } SD \text{ late}) + p(\text{Make on time and } SD \text{ late})$$
$$= p(SD \text{ late}) = 0.3, \text{ or}$$

$$p(\text{Buy late and } SD \text{ late}) + p(\text{Buy on time and } SD \text{ late})$$
$$= p(SD \text{ late}) = 0.3$$

We now must do some estimating based on reasoning about the project situation as we know it. "Make on time" and "Make late" have probabilities of 0.4 and 0.6, respectively. If these were independent of "*SD* late," then the joint probabilities would multiply out to the multiples of the probabilities:

$$\text{Make on time and } SD \text{ late} = 0.4 * 0.3 = 0.12$$

and

$$\text{Make late and } SD \text{ late} = 0.6 * 0.3 = 0.18$$

However, in our situation "*SD* late" conditions performance, so the probabilities are not independent. Intuitively, the joint probability of being on time should be more pessimistic (smaller) since the likelihood of the joint event is more pessimistic than each event acting independently. In that case, the joint probability of being late is more optimistic (more likely to happen):

$$p(\text{Make on time and } SD \text{ late}) \leq p(\text{Make on time}) * p(SD \text{ late}),$$

$$\text{Estimate: } p(\text{Make on time and } SD \text{ late}) = 0.1$$

and then:

$$\text{Estimate: } p(\text{Make late and } SD \text{ late}) = 0.2 = 0.3 - 0.1$$

We can make similar estimates for the "buy" situation. Multiplying probabilities as though they were independent gives:

$$p(\text{Buy late and } SD \text{ late}) = 0.2 * 0.3 = 0.06$$

and

$$p(\text{Buy on time and } SD \text{ late}) = 0.8 * 0.3 = 0.24$$

Following the same reasoning about pessimism as we did in the "make" case:

$$p(\text{Buy on time and } SD \text{ late}) \leq p(\text{Buy on time}) * p(SD \text{ late}),$$

$$\text{Estimate: } p(\text{Buy on time and } SD \text{ late}) = 0.23$$

and then:

$$\text{Estimate: } p(\text{Buy late and } SD \text{ late}) = 0.07 = 0.3 - 0.23$$

Table 4-5   Buy Calculations with Dependent Conditions

Project Situation: BUY	Probability of Situation Occurring
20 days and late *SD* decision	0.07
0 days and late *SD* decision	0.23
Total LATE SD decision	**0.3**
20 days and on-time *SD* decision*	0.14
0 days and on-time *SD* decision*	0.56
Total ON-TIME *SD* decision	**0.7**
Total *SD* decision	**1.0**
20 days given *SD* late = (20 days and *SD* late)/*SD* late	0.23
0 days given *SD* late = (0 days and *SD* late)/*SD* late	0.77
Total given *SD* late	**1.0**
20 days given *SD* on time = 20 days	0.2
0 days given *SD* on time = 0 days	0.8
Total given *SD* on time	**1.0**

* These events are independent so the joint probabilities are the product of the probabilities.

We now apply Bayes' Theorem to our project situation and calculate the question we started to resolve. The probability p(Make or Buy performance given *SD* late) is given in Table 4-5 and Table 4-6:

p(Make performance given *SD* late) = p(Make performance and *SD* late)/p(*SD* late)

p(Make 20 days late given *SD* late) = 0.2/0.3 = 0.67

p(Make 0 days late given *SD* late) = 0.1/0.3 = 0.33, and

p(Buy performance given *SD* late) = p(Buy performance and *SD* late)/p(*SD* late),

p(Buy 20 days late given *SD* late) = 0.07/0.3 = 0.23

p(Buy 0 days late given *SD* late) = 0.23/0.3 = 0.77

Notice the impact on the potential for being late with a buy. The probability of a 20-day delay has increased from 0.2 with no dependent conditions to 0.23

Table 4-6   Make Calculations with Dependent Conditions

Project Situation: MAKE	Probability of Situation Occurring
20 days and late **SD** decision	0.2
0 days and late **SD** decision	0.1
Total LATE SD decision	**0.3**
20 days and on-time **SD** decision*	0.42
0 days and on-time **SD** decision*	0.28
Total ON-TIME SD decision	**0.7**
Total SD decision	**1.0**
20 days given **SD** late = (20 days and **SD** late)/**SD** late	0.67
0 days given **SD** late = (0 days and **SD** late)/**SD** late	0.33
Total given SD late	**1.0**
20 days given **SD** on time = 20 days	0.6
0 days given **SD** on time = 0 days	0.4
Total given SD on time	**1.0**

* These events are independent so the joint probabilities are the product of the probabilities.

with dependent conditions. Correspondingly, the on-time prediction dropped from 0.8 to 0.77. For a make decision, the probability of delay went from 0.6 to 0.67.

Let us now compute the dollar value of the outcomes of the decision tables. Table 4-7 provides the illustration of this project scenario. Take care when looking at this table. The acquisition costs of the make, $125,000, or of the buy, $200,000, are not affected by the late or on-time decision, *SD*, of the sponsor. Acquisition costs are only affected by the sponsor's decision, *S*, to have the item in the WBS or not. The value of the delay, if any, is taken care of with the value of the timeliness of the decision, *SD*, times the probability of the decision itself, *S*.

Note further that the decision to make or buy is not changed by the effect of a late decision of the sponsor. "Buy" comes out more advantageous in the face of a dependent condition with the sponsor's decision. The upside and downside of a decision in favor of "Buy" are:

Upside of an on-time sponsor's decision is the "Buy" acquisition cost = $200,000

Downside of late sponsor's decision = $181,350 − ($200,000 + $200,000)
= −$218,650

Table 4-7 Decision with Dependent Conditions

Alternative ID	Description	Probability Sponsor Exercises Option	Probability of Sponsor Decision, SD, Late	Probability of 20-Day Schedule Delay	Face Value of Delay, D, @ $10,000 per Day	EV of Delay, D (p of SD * p of Delay * $Face Value)	EV of Acquisition Cost (p of Option * $Face Value * D)	Expected Value of Alternative
A	MAKE		0.3 Late 0.3 Late	0.67 Yes 0.33 No	$200,000 Yes $0 No	$40,200 $0		
A	MAKE	0.75 Yes	0.7 On time 0.7 On time	0.6 Yes 0.3 No	$200,000 Yes $0 No	$84,000 $0	= $125,000 * 0.75 = $93,750	= 0.75 * ($40,200 + $84,000) + $93,750 = $186,900
A	MAKE	0.25 No 0.25 No		0.6 Yes 0.4 No	$200,000 Yes $0 No	$0 $0	$0	$0
B	BUY		0.3 Late 0.3 Late	0.23 Yes 0.77 No	$200,000 Yes $0 No	$13,800 $0		
B	BUY	0.75 Yes	0.7 On time 0.7 On time	0.2 Yes 0.8 No	$200,000 Yes $0 No	$28,000 $0	= $200,000 * 0.75 = $150,000	= 0.75 * ($13,800 + $28,000) + $150,000 = $181,350
B	BUY	0.25 No 0.25 No		0.2 Yes 0.8 No	$200,000 Yes $0 No	$0 $0	$0	$0

Table 4-8 Summary of Important Points

Point of Discussion	Summary of Ideas Presented
Project policy for decisions	■ Quantitative decision making is most useful when there is a rational policy for obtaining the outcomes. ■ Rationality, used in this sense, means that the decision is a consequence of all the inputs having been applied systematically to a decision-making methodology.
Decision trees	■ The decision tree is a decision tool to be applied in a decision methodology. ■ The decision tree, and its cousin the decision table, sums up all the expected values of each of the alternatives being decided and makes available the expected values to the decision maker. ■ In applying the decision tree to decision making, the project manager gives consideration to risk by considering both the upside opportunity and the downside risk as well as the expected values of the alternatives.
Decisions with independent conditions	■ It is rare that project managers can make decisions without consideration for other activities or constraints going on in the project. ■ Independent conditions establish prerequisites but do not in and of themselves affect performance thereafter.
Decisions with dependent conditions	■ Dependent conditions affect performance or value. That is to say, the performance in a project work package is conditioned on the first decision made.
Bayes' Theorem	■ $p(A \mid B) = p(A \text{ and } B)/p(B)$. ■ The project manager usually is given or can estimate directly one of the three probabilities in Bayes' Theorem. To obtain the other two probabilities, usually another estimate or measurement must be made.
Utility	■ In situations where the decision making takes into account the absolute affordability of an opportunity, we call decision making of this type "risk averse." ■ Utility simply means that the decision maker's view of risk is either discounted or amplified compared to the risk-neutral view.

SUMMARY OF IMPORTANT POINTS

Table 4-8 provides the highlights of this chapter.

REFERENCES

1. Schuyler, John, *Risk and Decision Analysis in Projects, Second Edition,* Project Management Institute, Newtown Square, PA, 2001, chap. 5, p. 59.
2. Goodpasture, John C., *Managing Projects for Value,* Management Concepts, Vienna, VA, 2001, chap. 3, p. 39.

5

RISK-ADJUSTED FINANCIAL MANAGEMENT

*Value increases when the satisfaction of the customer augments
and the expenditure of resources diminishes.*

Robert Tassinari
Le Rapport Qualite/Prix, 1985

In Chapter 1, we discussed the idea of the balanced scorecard as one of the business scoring models driving the selection and funding of projects. On every scorecard there are quantitative financial measures that set the bar for project selection and for project success or failure. It is inescapable that project managers will be involved in financial measures and in the financial success of projects. Financial performance in projects, like every other aspect of project performance, is subject to uncertainty: uncertainty of performance by the project team; uncertainty of performance by vendors, suppliers, and partners; and ultimately, uncertainty of financial performance by project deliverables in the marketplace. Uncertainty, we know, is risk. In this chapter, we introduce the financial concepts most important to the project manager, but we introduce them in the context of risk adjustments that are made to provide a more realistic context for measurement and evaluation.

FINANCIAL STATEMENTS

Finance officers have long-established standards for reporting the numbers. The general body of knowledge for accounting standards is contained in the *Generally Accepted Accounting Principles* (GAAP), published and maintained by the accounting industry. Within your business, the controller (comptroller, if you are in the government) is the chief accountant. The controller interprets and applies the GAAP to the specifics of your company.

Financial information is more often than not presented on a set of "financial statements." We will discuss three of those statements that are of most use to the project manager. The statements are:

- **The expense statement**: Often called the "profit and loss" or "P&L" statement, the expense statement is where project financial expenses are "recognized" by the controller and recorded each period. We will learn that not all expenses on the expense statement are cash expenses, so to keep the books on the expense statement means keeping track of more than just the checks that are written. A common refrain is: "Cash is a fact, but profit is an opinion."[1] This reflects the thought that the expense statement is subject to much interpretation of the GAAP, whereas cash is tangible and well understood without ambiguity.
- **The balance sheet**: The balance sheet is a two-sided ledger that we studied in Chapter 3. It is a recording of a snapshot in time of the dollar value of all the assets, liabilities, and capital employed on the project.
- **The cash flow statement**: Actual cash going into or out of the company or project is recorded on the cash flow statement. It is on the cash flow statement that we actually see "sources and uses" of cash in the project.

The neat thing about these statements is that they actually all play together, something engineers and project professionals would call system integration, but accountants would call "balance" or "reconciliation." Even though one statement may measure flow and another may measure a value at a point in time, over the life of the project an entry on any one of these statements has a corresponding response on another statement. Collectively, and with their risk-adjusted partners, net present value and economic value add, the project financial statements provide a rich source of information about the performance of projects.

The chart of accounts was discussed in the chapter on the work breakdown structure (WBS). The chart of accounts is the controller's WBS of the business. The WBS of the project is just an extension of the WBS of the business, i.e., the chart of accounts. In this chapter, we will discuss the "trial balance" as a reporting tool for financial and project managers that is closely tied to the chart of accounts and the financial statements.

The Expense Statement

The expense statement, sometimes known as the income or P&L (profit and loss) statement, is an ordered list of the revenue and expense items for the project. The item categories and ordering of the categories is by account from the chart of accounts. Typically, there are accounts listed and expense entries for labor and labor benefits, purchased materials, travel, training, facility supplies and consumables, information services for data processing, networks and computer environments, vendor charges, facility rent and utilities, freight and fuel, capital depreciation expenses, general and administrative (G&A) expenses, sales and marketing expenses, legal and contract management expenses, taxes, and perhaps others, *but not deliverables*. It is very unlikely that you will see a project deliverable on the controller's expense statement for the project. The expense statement is therefore a "view" of the expenses from the controller's point of view.

Table 5-1 illustrates a project P&L.

The Expense Statement and the Work Breakdown Structure

From the discussion in Chapter 2, we know that the project expenses on the WBS are typically presented from a "deliverables point of view" since the mission of the project manager is to provide the deliverables for not more than the resources committed to the project. Therefore, at the project level, the expense statement may have to be "mapped" to the project WBS. For example, there may be an expense item for travel and subsistence on the expense statement provided by the controller. The travel and subsistence within each WBS element should roll up to the figures in the expense statement for the same things, in this case travel and subsistence. If expenses within the project WBS are coded and identified according to the expense statement, it can be a simple matter for the project administrator to extract and add together these elements to "balance" or "reconcile" the expense statement with the WBS. Figure 5-1 shows a simple case of relating the expense statement to the WBS.

Most large companies run their business accounting on an "accrual basis," rather than on a cash basis. The consequence of the accrual method is that expenses can be reserved or recognized before any cash changes hands. Accrual accounting thus leads us to the fact that not all expenses are actually cash; they may only be an accrual that is being "recognized" in a particular period. For example, taxes are typically accrued each month as a recognized expense on

Table 5-1   P&L Statement for Project

Statement Item	$0.00
Revenue from operations	
(Special note: project deliverables not operational)	$0.00
Direct expenses	
Fixed expenses	
Rent of project facilities	$2,000.00
Utilities of project facilities	$250.00
Project management staff labor compensation	$80,000.00
Project management staff compensation benefits	$16,000.00
Network and communications chargeback	$350.00
Total fixed expenses	**$98,600.00**
Variable expenses	
Work package labor compensation	$850,000.00
Work package compensation benefits	$170,000.00
Office supplies	$500.00
Work package purchased materials	$45,000.00
Travel and subsistence	$10,000.00
Training for staff	$5,000.00
Rental and operating leases	$3,500.00
Total variable expenses	**$1,084,000.00**
Total direct expenses	**$1,182,600.00**
Indirect expenses	
Indirect allocation of direct support expenses @ 100% of labor compensation	$930,000.00
G&A expenses (% direct)	
Independent R&D @ 2%	$23,652.00
General executive management @ 15%	$177,390.00
Legal, HR, finance, contracts, IT @ 12%	$141,912.00
Selling expenses @ 3%	$35,478.00
Total indirect expenses	**$1,308,432.00**
Indirect rate (indirect/direct)	111%
Depreciation of capital assets	
Special tools and facilities for project	$30,000.00
Software over $25,000	$525.00
Capital leases for special vehicles	$1,200.00
Total depreciation	**$31,725.00**
Total operating income (expense)	**($1,340,157.00)**

the expense statement, but they are paid each April. The cash flow will be seen on the April cash flow statement even though "expenses" have been seen each period on the expense statement. In April, the cash flow will reconcile or balance with the cumulative expense statement insofar as taxes are concerned. Similarly, benefits, like vacation, are accrued as expenses each period. Some-

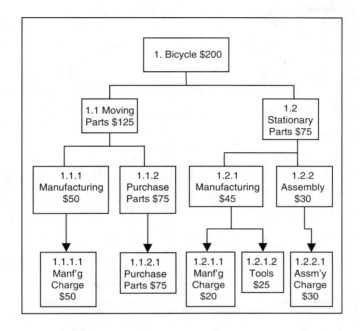

Expense Statement for Bicycle

Direct Expenses

Direct Labor	$60
Purchased Parts	$65
Tools	$20

Indirect Expenses

Labor Overhead	$40

General & Administrative

G&A on Purchases	$15
Total for Project Bicycle	**$200**

Direct Labor [DL] + Labor Overhead = WBS 1.1.1.1 + 1.2.1.1 + 1.2.2.1
Purchased Parts + Tools + G&A = WBS 1.1.2.1 + 1.2.1.2

Figure 5-1   Expense Statement Mapping to the WBS.

times the project manager sets up an accrual for a vendor or subcontractor's expenses so that their expenses are "smoothed" into each period. Then, when the vendor invoice is paid, the cumulative expense statement and the cash flow statements will reconcile and balance. Figure 5-2 shows an example of the process described.

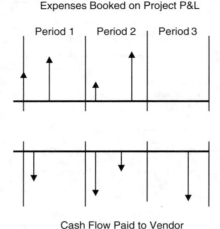

Figure 5-2 Cash Flow and Expense Reconciliation.

The Balance Sheet

In Chapter 3 we discussed the connection between the balance sheet and the expense statement. Expenses are logged on the "T" charts and totals moved to the balance sheet at the next "snapshot in time." The most important aspect of the balance sheet insofar as the project manager is concerned is the "capitalized expense" that is shown on the balance sheet. Large material purchases, and in some cases labor expenses, both internal and supplier provided, as allowed by the GAAP, are often "capitalized." "Capitalized" is a verb that has been coined to capture the idea that certain cash expenses should not be recognized on the expense statement until the item that was purchased is put into use. The GAAP idea is to align use and cost of use in the same accounting period. The balance sheet is where the unrecognized expense is maintained until the time comes to "expense" it to the expense statement. The process of expensing the balance sheet is called "depreciating," and the expense is called "depreciation expense." For example, if a truck is bought for the project in June and depreciation begins in September, when the truck goes into use on the project, there is no actual cash expense in September. The cash went out of the business in June when the truck was purchased. Depreciation is one of the prominent "noncash" expenses on the expense statement. Accruals, already discussed, are the other prominent noncash expenses.

The Balance Sheet and the Work Breakdown Structure

How would the project team handle the truck example: purchase a truck for cash in June and then put the truck into service in September when depreciation begins? Obviously the work package schedule would show the purchase activity in June and the service activity beginning in September. Regarding the financial part of the transaction, a common practice is for the project manager to maintain a capital budget for the capital items, like a truck, that are to be purchased for the project and for the work package manager to maintain an expense budget. (We will discuss some of the special factors in capital budgeting in subsequent paragraphs of this chapter.) The capital budget would have the schedule and record of the cash purchase; the expense budget would begin in September for the truck and show the depreciation expense in the work package. Each period, the balance sheet would be reduced by the amount depreciated onto the expense statement. When depreciation is completed, the sum of the depreciation expenses should equal the initial cash purchase.

The Cash Flow Statement

Now we come to the cash and to the flow of cash. As described by Robert Higgins in his book, *Analysis for Financial Management,*[2] the cash flow statement is commonly thought of as the place to put down the sources of cash and uses of cash in the project. Viewed this way as a double entry system, the sources ought to balance the uses. Flow refers to a change over time. As such, a cash flow statement is not a statement of cash on hand, but rather the change in cash over the reporting period.

There are only two ways a company can generate cash: decrease an asset or increase a liability. Decreasing the accounts receivable asset account brings cash into the company that is recorded on the P&L as revenue; selling a building or a truck brings cash into a business. Taking cash out of a checking account brings cash into a company. This last example is often confusing. How can reducing the cash balance of a company's checking account be a source of cash for the company? Think of it this way: reducing the balance in the asset account puts cash in the hands of the company's management just as if you had cashed a check on your personal account at a bank. The cash value of the checking account is no more actual cash than the cash value of the truck.

Correspondingly, the only two uses of cash are to increase an asset or decrease a liability. Paying vendors reduces the accounts payable liability account, as does paying off a loan. Adding to the cash balance of a checking account or acquiring a capital asset, like a truck, increases assets and is a use of cash.

Table 5-2 Sources and Uses

Sources of Project Cash	$000
Reductions in checking cash	$38.5
Increase notes (debt) from project investor	$5
Increase current accounts payable for project purchases	$4
Increase accrued benefits on project staff	$35
TOTAL sources of CASH	**$82.5**
Uses of Project Cash	**$000**
Increase short-term notes to project supplier	$15
Increase prepaid licenses	$10
Increase capital assets for project	$20
Reductions in accrued labor for staff	$37.5
TOTAL uses of CASH	**$82.5**

Table 5-2 shows an example of a cash flow statement presented as sources and uses. Another form of the cash flow statement arranges the items into three categories: cash from operations; cash from investments in property, plant, and equipment; and cash from financing activities like stock sales. Even so, the sum of the total uses must balance the sum of the total sources.

Unfortunately, there is no single definition of cash or cash flow, but there are several in common use, some of which will be important to project managers:

- **Net cash flow** is defined as "net income from the expense statement plus or minus noncash adjustments."[3]
- **Net cash flow from operations** is defined as net cash flow plus or minus the changes in current liabilities and assets.
- **Free cash flow** is defined as the cash available to distribute to shareholders or owners.
- **Discounted cash flow** is taken to be the present value of *net cash flow* or *net cash flow from operations*.

For projects, we will be concerned with the present value of the *net cash flow from operations* for net present value calculations and *net cash flow* for economic value add calculations.

The Cash Flow Statement and the Work Breakdown Structure

The WBS is not usually reconciled directly with the cash flow statement. Ordinarily the project manager manages the capital budget, whereas the WBS reflects the expense budget. The project manager's practice may be to reconcile the capital budget with the WBS work packages for the reporting period. However, if the project WBS is on a cash-accounting basis, then the WBS provides the sources and uses of cash in the project.

The Trial Balance for Project Managers

The controller will undoubtedly provide a "trial balance" to the project manager each month. The trial balance is a report of debits and credits by account, typically summed for each account so that at report time a specific account will show a net value in the debit column or a net value in the credit column, but not in both columns at once. Recall that there is no such thing as a "negative debit" because a "negative debit" is recorded as a positive credit. The debit or the credit amount is a report of the value of the account on the report date. The trial balance follows the same protocol as the balance sheet: asset accounts are debited to increase their value and credited to decrease their value; just the opposite is done for liability and capital accounts.

Naturally, the debits and credits of the trial balance should balance. The project manager is often called on to reconcile and correct the account values shown on the trial balance. Table 5-3 illustrates an example.

The Trial Balance and the Work Breakdown Structure

Everything on the WBS must roll up to some account on the chart of accounts. Assuming that the project administrator has a mapping of the WBS accounts to the chart of accounts, the WBS can be reconciled to the trial balance using pivot queries in a spreadsheet.

Table 5-3   Trial Balance for Project

Expense Account	Equity Account	Capital Account	Debit	Credit
Prepaid expenses			$500,000	
Accrued compensation				$250,000
Travel and subsistence			$300,000	
Checking			$300,000	
Communications			$50,000	
Rent and utilities			$550,000	
	Paid in stock			$1,000,000
	Long-term debt			$250,000
		Accumulated depreciation		$200,000
		Capital equipment	$300,000	
	Total debits and credits		$1,700,000	$1,700,000

CAPITAL BUDGETING

Capital budgeting is about how to budget and spend cash for the big-ticket items on the project. Spending cash creates cash flow. The cash flow statement is one of the important tracking tools for the capital budget. Capital budgeting is closely related to the concept of *discounted* cash flow (DCF), a methodology to assign risk (that is, a discount) to cash flows that will occur in the future. In this section we address the capital budgeting per se and address its close cousin, DCF, in the next section.

Capital Budgeting for Projects

Capital budgets refer to those project budgets for which cash is paid out now, in the present during the project execution, but for which the expense will be recognized in the future when the item is put into use. The principle at work is "alignment": use and the cost of use should align in the same period. Expensing could begin during project execution if the capital purchase is to be used for the project itself, or expensing could be deferred until the capital item is to be used for operations after project completion. Expensing the capital item "relieves" the balance sheet amount for the item each time an expense is recorded on the expense statement. When the balance sheet amount is fully relieved (that is, the amount on the balance sheet is $0), then expensing ends. Table 5-4 provides an example. The controller will make the decision about what project items to make capital purchases and when the expensing of those items will begin.

So far, our discussion has been about paying cash for a capital item. It is possible to lease a capital item and thereby create a "capital lease." A capital lease shows up on the balance sheet as a liability, just like a purchased item would show as an asset. The lease payments are expensed, thereby relieving the balance sheet liability. There are several tests the controller applies to determine if a lease is a capital lease or an "operating lease." The latter is expensed just like a rental item or an item bought on credit. The controller is the ultimate decision maker on whether a lease is a capital lease or an operating lease.

Capital Structure and Projects

Going back to the discussion of the balance sheet in Chapter 3, we know that assets on the left side are "paid for" or "financed" by liabilities on the right side. Owners, shareholders, debt holders, and suppliers are the creditors of the business. The relative weight of debt and owner capital paid in is called the "capital structure" of the company. Generally speaking, the long-term debt (like capital

Table 5-4   Expensing the Balance Sheet

Item	Year 0	Year 1	Year 2	Year 3	Year 4
Balance sheet capital employed, crane with truck	$500,000	$375,000	$250,000	$125,000	$0
Depreciation to the P&L statement, *straight line method**	$0	$125,000 = $500,000/4	$125,000 = $500,000/4	$125,000 = $500,000/4	$125,000 $500,000/4
Balance sheet capital employed, software license	$500,000	$300,000	$150,000	$50,000	$0
Depreciation to the P&L statement, *sum of years method* (4 + 3 + 2 + 1 = 10)*	$0	$200,000 = (4/10) * $500,000	$150,000 = (3/10) * $500,000	$100,000 = (2/10) * $500,000	$50,000 = (1/10) * $500,000

* Notes: In the *straight line method,* an equal amount is expensed to the P&L each period. In the *sum of years method,* the number of years is added cumulatively to find the denominator; the numerator is the "year number."

leases, notes and bonds, and capital paid in for stock or partnership) finances the long-term capital purchases; short-term debt (such as accounts payable to suppliers) finances the short-term assets (like accounts receivables).

For project managers, the importance of the capital structure is this: there is a "cost of capital" that is passed along to the project. For the most part, the cost of capital is not a real expense that shows up on an expense statement, but it is an "opportunity cost" that creates competition for capital. If the project loses out in the capital competition, the project is starved of the resources it needs or the project is never approved in the first place.

Opportunity Cost for Projects

The opportunity cost works as follows for projects: If a company has investment dollars that can be made available to projects, which projects should get what amounts? The decision is usually made on the basis of benefit returns to the company. The ratios in play are the ROI (return on investment), the net present value (NPV), and the economic value add (EVA). We will define these for the project manager and demonstrate their application to projects in subsequent paragraphs.

Suffice it to say, benefit returns are risky because they are earned in the future. Therefore, benefit returns must be risk adjusted before they are plugged into the formula. The opportunity cost is then the difference in returns, after risk

Table 5-5   Opportunity Cost for Projects

Project Manager's Responsibility			Project Sponsor's Responsibility		
Capital Employed	Expenses	Confidence in Capital and Expense	Benefits Over Three Years	Confidence in Benefits	Net Risk Adjusted Return
Project A					
$350,000 (depreciate over three years)	$125,000 (one year)	80%	$650,000 cumulative	75%	Compared to B higher cost risk, same benefit risk
Project B					
$50,000	$300,000	90%	$525,000	75%	Compared to A lower cost risk, same benefit risk

Project A Benefit − Cost = $650 − $475 = $175
Project B Benefit − Cost = $525 − $350 = $175

Opportunity Cost A = Project A − Project B higher risk
Opportunity Cost B = −Project A + Project B lower risk

Without considering risk, the opportunity cost of Project A vs. Project B is $0.

adjustment, between one project opportunity and the next most favorable opportunity that is competing for the same capital.

The role of project managers in the capital competition is twofold: provide risk management so that the returns are maximized to the extent possible, and manage capital budgets to minimize capital expenditures. Those two activities will maximize the returns and minimize the opportunity cost of the project.

Consider an example project situation as shown in Table 5-5. There we see two projects, each with different demands on capital and expense, but each with an equal face-value opportunity for net benefits, $175,000. If not for considering the confidence of obtaining the returns, there is no opportunity cost between these two projects. However, our confidence in one project's return is higher than the other. On a risk-adjusted basis, there is a "cost" of selecting the more risky project. The cost we speak of is an opportunity cost of picking one over the other. To ensure the selection of the more favorable project, the decision policy must embrace the concept of opportunity cost. The objective of the project team is to make the risk factors as favorable as possible in order to create the greatest competitive advantage for the project.

DISCOUNTED CASH FLOW

The concept of DCF for projects often governs whether or not a project will be selected to go forward, or whether or not a change in scope requiring new resources will be approved. Those are two good reasons why project managers should be familiar with the concept. The controller's office usually makes the DCF calculations for the project manager. However, the project manager often influences the risk factors that go into determining the discount rate. Thus, the project manager is not entirely a passive partner in the DCF deliberations.

The Discount Rate

The discount rate, sometimes called an interest rate, but also called the cost of capital rate or factor, is the discount applied to future cash flows to account for the risk that those flows may not happen as planned or to create "equivalence" with another investment opportunity.[4] Discounting gives us a present-time feel for the value of future flows, having taken risk and alternate opportunities into account.

Many things can be considered in determining the discount rate: real interest that could be earned on an alternate opportunity, the risk of inflation, the risk that the market will not be accepting of the project deliverables, the risk that customers will not have the capacity to pay in the future because of some mishap in the economy, the risk that the project will not be completed on time in order to exploit a market opportunity, or that the project will consume more capital than planned.

It is not uncommon for different discount rates to be applied to different projects in the same company because of the different risk factors faced by each project. Ordinarily, to make discounting practical, all projects of similar type are given the same discount factor, such as all pharmaceutical projects discounted at one rate and all real estate projects discounted at another rate.

Net Present Value and Net Future Value

You may recognize that discounting is the inverse of the familiar idea of compounding. Compounding begins with a present value and forecasts a future value based on an interest rate or capital factor rate. Discounting begins with a forecasted future value to which a discount factor is applied to obtain a present value of the amount. In the same project, the compounding factor and the discount rate are the same rate. Therefore, it is relatively easy to work from the present to the future or from the future back to the present.

Most of us who have had a savings or investment account are familiar with the compounding formula, so let's begin with compounding as a lead-in to discounting. Let's use "k" as the compounding (or discounting factor) and compute the values at the *end* of the compounding period:

$$\text{Future value (FV)} = \text{Present value (PV)} * (1 + k)^N$$

where N is the number of periods to be compounded. N takes on values from N = 0 to some value "m".

To take a simple numerical example, if "k" = 8% and "N" = 3, then we can calculate the future value:

$$FV = PV * (1 + 0.08)^3$$

$$FV = PV * 1.2597$$

Thus, if we had an opportunity to invest $10,000 for three years, we have an expectation that $12,597 will be returned to us at the end of three years, given that the compounding factor is 8%. The return on our investment is the net of the investment and the total return: $12,597 − $10,000 = $2,597.

If we had other opportunities to evaluate, the opportunity costs would be the difference in returns between each opportunity. The factor 1.2597 is called the future value factor. *Future value factors are distinguished by always being a number equal to or larger than 1.* Future value factors are easily calculated in Excel® using the "power" function or they can be found in future value tables in finance books. Table 5-6 is an abridged collection of future value factors.

Now, about discounting: discounting begins in the future with forecasted flows; the DCF factor "k" is used to find the present value. We solve for present value using the future value formula given above:

$$PV = FV/(1 + k)^N$$

where N is the number of periods to be compounded.

The present value factors are the inverse of the future value factors. For instance, for m = 3, the present value factor using 8% is 1/1.2597, or 0.7938. *All present value factors will be numbers less than or equal to 1.* Table 5-7 is an abridged example of present values.

Using the 8% factors and m = 3, suppose we had a forecast for future flows due to a present investment of $10,000 as follows:

N = 0, $10,000 present-time investment outflow

Table 5-6   Future Value Factors

Discount Rate	Year 0	Year 1	Year 2	Year 3	Year 4
5%	1	1.05	1.1025	1.157625	1.215506
7%	1	1.07	1.1449	1.225043	1.310796
9%	1	1.09	1.1881	1.295029	1.411582

These factors are easily calculated using a spreadsheet. The formula in any particular cell is: Factor = $(1 + \text{discount rate})^N$ where N is the number of the year, 0 to 4.

In Excel, the "power" function can be used to calculate the Factor equation. There are two arguments in "power": the first is (1 + discount rate), and the second is N.

and future forecasted inflows:

$$N = 1, \$3,000, k = 1.08, 1/k = 0.9259$$

$$N = 2, \$6,000, k^2 = 1.08^2, 1/k^2 = 0.8573$$

$$N = 3, \$7,000, k^3 = 1.08^3, 1/k^3 = 0.7938$$

The present value of these flows given a discount of 8% is given by:

$$PV(\text{inflows}) = \$3,000 * 0.9259 + \$6,000 * 0.8573 + \$7,000 * 0.7938 = \$13,478$$

NPV of return = –$10,000 + $13,478 = $3,478 at the end of three periods.

Figure 5-3 provides a graphical presentation of the cash flows. It is usually simpler to calculate the NPV directly by entering all "outflows" as negative numbers and all "inflows" as positive numbers. In the figure, outflows are

Table 5-7   Present Value Factors

Discount Rate	Year 0	Year 1	Year 2	Year 3	Year 4
5%	1	0.952381	0.907029	0.863838	0.822702
7%	1	0.934579	0.873439	0.816298	0.762895
9%	1	0.917431	0.84168	0.772183	0.708425

These factors are easily calculated using a spreadsheet. The formula in any particular cell is: Factor = $1/(1 + \text{discount rate})^N$ where N is the number of the year, 0 to 4.

In Excel, the "power" function can be used to calculate the denominator in the Factor equation. There are two arguments in "power": the first is (1 + discount rate), and the second is N.

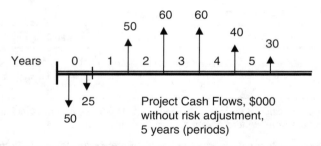

Project Cash Flows, $000 without risk adjustment, 5 years (periods)

			Years				
0	1	2	3	4	5	Total	
−$75.0	$50.0	$60.0	$60.0	$40.0	$30.0	**$165.0**	**Net Future Value**
−$75.0	$47.2	$53.4	$50.4	$31.7	$22.4	**$130.0**	**Net Present Value**
1	0.943396	0.889996	0.839619	0.792094	0.747258		PV Factor @ 6%

Figure 5-3   NPV Example.

arrows pointing down and the inflows are arrows pointing up. With this convention, the above would be written as:

$$NPV = PV \text{ (all inflows)} - PV \text{ (all outflows)}$$

$$NPV = PV \text{ (all inflows} - \text{all outflows)}$$

At 8% discount rate:

$$NPV = -\$10{,}000 + \$3{,}000 * 0.9259 + \$6{,}000 * 0.8573 + \$7{,}000 * 0.7938$$
$$= \$3{,}478$$

NPV is our first risk-adjusted measure of project financial performance. If the outflows are the cash expended on the project and the inflows are the cash received because of the project, then in the case illustrated above it makes sense to do the project because the NPV ≥ $0. If the NPV is negative, then more money is going out of the business than is coming into the business on a risk-adjusted basis; it makes no financial sense to do projects of negative NPV:

Decision policy:
Only projects with NPV ≥ $0 will be selected for execution.

Internal Rate of Return

Now what about this question: Given that the future flows are forecasted, as they were in the example we have just studied, what is the discount factor that makes the NPV exactly $0? We are interested in that factor, which we will call the IRR (internal rate of return), because any discount factor that might be imposed by the controller that is higher than the IRR would cause the NPV to be negative and the project would not be approved.

$$\text{IRR} = \text{Discount rate for which NPV} = 0$$

We cannot solve for the IRR directly. The IRR can only be solved iteratively. For instance, for the project just discussed, using the present value factor tables, we find that at a discount of 24%, the NPV is slightly negative. At 23%, the NPV is slightly positive, meaning the IRR is between 23 and 24%. IRR can be solved in Excel® using the IRR function that solves iterative equations. The exact solution is 23.598%.

In some companies, the IRR is called the "hurdle rate." No project can be approved with a discount above the hurdle rate. *The IRR is the upper bound of the discount factor for a positive NPV.*

Decision policy: The project is acceptable if k < IRR.

When k = IRR, the project is usually not accepted.

Benefit/Cost Ratio

The benefit/cost ratio (BCR) is a figure of merit that is often used to evaluate projects. Project managers may be asked to participate in calculating the BCR by evaluating the risks in the project that affect cash flows. The BCR is defined as:

$$\text{BCR} = (\text{PV of all cash inflows})/(\text{PV of all cash outflows})$$

Defined as above, if BCR > 1, then the project has greater inflow than outflow, the NPV will be positive, and, all other things being equal, the project should be on a list of good candidates:

Decision policy: The project is acceptable if BCR > 1.

Break-Even Point

Using the DCFs, the break-even point is when the cumulative project DCFs go from cash negative to cash positive. In equation form, the break-even point occurs when:

$$\sum \text{PV of discounted cash outflows} = \sum \text{PV of discounted cash inflows}$$

Economic Value Add

EVA is a risk-adjusted quantitative measure of project performance. Unlike the previous measures, EVA is focused on earnings.* The idea of EVA is that a project should earn more in profits than the cost of the project's capital employed. Remember that capital employed is the liability or equity (resources "owned" by creditors and owners) that finances the expenses of the project. If the project were less profitable than the cost paid for its capital employed, then the creditors and owners would do better to employ their capital elsewhere. Such a competitive rationale should be a component of any rational decision policy.

When working with EVA we use the same risk factors and notation as already developed. The cost of capital factor (CCF) is the discount rate, "k":

The cost of capital employed ($CCE) = k * $Capital employed

Thus, if a project absorbs $100,000 in capital for a year, and the risk factor, CCF, is 8%, then the CCE is $8,000. The project's earnings must exceed $8,000 or else more is being spent on capital than is being earned on the same capital. *A special note: the time frame for comparison of earnings and CCE should be identical or else each is subject to different risks.* It is common practice to discount all figures to present time for a common comparison.

The first step in looking at EVA is to get a handle on earnings. Earnings are profits and they are portrayed on the P&L. Typically, the P&L would show:

(Revenues – Cash expenses – Noncash expenses) * (1 – Tax rate)
= Earnings after tax (EAT)

Immediately we see that noncash expenses save real cash outlays on taxes by subtracting from taxable revenue. For our purposes, we will assume the noncash expense is depreciation of capital assets and that the revenue is from the deliverables of the project.**

If we then sum up the EAT for each period and compare the summed EAT to the CCE, we have the EVA for the project.

$$EVA = EAT - k * CCE$$

---

* P.T. Finegan first wrote about EVA in the publication *Corporate Cashflow*.[5] Shawn Tully[6] made EVA popular in a *Fortune* magazine article after Finegan wrote about EVA.
** If the project does not generate revenue, but generates cost savings instead, the cost savings can be plugged in since they also create increased earnings.

To put EVA in a project context, consider Table 5-8. We assume a $500,000 capital investment in the project and a five-year straight-line depreciation of $100,000 per year.* Our capital investment on the balance sheet is relieved ("relieved" is accounting terminology for "reduced") by a depreciation expense each year; each year the capital employed in the project goes down accordingly, and the CCE is less each year as well. Each year we multiply the investment balance on the balance sheet by the cost of capital factor, k, to calculate the cost of capital for that year. Discounting by $1/(1 + k)^N$ each year provides the present value of the cost of capital employed (PV CCE).

Now in Table 5-9 we calculate the EVA. For purposes of this example, let's assume the project business case proposes an earnings figure, before noncash additions, of $50,000 per year. That $50,000 is the earnings figure before any risk adjustments. To find the EVA, we simply make the risk adjustments by finding the present value of the EAT and subtracting the PV CCE, and that provides the PV EVA.

We see in this example that the EVA is comfortably positive, so this project earns more than it costs to employ the capital.

Economic Value Add and Net Present Value Equivalence

Fortunately for project managers, NPV and EVA are exactly equivalent. NPV is computationally much more straightforward, so EVA–NPV equivalence is a very big convenience indeed. Let's see how this equivalence works in the example project. Table 5-10 shows the calculations.

First, we must reorient ourselves to cash flow rather than earnings. Tom Pike's ditty — "*Cash is a fact but profit is an opinion*" — jumps to mind. To show equivalence between NPV and EVA, we must find the cash flow from cash earnings. Remember that we define cash earnings as *net cash flow* (NCF). Also recall the definition previously given of *net cash flow*: the after-tax earnings with the noncash expenses on the expense statement added back in:

$$NCF = EAT + \text{Noncash expense}$$

$$NCF = EAT + \text{Depreciation}$$

From this point the calculations are straightforward: add the EAT and the depreciation together to obtain NCF, calculate NCF present value, and the result

---

* Depreciation is not always uniformly the same figure each year. There are "accelerated" depreciation methods that take more expense in the early years and less in the later years. The controller will make the decision about which depreciation formula to follow.

Table 5-8 Depreciation in EVA Example

Present	1	2	3	4	5	Total	
$0.00	$100,000.00	$100,000.00	$100,000.00	$100,000.00	$100,000.00	$500,000.00	Depreciation
$500,000.00	$400,000.00	$300,000.00	$200,000.00	$100,000.00	$0.00		Capital employed
	0.08	0.08	0.08	0.08	0.08		Discount rate, "k"
	$40,000.00	$32,000.00	$24,000.00	$16,000.00	$8,000.00	$120,000.00	CCE
	$37,037.04	$27,434.84	$19,051.97	$11,760.48	$5,444.67	$100,729.00	PV of CCE

Present = Period 0.
Capital employed = nondepreciated value of asset remaining.
PV of CCE = present value of the cost of capital employed.

Table 5-9 EVA of Project

Present	1	2	3	4	5	Total	
	$50,000	$50,000	$50,000	$50,000	$50,000	$250,000	Business case EAT
	$46,296.30	$42,866.94	$39,691.61	$36,751.49	$34,029.16	$199,635.50	PV of EAT
	$37,037.04	$27,434.84	$19,051.97	$11,760.48	$5,444.67	$100,729.00	PV of CCE
$0.00	$9,259.26	$15,432.10	$20,639.64	$24,991.01	$28,584.49	$98,906.50	PV of EVA
	0.08	0.08	0.08	0.08	0.08		Discount rate, "k"

PV of EAT = present value of earnings after tax.
PV of CCE = present value of the cost of capital employed.
PV of EVA = present value of economic value add.

Table 5-10 EVA–NPV of Project

EVA of Project

Present	1	2	3	4	5	Total	
	$50,000.00	$50,000.00	$50,000.00	$50,000.00	$50,000.00	$250,000.00	Business case EAT
	$46,296.30	$42,866.94	$39,691.61	$36,751.49	$34,029.16	**$199,635.50**	PV of EAT
$0.00	$37,037.04	$27,434.84	$19,051.97	$11,760.48	$5,444.67	**$100,729.00**	PV of CCE
	$9,259.26	$15,432.10	$20,639.64	$24,991.01	$28,584.49	**$98,906.50**	PV of EVA
	0.08	0.08	0.08	0.08	0.08		Discount rate, "k"

PV of EAT = present value of earnings after tax.
PV of CCE = present value of the cost of capital employed.
PV of EVA = present value of economic value add.

NPV of Project

Present	1	2	3	4	5	Total	
	$50,000.00	$50,000.00	$50,000.00	$50,000.00	$50,000.00	$250,000.00	Business case EAT
	$100,000.00	$100,000.00	$100,000.00	$100,000.00	$100,000.00	$500,000.00	Depreciation
	$150,000.00	$150,000.00	$150,000.00	$150,000.00	$150,000.00		NCF
	0.08	0.08	0.08	0.08	0.08		Discount rate, "k"
$0.00	$138,888.88	$128,600.82	$119,074.84	$110,254.48	$102,087.48	**$598,906.50**	PV of NCF
						–$500,000.00	PV of investment
						$98,906.50	NPV

PV of NCF = present value of net cash flow.

is the present value of the cash inflows from earnings. Then subtract the present value of the outflows. The result is the NPV. We see that, to the penny, the EVA and the NPV are the same, though the calculations for NPV are usually much simpler since cash is much easier to measure and track than EAT.

$$\text{NPV (NCF from operations)} = \text{EVA (EAT)}$$

SUMMARY OF IMPORTANT POINTS

Table 5-11 provides the highlights of this chapter.

Table 5-11   Summary of Important Points

Point of Discussion	Summary of Ideas Presented
Financial statements	■ The general body of knowledge for accounting standards is contained in the *Generally Accepted Accounting Principles*. ■ Four statements for project managers are: the P&L expense statement, the cash flow statement, the balance sheet, and the trial balance.
P&L statement	■ The expense statement, sometimes known as the income or P&L statement, is an ordered list of the revenue and expense items for the project. ■ Expenses within the project WBS are coded and identified according to the expense statement.
Balance sheet	■ The balance sheet is where the unrecognized expense is maintained until the time comes to "expense" it to the expense statement.
Cash flow statement	■ The cash flow statement is commonly thought of as the place to put down the sources of cash and uses of cash in the project. ■ There are only two ways a company generates cash: (1) decrease an asset or (2) increase a liability.
Discounted cash flow	■ DCF is taken to be the present value of *net cash flow* or *net cash flow from operations*. ■ The discount rate, sometimes called an interest rate, but also called the cost of capital rate or factor, is the discount applied to future cash flows to account for the risk that those flows may not happen as planned. ■ IRR = discount rate for which NPV = 0.
Trial balance	■ The trial balance is a report of debits and credits by account.
Capital budgeting	■ Capital budgeting is about how to budget and spend cash for the big-ticket items on the project. ■ Capital budgets refer to those project budgets for which cash is paid out now, in the present during the project execution, but for which the expense will be recognized in the future when the item is put into use.

Table 5-11   Summary of Important Points (continued)

Point of Discussion	Summary of Ideas Presented
Opportunity cost	■ The opportunity cost of the difference in returns, after risk adjustment, between one project opportunity and the next most favorable opportunity that is competing for the same capital.
Net present value	■ Present value (PV) = Future value/$(1 + k)^N$. ■ NPV = PV (all inflows) − PV (all outflows). ■ Decision policy: Only projects with NPV $\geq$ \$0 will be selected for execution.
Economic value add	■ EVA is a risk-adjusted quantitative measure of project performance. ■ A project should earn more in profits than the cost of the project's capital employed. ■ EVA = EAT − k * CCE. ■ NPV (net cash flow from operations) = EVA (after-tax earnings).

REFERENCES

1. Pike, Tom, *Retool, Rethink, Results,* Simon & Schuster, New York, 1999.
2. Higgins, Robert C., *Analysis for Financial Management,* Irwin McGraw-Hill, Boston, MA, 1998, chap. 1, pp. 16–21.
3. Ibid., p. 19.
4. Ibid., p. 238.
5. Finegan, P.T., Financial incentives resolve the shareholder-value puzzle, *Corporate Cashflow*, pp. 27–32, October 1989.
6. Tully, S., The real key to creating wealth, *Fortune*, pp. 38–50, September 1993.

EXPENSE ACCOUNTING AND EARNED VALUE

*Every individual endeavors to employ his capital
so that its produce may be of greatest value.*

Adam Smith
The Wealth of Nations, 1776

Most project managers keep track of two financial measures for their project: the dollar amount budgeted and the dollar amount spent. If the project manager spends less than budgeted, then very often the project is considered a success, at least financially:

If: \$Budget – \$Spent ≥ \$0, Then: OK; Else: Corrective action required

However, the two measures of budget and actual expenditures taken together as one pair of financial metrics do not provide a measure of value obtained and delivered for the actual expenditures. The fact is that all too often the money is spent and there is too little to show for it. Thus, in this chapter we will "follow the money" a different way and introduce the concept of "earned value," which often draws a different conclusion about project financial success:

If: \$Value delivered – \$Spent ≥ \$0, Then: OK, Else: Corrective action required

Before getting to the earned value concept, however, we will revisit the P&L (profit and loss) statement discussed in Chapter 5 to understand the various expense items that might show up on an earned value report in the categories of $Spent and $Value delivered.

THE EXPENSE STATEMENT

The P&L expense statement is one of the three most important financial statements that the controller will provide to the project manager. The other two financial statements that are useful to project managers, as were discussed in Chapter 5, are the cash flow statement and the balance sheet. The project manager has little to say about the expense categories on the P&L; the controller usually defines the expense categories when the chart of accounts is put together. On the other hand, the project manager has nearly full freedom to create the work breakdown structure (WBS) and define the expense categories on the WBS.*

Although the WBS is traditionally thought of as the document that defines the scope, and all the scope, for the project, in fact it can also serve as an important financial document, connecting as it does to the chart of accounts. To employ the earned value methodology, we must have a complete WBS; to dollar-denominate the earned value reports and also allocate the budget to the WBS, we must understand the chart of accounts, or at least the chart of accounts as it is represented on the P&L statements. Since it is the P&L by which managers govern and are measured for success, the various tools must all correlate and reconcile.

Let us begin this chapter by discussing more thoroughly the nature of the expenses that will be on the P&L. We will look at how these expenses can be traced to the WBS, and then from the WBS back to the P&L.

Direct and Indirect, Fixed and Variable Expenses in Projects

We know from Chapter 5 that the P&L records the project expenses each month. The P&L does not necessarily indicate the cash flow, and not all expenses on

---

* The exception to the project manager creating the WBS occurs when the project is on a contract for a customer who chooses to define the WBS. Typically, the customer will define the WBS down to the second or third level. To the customer, this WBS is the contractor WBS (CWBS). The contractor uses this CWBS, but extends it to lower levels to encompass the project detail of the implementing organization. Further explanation of this concept can be found in MIL-HDBK-881, Department of Defense Handbook Work Breakdown Structure, January 1998, Chapter 3.

the P&L are cash. Depreciation and various P&L accruals for taxes, compensation, and benefits are not cash. Expenses, like payments to a vendor, are "recognized" according to the business rules of your business. The expense recognition might be at a different time from when the credit is made to the accounts payable liability account (the usual expense "recognition trigger"), or different from the time the vendor check is mailed after the liability is created, and different yet from when the check clears the banking system and is credited to the checking account. Thus, timing may be an issue for the project manager as the project manager reconciles expenses between the controller reports and the project reports.

In larger companies, the expense recognition rules tend toward recognizing expenses as soon as the expense obligation is created. Actually paying the cash is not so important to the project per se. The company treasurer or chief financial officer usually sets policies for actually paying the cash to the vendor since there can be some financing income from the checking account "float."

The controller may choose to categorize expenses and show those categories on the expense statement. For instance, expenses that are for the express benefit of the project, and would not be incurred if not for the project, are usually called "direct expenses." Project travel is a good example of direct expenses.

However, many expenses of the company, such as executive and general management expenses, are present whether or not there is a project. The controller may make an allocation of these expenses to the project. Expenses such as these are called "indirect" or "overhead" expenses. Project managers can think of them as an internal "flat tax" on the direct expenses since the allocation is often made as a fixed percentage of the direct expenses.

Other expenses may simply be assigned to the project as a means to account for them on the company's overall P&L. For example, if a paint shop is needed by the project, and no other projects are using the paint shop, its expenses may be assigned to the project. If not for the project, perhaps the paint shop would be closed.

Expenses can also be categorized as fixed or variable. Fixed expenses are not subject to the volume of work being done. For instance, the project manager's compensation is usually a fixed expense each period. Fixed expenses are incurred each expense period regardless of the work being done. Fixed expenses are sometimes called "marching army" expenses because they are the cost of running the project even when there is little going on. Obviously, the cost of the "marching army" represents a significant risk to the project manager's plan to execute the project on budget. One strategy to mitigate "marching army" expense risk is to convert fixed expenses to variable expenses whenever possible.

Variable expenses track the workload: more work, more expense. For example, the number of painters in the paint shop may be variable according to workload. The risk associated with variable costs is the setup and teardown costs, even if the cost item is software system engineers rather than painters. If the same system engineers do not return to the project when needed, then the setup and training costs for new system engineers may be prohibitive. Thus, the project manager may elect to convert a variable category to a fixed category and bear the risk of the "marching army" of system engineers as a better bet than the recruiting of a variable workforce of system engineers.

Variable Expenses and Lean Thinking

Lean Thinking[1] is the name of a book by James Womack and Daniel Jones* and a concept of optimizing variable activity and expense. The essence of the concept is to create "flows" of activities leading to valuable deliverables. Minimizing batch cycles that cause interruption in the value stream and require high cost to initiate and terminate creates flows. Initiation and termination costs are "nonvalue add" in the sense that they do not contribute to the value of the deliverable. For example, if a project deliverable required painting, say the color red, should all red painting wait until all red painting requirements are ready to be satisfied in a red paint batch, or could a specific deliverable be painted red now and not be held up for others not ready to be painted?

What about sequential development? A familiar methodology is the so-called "waterfall" in which each successive step is completed before the next step is taken. The objective of the waterfall is to obviate scrap and rework if new requirements are discovered late. As an example, in the waterfall methodology all requirements are documented on one step of the waterfall before design begins on the next successive step. Each step is a "batch." Flow in the value stream is interrupted by stopping to evaluate whether or not each step is completed, but "marching army" variable costs are minimized: once the requirements staff is finished, they are no longer needed, so there is no subsequent nonvalue add to bringing them back on the project.

Lean thinking applied to project cost management has many potential benefits. If the cost to initiate the batch work could be made negligible, whether painting or developing, project managers would plan the project exclusively around the requirements for deliverables and not around the deliverables as influenced by the requirements of the process itself. Many fixed costs could be converted easily to variable expenses, nonvalue-add variable costs could be reduced, and the overall cost to the project would be less.

---

* James Womack and Daniel Jones are probably best known for their groundbreaking study of just-in-time quality manufacturing at Toyota that was documented in their famous book with co-author David Roos, *The Machine That Changed the World.*

Table 6-1   Standard Costs Example

Labor Code	Labor Category	Standard Cost, $/hour	Actual Compensation, Range $/hour
1001	Programmer	$22.25	$20.10–$26.00
1002	Lead Programmer	$26.50	$24.90–$30.25
1003	Senior Programmer	$31.25	$27.00–$38.00
1004	Systems Programmer	$40.00	$33.50–$50.25
2001	Welder	$12.25	$10.10–$16.00
2002	Senior Welder	$16.50	$14.90–$20.25
2003	Welding Specialist 1	$21.25	$17.00–$28.00
2004	Welding Specialist 2	$30.00	$23.50–$40.25

Standard Costs and Actual Costs

There is yet one more way to show costs on the expense statement: manage to standard costs rather than actual costs. Simply put, standard costs are average costs. The controller sets the period over which the average is made, determines any weighting that is to be applied in the averaging process, and selects the pool of participants in the average. Table 6-1 provides an illustration of how standard costs are applied to labor categories.

In some businesses, the project is charged the standard cost for, for example, a welder or forklift operator rather than the actual cost. The controller's office manages the variance between the sum of the standard costs and the sum of the actual costs on the project. Sometimes this variance is charged to the project and sometimes it goes into the indirect cost pool and therefore is liquidated by charge back to projects in the overhead rate. Thus, the variance to standard cost could become a project expense over which the project manager has some control with other project managers if more than one project is contributing to the standard cost pool. However, even more problematic for the project manager, the standard cost variance could be passed to a customer if the customer has contracted for the project on a cost-reimbursable contract. Such arrangements are common in federal government contracting, especially in the defense sector.*

---

* As an example of standard costs in reimbursable-cost-type contracts, consider the situation in which a customer contracts for a project and the proposal for the work is prepared by the project manager using standard costs. As named individuals are assigned by the project manager to do contracted work, the compensation of the named individuals may be more or less than the standard costs for their labor category. The variance to standard costs, either favorable or unfavorable, would be passed to the customer on a cost-reimbursable contract. On the other hand, if the contract is fixed price standard cost, then the variance to standard cost is absorbed by the project and is not passed to the customer.

Cost Categories on the Profit and Loss Statement

Cost categories on the P&L can be interlaced in a hierarchy according to the view most advantageous to managers. Direct expenses could be divided into fixed and variable, or you could turn it around so that fixed expenses could be divided into direct and indirect. At the bottom line, the sum total is indifferent to the management's selection of the cost hierarchy.

APPLYING THREE-POINT STATISTICAL ESTIMATES TO COST

The P&L statement that we have just discussed is deterministic. The P&L statement is a product of the business accounting department. The P&L is not based on statistics. However, the project cost estimates are probabilistic and require three-point estimates of most pessimistic, most optimistic, and most likely, as was discussed in the chapter on statistical methods. Once the three-point estimates are applied to a distribution and the expected value determined, the expected value could then be used in the earned value concept, which will be discussed in the balance of this chapter.

Statistical Distributions for Cost

We actually use the same statistical distributions discussed earlier for all probabilistic problems in projects, whether cost, schedule, or other. It is up to the project manager and the project team to select the most appropriate distribution for each cost account on the WBS. Often the project manager applies three-point estimates only to selected cost accounts on the WBS simply because of the "80–20" rule (80% of problems arise from 20% of the opportunities).

The Uniform distribution would be applied when there is no central tendency around a mean value. There may indeed be some cases where the cost is estimated equally likely between the pessimistic and optimistic limits. However, if there is a central tendency and the likelihood of pessimistic or optimistic outcomes is about equal, then the Normal distribution would be appropriate. We know, of course, that the BETA and Triangular distributions are applicable when the risk is asymmetrical.

Three-Point Estimates

When doing the cost estimates leading to the summarized project cost, three-point distributions should be applied to the WBS. We will discuss in Chapter 7 that the ultimate cost summarization at the "top" of the WBS will be approximately Normal regardless of the distributions applied within the WBS. The fact that the final outcome is an approximately Normal distribution is a very significant fact and a simplifying outcome for the project manager. Nevertheless, in spite of the foregone result of a Normal distributed cost summation, applying three-point estimates to the WBS will add information to the project that will help establish the degree of cost risk in the project. The three-point estimates will provide the information necessary to estimate the standard deviation and the variance of the final outcome and quantify the risk between the project side and the business side of the project balance sheet.

THE EARNED VALUE CONCEPT

The earned value concept is about focusing on accomplishment, called earnings or performance, and the variance between the dollar value and the dollar cost of those accomplishments. Perhaps focusing on the dollar value of accomplishment is what you thought you have always been doing, but that probably is not so. More often, the typical financial measure employed by project managers is the variance between period budget and period cost. Such a variance works as follows: if we underspend the budget in a period, regardless of accomplishment, we report a favorable status, "budget less cost > $0," for the period. Such would not be the case in the earned value system: if accomplishment does not exceed its cost, the variance of "accomplishment less cost < $0" is always reported as an unfavorable status.

The earned value concept is not exclusively about minimizing the variance and interchanging the word *value* for the word *budget* in the equations. All of that calculation is historical and an explanation of how the project got to where it is at the time the variance is measured. Earned value also provides a means to forecast performance. The forecast is a tool to alert the project manager that corrective action may be required or to expose upside opportunity that might be exploited. For instance, if the forecast is for an overrun in cost or schedule, then obviously the project manager goes to work to effect corrections. However, if the cost or schedule forecast is for an underrun, then what? Such an underrun may present an opportunity to implement a planned phase earlier or bring forward deferred functionality. Whether or not the opportunity is acted on, the earned value forecast identifies the possibility to the project team.

Earned Value Standards and Specifications

The earned value system has been around since the late 1960s in its formal state, but the idea of "getting your money's worth" is a concept as old as barter. A brief but informative history of the earned value system is provided by Quentin Fleming and Joel Koppelman in their book, *Earned Value Project Management, Second Edition.*[2] Earned value as it is known today originated around 1962 in the Department of Defense, originally as an extension of the scheduling methodology of the era, PERT,* but became its own methodology in 1967 with the introduction of the Cost/Schedule Control Systems Criteria[3] (C/SCSC for short, and pronounced "c-speck") into the Defense Department's instructions (DoDI) about systems acquisition.** The Defense Department C/SCSC has evolved over time to the present ANSI/EIA 748 standard.*** Along the way, some of the acronyms changed and a few criteria were combined and streamlined, but nothing has changed in terms of the fundamentals of earning value for the prescribed cost and schedule.

In the original C/SCSC, the requirements for measuring and reporting value were divided into 35 criteria grouped into five categories.[4] The ANSI/EIA 748 has fewer criteria, only 32, but also the same five categories, albeit with slight name changes. The five categories are explained in Table 6-2. Quentin and Koppleman[5] provide detail on all of the criteria from both standards for the interested reader.

Earned Value Measurements

Earned value measurements are divided roughly between history and forecast. The history measures by and large involve *variances.* Variances are computed by adding and subtracting one variable from another:

$$\$Variance = \$Expectation\ of\ performance - \$Actual\ performance$$

---

* PERT is an acronym for Program Evaluation Review Technique. PERT is a network scheduling methodology that employs expected value for the duration estimate. The expected value is estimated from three-point estimates of duration applied to the BETA distribution. The α and β parameters of the BETA distribution are such that the distribution is asymmetric with the mode closer to the optimistic value than to the pessimistic value.

** In 1967, the earned value standard was under the executive control of the DoD comptroller (the chief accountant) because it was seen chiefly as a financial reporting tool. Not until 1989 did the executive control pass to the systems acquisition chief in the Pentagon, thereby recognizing the importance of the tool to the overall management of the project.

*** ANSI/EIA is an acronym for two standards organizations: the American National Standards Institute and the Electronic Industries Association. The ANSI/EIA 748 standard can be obtained, for a fee, from the sponsoring organizations.

Table 6-2 Earned Value Management Categories

Category	General Content and Description	Number of Criteria in Category
Organization	Define the WBS, the program organizational structure, and show integration with the host organization for cost and schedule control.	5
Planning, scheduling, and budgeting	Identify the work products, schedule the work according to work packages, and apply a time-phased budget to the work packages and project. Identify and control direct costs, overhead, and time and material items.	10
Accounting considerations	Record all direct and indirect costs according to the WBS and the chart of accounts; provide data necessary to support earned value reporting and management.	6
Analysis and management reports	Provide analysis and reports appropriate to the project and the timelines specific to the project.	6
Revisions and data maintenance	Identify and manage changes, updating appropriate scope, schedule, and budgets after changes are approved.	5

Forecasts require performance *indexes*. Indexes are ratios of one variable divided by another of like dimension. Indexes are historical; numerator and denominator both come from past performance. These indexes, which are dimensionless, are used as a factor to amplify or discount remaining future performance. Forecasts are computed by multiplying performance remaining by a historical performance factor that amplifies or discounts remaining performance based on performance to date:

$$\$Forecast = \$Performance\ remaining$$
$$* \ Historical\ performance\ factor$$

Historical performance factor = Value obtained/Value expectation

It is evident from the components of variance and forecast that three measures are needed to construct an earned value system of performance evaluation:

- **Planned value (PV)**: The dollar value planned and assigned to the work or the deliverable in the WBS. PV is the expectation project sponsors have for the value embodied in the project. PV is a quantity on the left side, or sponsor's side, of the project balance sheet. PV assignments are made by decomposing the overall project dollar value, in other words the budget, into dollar values of the lowest work package. PV assignments are made before work begins; the aggregate of the PV assignments makes up the dollar value of the performance measurement baseline (PMB) that is, in turn, the budget for the project. The PMB is on the right side of the project balance sheet and should reconcile with the PV on the sponsor's side. If there is a mismatch, the difference is made up in risk.

$$\Sigma \text{ (All PV \$assignments)} = \$PMB$$

$$\Sigma \text{ (All PV \$assignments)} = \text{Project manager's \$budget for the project}$$

$$\$\text{Value of the project} = \Sigma \text{ (All PV assignments)} + \$Risk$$

- **Actual cost (AC)**: The cost of performance to accomplish the work or provide the deliverable on the WBS. AC should reconcile with the expenses reported on the project P&L. Now is where our discussion of depreciation, fixed and variable, and direct and indirect costs comes into play. In the category of "Accounting Considerations" in the ANSI/EIA 748 standard, criteria 16–19 (of 32 criteria) address handling direct and indirect costs. Generally, the criteria can be interpreted as requiring direct costs to be identified at the work package level, with indirect costs allocated appropriately. Such guidance can be applied two ways: either the work package manager tracks indirect costs or the project manager tracks indirect costs at the project level. The important idea for the cost account and work package managers is to have a consistent approach that can be used to systematically align with the project P&L.
- **Earned value (EV)**: A measure of the project value actually obtained by the work package effort. EV could be more than, equal to, or less than the PV for the work package for the period being measured. Of course, the same could be said for the AC: AC could be more than, equal to, or less than the PV.

The acronyms PV, AC, and EV are new with the ANSI/EIA 748 standard. The old acronyms that they replace, along with other comparisons between the old and new standards, are given in Table 6-3.

The Bicycle Project Example

As a simple example to illustrate the principles explained so far, let us assume the following project situation. The project is to deliver a bicycle to the project

Table 6-3   Earned Value Acronyms

ANSI/EIA 748 Standard	DoD C/SCSC Standard	Description
Planned Value, PV	Budgeted Cost of Work Scheduled, BCWS	The time-phased budget for the project that is allocated to the cost accounts on the WBS.
Earned Value, EV	Budgeted Cost of Work Performed, BCWP	The dollar value of the work accomplished in each cost account in the evaluation period, whether the work is scheduled for that period or not. The dollar value of the work is found in the PV for the cost account.
Actual Cost, AC	Actual Cost of Work Performed, ACWP	The dollar value paid for the work accomplished in each cost account in the evaluation period, whether the work is scheduled for that period or not. The dollar value of the payment is independent of the dollar value of the work as set in the PV for the cost account.
Cost Performance Index, CPI	Cost Performance Index, CPI	An index of efficiency relating how much is paid for a unit of value. Optimally, $1 is paid for $1 of value earned, CPI = 1.
Schedule Performance Index, SPI	Schedule Performance Index, SPI	An index of efficiency relating how much value that is scheduled to be accomplished really is accomplished. Optimally, $1 of scheduled value is earned in the period scheduled for that $1, SPI = 1.
Cost Variance	Cost Variance	A historical measure to indicate whether the actual cost paid for an accomplishment exceeds, equals, or does not exceed the value of the accomplishment. Variance = EV − AC.
Schedule Variance	Schedule Variance	A historical measure to indicate whether value is being accomplished on time. This variance can also be thought of as a "value variance." Variance = EV − PV.

sponsor. Let us say that the sponsor has placed a value on the bicycle of $1,000 (PV = $1,000). Within the $1,000 value, we must deliver a complete and functioning bicycle that conforms to the usual understanding of a bicycle: frame, wheels, tires, seat, brakes, handlebars, chains and gears, pedals and crank, all assembled and finished appropriately.

Ordinarily, the project manager will spread the $1,000 of PV to all of the bicycle work packages in the WBS. The sum of all the PV of each individual work package then equals the PV for the whole project. We call the distributing of PV into the WBS the PMB. For simplicity, we will skip that step in this example.

What happens if at the end of the schedule period all is available as pre-scribed except the pedals? Because of the missing pedals, the project is only expensed $900 (AC = $900). How would we report to the project sponsor? By the usual reckoning, we are okay since we have not overspent the budget; in fact, we are $100 under budget (Variance to budget = $1,000 – $900 = $100). The variance to budget is "favorable." If we have not run out of time, and the bicycle is not needed right away, perhaps we could get away with such a report.

In point of fact, we have spent $900 and have no value to show for it! If the pedals never show up, we are not $100 under budget; we are $900 out of luck with nothing to show for it. A bicycle without pedals is functionally useless and without value. We should report the EV as $0, PV as $1,000, and the AC as $900. Our variances for the first period are then:

$$\text{Planned value}_1 = PV_1 = \$1,000$$

$$\text{Cost variance}_1 = EV_1 - AC_1 = \$0 - \$900 = -\$900 \text{ (unfavorable)}$$

$$\text{Value variance}_1 = EV_1 - PV_1 = \$0 - \$1,000 = -\$1,000 \text{ (unfavorable)}$$

Now here is an interesting idea: *the value variance has the same functional effect as a schedule variance.* That is to say, the value variance is the difference between the value expected in the period and the value earned in the period. So, in the case cited above, the project has not completed $1,000 of planned work and thus is behind schedule in completing that work. We say in the earned value management system that the project is behind schedule by $1,000 of work planned and not accomplished in the time allowed.

$$\$\text{Schedule variance} = \$\text{Value variance} = EV - PV$$

$$\$SV = EV - PV$$

What is the reporting if in the next period the pedals are delivered, the project is expensed $100 for the pedals, and the assembly of the bicycle is complete in all respects? The good news is that the project manager can take credit for earning the value of the bicycle. The EV is $1,000 in the second period. The PV for the second period is $0; baselines do not change just because there is a late-performing work package. We did not intend to have any work in the second period, so the PV for the second period is $0. The project AC in the second period is $100. We calculate our variances as follows:

$$\text{Cost variance}_2 = EV_2 - AC_2 = \$1,000 - \$100 = \$900 \text{ (favorable)}$$

$$\text{Value variance}_2 = EV_2 - PV_2 = \$1,000 - \$0 = \$1,000 \text{ (favorable)}$$

$$\text{Schedule variance}_2 = EV_2 - PV_2 = \$1,000 - \$0 = \$1,000 \text{ (favorable)}$$

As a memory jogger, note the pattern in the equations. The EV is always farthest to the left, and both the AC and the PV are subtracted from EV.

Now, let's take a close look at this second period. The second period was never in the plan, so the PV for this period is $0. However, any value earned in an unplanned period always creates a positive value or schedule variance in that period. The cost variance does not have a temporal dependency like the PV. The cost variance is simply the difference between the claimed value and the cost to produce it. The cost variance in an unplanned period might be positive or negative. Overall, the project at completion, considering Period 1 and 2 in tandem, has the following variances:

$$\text{Project variances} = \Sigma \text{ (All period variances)}$$

$$\text{Value (schedule) variance} = -\$1,000_1 + \$1,000_2 = \$0$$

$$\text{Cost variance} = -\$900_1 + \$900_2 = \$0$$

Earned Value Equations for Variances and Indexes

From the bicycle example, we have developed some experience with the two most important earned value equations that address project history: the cost variance and the schedule or value variance. Table 6-4 provides all the equations associated with the earned value measurements that are important to project managers. You can see that they are quite simple mathematically. In this table you will find not only the equations that address history but also the equations necessary to understand the potential outcome of the project. You will also see some of the other acronyms associated with the process; for instance, ETC stands for estimate to complete and EAC stands for estimate at completion.

It is self-evident from Table 6-4 that the mathematics are not the challenging part of the earned value process. The equations are simple formulas involving relatively few and easily understood variables. The challenges arise, as is often

Table 6-4 Earned Value Equations

Metric	Equation	Comment
Cost variance	$CV = EV - AC$	Historical measurement of past cost performance.
Schedule variance	$SV = EV - PV$	Historical measurement of past scheduled work accomplishment performance; can also be viewed as a variance on value.
Cost performance index (CPI)	$CPI = EV/AC$	Index of cost efficiency of past cost performance. A figure less than 1 indicates more actual cost is being paid than is value being earned.
Schedule performance index (SPI)	$SPI = EV/PV$	Index of scheduled-work efficiency of past scheduled performance. A figure less than 1 indicates more actual time is being consumed than was planned for the value earned. Can also be thought of as an index on value accumulation in the project.
COST estimate to complete (ETC)	$ETC = PVR/CPI$	ETC is equal to remaining or unearned value normalized to the historical cost performance. A CPI less than 1 will inflate the ETC to greater than the remaining budget. PVR = PV remaining.
COST estimate at completion (EAC)	$EAC = AC + ETC$	EAC is the total forecasted funds needed to do the project.
To complete performance index (TCPI)	$TCPI = PVR/ETC$	TCPI less than 1 means the project will overrun the remaining budget for the work remaining.
SCHEDULE estimate to complete (STC)	$STC = (SR)$ $* (EVR)/(PVR)$	SR = schedule remaining. EVR = EV remaining.
SCHEDULE estimate at completion (SAC)	$SAC = STD + (SR)$ $* (EVR)/(PVR)$	STD = schedule to date.

the case, from application of theory to real practice. We will address these practice problems in the subsequent paragraphs.

PREPARING THE PROJECT TEAM FOR EARNED VALUE

From the bicycle example and the equations presented in Table 6-4, it is somewhat evident what must be done to prepare the project team for earned value. The most critical steps are:

- Prepare a complete WBS for the project. Without a complete WBS, the PMB cannot be adequately prepared. Earned value is measurement of accomplishment against a baseline. Without the baseline, there can be no meaningful measurement. In the chapter on estimates, we discussed in detail how to decompose the sponsor's value estimate into the WBS. In the earned value system, the sponsor's value estimate becomes the planned value of the project.
- Set up the project rules for sizing the cost accounts work packages. Work packages are the smallest units of work on the WBS and are collectively rolled into cost accounts. Cost accounts are typically the lowest level on the WBS where formal cost tracking and allocation are made. Sizing the cost account means deciding how large in dollars a cost account should be before it is too large for effective management and needs to be subdivided into multiple cost accounts. There are no fixed rules. On some smaller projects, $50,000 or less may be a cost account; however, on larger projects, so small an amount may be impractical. The project manager and the project team make these decisions.
- Provide a means to collect and report actual cost. Collecting and reporting actual cost is the most difficult part of applying earned value. Outside of the contractor community that serves the Department of Defense, there are few businesses that invest in the means to collect actual cost beyond direct purchases. Most projects are run with salaried labor for which project-level timekeeping is not available. Without actual cost, there is little that can be done with the quantitative metrics of earned value, although the concept of focusing on accomplishment remains valid.
- Set up the project rules for claiming earned value credit. Earned value credit rules must be set up in advance and made known to the cost account and work package leaders.

Dollar Sizing the Cost Account

Apart from any qualitative management considerations regarding effective control of cost accounts, there are some quantitative implications to "large" and "small" accounts. The quantitative implications arise from the variance estimates that are a direct consequence of the distance between the most pessimistic dollar value and the most optimistic dollar value of a cost account probability distribution. The larger the account, the greater is the pessimistic–optimistic distance and the greater is the amount at stake in dollars.

The concept of larger dollar risk with larger cost accounts is intuitive but has a statistical foundation. The statistical foundation can provide guidance to the project manager regarding practical approaches to subdividing cost accounts to mitigate risk. It turns out that the same phenomenon occurs in scheduling with "long" tasks. Indeed, when you think about it, planning involves not only sizing the cost accounts for dollars, but also sizing for schedule. In fact "right sizing" for dollars may well lead the project manager toward "right sizing" for schedule. Because of the coupling between right sizing for cost and right sizing for schedule, we will defer the quantitative discussion until Chapter 7.

Rolling Wave Planning

We have all faced the planning problem where activities in the future, beyond perhaps a near-term horizon of a few months or a year, are sufficiently uncertain that we can only sketch out the project plan beyond the immediate horizon. Such planning has a name: rolling wave planning. Rolling wave planning simply means that the detail down to the cost account is done in "waves" or stages when the project activities, facilities, tools, staffing, risks, and approach become more known. In effect, rolling wave planning is conditional planning. The "if, then, else" direction of the project in the future depends on outcomes that will only become known as the project proceeds.

Whether the large cost account is a result of rolling wave planning or is simply a planning outcome of the WBS and the schedule network, the statistical implications are similar. The quantitative aspects of rolling wave planning are discussed with the material on schedule planning in Chapter 7.

Project Rules for Claiming Earned Value Credit

There are three rule systems generally applied to earned value systems: (1) all or nothing, such as was applied in the bicycle project example; (2) some number of discrete steps like 0, 50, or 100%; and (3) continuous estimates of credit from 0 to 100% complete with any number in between being acceptable. Practice has shown that the continuous method dilutes the value of the earned value method since the tendency to be "90% complete" for most of the timeline is very prevalent.

Of course it is not enough to simply have a rule without also considering when a work package task begins and ends. When does the clock begin running and the expenses start accumulating for the actual cost, and, just as important, when does the accumulation of expenses end so that a variance can be calculated? Just looking at the project network diagram to find the task dependencies

Table 6-5   Earned Value Claim Rules

Claim Parameter	Application	Explanation
Task started	Time-Centric Earned Value	Predecessor events that establish the prerequisites of the task are done and the current task has begun expending effort.
Task completed	Time-Centric Earned Value	All work necessary to complete the successor dependencies is complete and the business value of the task is accomplished.
All work performed	EAI Standard Earned Value	All work necessary to complete the successor dependencies is complete and the business value of the task is accomplished.
Partial credit for work performed	EAI Standard Earned Value	All work necessary to meet the standing criteria for partial credit is complete and the business value of the task up to the partial complete level is accomplished.
Standard units of work	Either Earned Value System	A "standard" unit of work measured in business value such that each WBS work package is measured in so many standard units. Earnings accrue for each unit completed.

may not be enough, though the network diagram is the place to start. Table 6-5 offers a few definitions that are helpful in establishing the earned value measurement system.

The Earned Value Claims Process

In point of fact, a process should be established for claimants to make their claims for value earned. Typically, the project manager holds a "value review" each period to receive the value claims for evaluation. By means of web-based project tools, video- and teleconferences, e-mail, and actual meetings, there is usually ample opportunity to receive this information. Once received, the earnings claims must be validated and accepted. Applying the claim rules may change the earnings claim as originally submitted. Once the claim is validated, the actual cost from the P&L can be applied to the work package deliverables. Then variances are calculated and forecasts are made.

If the forecast is not favorable, the project manager can take several different actions depending on the severity of the variance:

■ Plan to mitigate the variance with offsetting positive variances in other work packages.

- Rebaseline the remaining project by re-estimating the remaining work using the history of past work to obtain a more realistic ETC and EAC. The estimating techniques discussed in other chapters would come into play at this point.
- Correct root cause problems that might be centered in staffing, training, tools, methods, facilities, vendors, specifications and procedures, or the like that are impacting performance on the PMB.

Rebaselining the Performance Measurement Baseline

The time may arise when the PMB no longer represents the plan that the project team is working to complete and the variances being reported are therefore not meaningful. In that event, the project manager, in consultation with the project sponsor, will rebaseline the project. Some rules should be decided in advance regarding how rebaselining is to be done. The following are the usual steps:

- Make a clear demarcation of the scope that is to be baselined in the second baseline.
- For the scope in the first baseline, set $EV_{baseline1} = PV_{baseline1}$. All unearned planned value goes to the second baseline and applies to the scope moved to the second baseline. Note that setting the planned value equal to the earned value at the end of PMB 1 resets the schedule and value variance to \$0. The cost variance remains unchanged in PMB 1 and for the project as a whole.
- The planned value moved to the second baseline is then decomposed into a second WBS and a second PMB is fashioned. The second WBS does not need to be structured the same as the first WBS, but the scope that moves should be mapped from WBS_1 to WBS_2.

APPLYING EARNED VALUE

Presuming the project team has been initiated into the earned value system and the rules for claims and reporting have been established, the project manager is ready to apply earned value to the project. The following examples provide some of the situations likely to be encountered.

Two-Task Example

With the earned value equations in hand, we can now turn to applying them to project situations. We must first establish a ground rule for taking credit for accomplishment. For the moment, the rule is the simplest possible: 100% earned

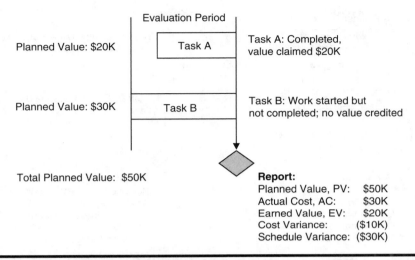

Figure 6-1 Two-Task One-Period Example.

value is given for 100% task completion; else, no credit is given for a partial accomplishment. This is the rule we applied in the bicycle example.

Look now at Figure 6-1. The planned value for the two tasks, A and B, is $50,000. Only Task A is completed, so under the "all-or-nothing" credit rule, no EV is claimed for Task B. Using the equations in Table 6-4, we calculate the report as shown in Figure 6-1. We see that we are $30,000 behind schedule. This means that $30,000 of work planned for the period was not accomplished and must be done at a later time. We are $10,000 over cost, having worked on Task B and claimed no credit and finished Task A for an unspecified cost for a total actual cost of $30,000.

Now in Figure 6-2, we see that we complete Task B, claim $30,000 of earned value, and calculate the variances for Period 2. Of course since there was no planned value and a big earned value, we get a positive schedule variance. Overall from the two periods combined, we get the following performance record for Tasks A and B:

$$PV = \$50,000, \ EV = \$50,000, \ AC = \$60,000$$

$$\text{Schedule variance at the end of Period 2: } EV - PV = \$0$$

$$\text{Cost variance at the end of Period 2: } EV - AC = -\$10,000$$

We are on schedule at the end of Period 2 but carry a cost variance along for the rest of the project. The project manager now begins to analyze where in the

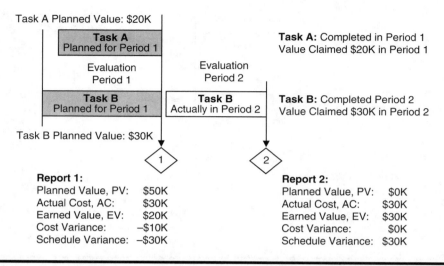

Figure 6-2   Two-Task Two-Period Example.

project there might be a $10,000 positive variance in another work package that could offset the cost variance from the Task A and B experience.

Three-Task Example

Now as it might happen, and often does, as the work package manager is working on a pair of tasks such as we just analyzed, along comes Task C. Task C is unplanned for the current period; Task C is planned for Period 2. Nonetheless, the decision is made to work on Task A and C and let Task B go to the next period. This situation is illustrated in Figure 6-3. Only Task A is completed in Period 1. Work is started in Period 1 on Task C, but not completed; Task C will be completed in Period 2. Task B is deferred to Period 2.

Penalty Costs and Opportunity Costs in Earned Value

You might have observed from the bicycle project that the value variance to the project sponsor for the one-period delay as measured in earned value is $0. By definition, the schedule variance is also $0. But in calendar terms, the project is one period late. Is it not reasonable to assign a variance to a late delivery? If the late delivery has no dollar consequence, then the late delivery has no influence on the earned value metrics. But one of the principal objectives of the earned value method is to influence project manager decision making and performance. Without consequences, the project manager will focus elsewhere.

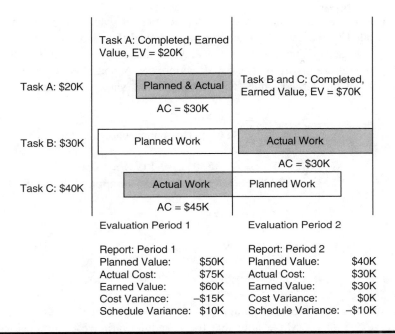

Figure 6-3 Three-Task Two-Period Example.

If there are dollar consequences to the late delivery, then those dollar penalties are incorporated into the period earned value or the period cost, depending on whether the dollar penalty is an opportunity cost (value) or an expensed cost (cost).

Consider this project situation: delivery of the bicycle one period late requires payment of a late delivery penalty of $500 to the ultimate customer. Such a payment is a "hard" cost expense. The $500 is expensed to the project and becomes a part of the project cost. The value of the bicycle to the sponsor remains the same, PV = $1,000. The variances now are for the whole project:

$$PV \text{ of bicycle} = \$1,000$$

$$AC = \$1,500 = \$1,000 \text{ cost} + \$500 \text{ penalty}$$

$$EV = \$1,000$$

$$\text{Cost variance} = EV - AC = \$1,000 - \$1,500 = -\$500$$

$$\text{Schedule or value variance} = EV - PV = \$1,000 - \$1,000 = \$0$$

A late delivery also may present a depreciation of value requiring a discount to be applied to the earned value. We have studied the discount issues in prior chapters. Let us say that a one-period delay requires a 5% discount of value. No dollar penalties are involved. The 5% discount is an opportunity cost requiring an adjustment of the earned value. The bicycle project variances would then be:

$$PV = \$1,000$$
(The performance baseline does not change)

$$EV = (1 - 0.05) * \$1,000 = \$950$$
(Opportunity cost is applied to the EV)

$$AC = \$1,000$$

$$\text{Cost variance} = EV - AC = \$950 - \$1,000 = -\$50$$

$$\text{Schedule or value variance} = EV - PV = \$950 - \$1,000 = -\$50$$

In subsequent tables and paragraphs the "value variance" will be called the "schedule variance." Make note that the schedule variance is dimensioned in dollars rather than hours, days, or weeks.

Graphing Earned Value

Let's turn our attention from numbers to graphs. Sometimes the graphical depiction is very instructive and more quickly grasped than the numbers. For the moment, let us consider the project situation as depicted in Figure 6-4. The equations from Table 6-4 have been used to draw some curves. To make it simple, the curves are actually straight lines. There is no loss of generality for having straight lines for purposes of variances. However, the slope of the cumulative line at the point of evaluation affects the forecast, so just connecting some widely spaced points may create errors in the forecast.

In Figure 6-4, we see a project already under way with a vertical line drawn at the evaluation point. The curves are the aggregated sums of all the work packages in the WBS up to the evaluation point. The PMB extends for the whole project. Thus, these curves represent the project situation overall. At a glance, the experienced project manager can see that the earned value curve is below the actual cost curve, so there is a cumulative unfavorable cost variance to the earned value. The earned value curve is also below the PMB, so there is a schedule variance as well.

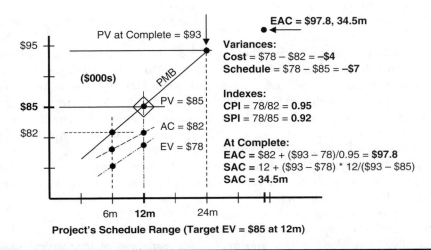

Figure 6-4   Project Example 1.

EV curve **below** AC means: *unfavorable cost* variance

EV curve **below** the PMB or PV means: *unfavorable schedule* variance

Forecasting with Earned Value Measurements

Let us return to the bicycle now that we have a more complete set of equations to work with from Table 6-4. At the end of Period 1, we could make some forecasts:

$$\text{Schedule performance index (SPI)} = EV_1/PV_1 = \$0/\$1{,}000 = 0$$

$$\text{Forecast of schedule} = (PMB - EV_1)/SPI = \text{indefinite}$$
$$\text{(on account of divide-by-0)}$$

$$\text{Cost performance index (CPI)} = EV_1/AC_1 = \$0/(-\$900) = 0$$

$$\text{Forecast of cost} = (PMB - EV_1)/CPI = \text{indefinite}$$

What to make of these forecasts? With no earnings, it is impossible to measure an earnings trend and therefore forecast the future from the past. What should the project manager do in such a case? With no guidance from the earned value forecast, the project manager could forecast the future or rebaseline by re-estimating the remaining work.

We can use the curves in Figure 6-4 to do some elementary forecasting. Doing so will give us a feel for the problem. Unlike the bicycle case, where the earned value was $0 and the forecast was indefinite, there are cumulative earnings for the project shown in Figure 6-4. The project manager can make a prediction by extending the cumulative earned value line until it intersects with the dollar value of the planned value at completion. At this intersection, the cumulative project earned value equals the cumulative value of the project. The extended time on the horizontal axis at the point where the cumulative earned value equals the planned value at completion is the schedule at completion.

The project manager must be careful at this point. The slope of the extension must match the slope of the cumulative earned value curve at the point of evaluation. The slope is the ratio of a small increment of the vertical scale divided by a small increment of the horizontal scale. On the figure we are working with, the horizontal scale is time, so the slope is:

$$\Delta EV / \Delta T, \text{ where } \Delta \text{ means "small increment of"}$$

This slope, $\Delta EV / \Delta T$, tells us we are earning value at a certain rate of so many dollars, $\$\Delta EV$, per time unit, ΔT. If the remaining value to be earned is $PV_{remaining}$, then the time required to earn that much value is:

$$\text{Remaining time} = \Delta T * PV_{remaining} / \Delta EV$$

A numerical example would probably be helpful at this point. Suppose there is $10,000 of remaining value to be earned on a project in the remaining periods. Let us say that in the last reporting period the earned value was $1,000, but that overall the earnings to date have been $24,000 over six periods. On average, the $EV/period is $24,000/6 = $4,000/period. Using this average, we could forecast that 2.5 periods remain to earn the remaining $10,000. Using our formula: 2.5 = 6 * $10,000/$24,000.

However, in the last period, earnings have slowed to $1,000/period. Thus, applying the formula to the performance as of the last period to find out how many remaining periods there are, we have: 10 = 1 * $10,000/$1,000. Which forecast is correct, 2.5 periods or 10 periods? It depends. It depends on the judgment of the project manager regarding whether or not the performance in the last period is representative of the future expectations. If the last period is not representative, then the overall average that uses much more information should be used. When working with statistics like average, in general the more information incorporated, the better is the forecast.

Estimate at Completion, Estimate to Complete

There is a simple formula that ties the EAC and ETC together:

$$EAC = ETC + AC \text{ to date}$$

The actual cost to date is obtained right off the P&L. However, the ETC is somewhat problematic. There are three ways to calculate ETC:

- Apply the earned value formula: $ETC = PV_{remaining} * AC_{to\ date}/EV_{to\ date}$
- Re-estimate the ETC and then rebaseline the remaining planned value as described elsewhere
- $ETC = PV_{remaining}$

Of course, all three methods will provide a different answer. Which to use is a decision to be made by the project manager considering the situation of the project.

TIME-CENTRIC EARNED VALUE

What we have discussed to this point is the traditional and most robust form of earned value. Whenever the resources are available to apply the method, it should be done because it focuses on the accomplishments that lead to project value being delivered as promised. However, the collection and reporting of actual cost is often impractical, thereby rendering the quantitative measures unobtainable. In that event, there is an alternative, though less robust, earned value method named "time-centric earned value,"* first described to the industry in the author's presentation[6] with James R. Sumara to the PMI® National Symposium in 1997.

---

* The original work on "time-centric earned value" was done by the author and colleague James Sumara while working with the Lanier Worldwide business unit of Harris Corporation in the mid-1990s. Although the traditional earned value system was well known and practiced at Harris, the Lanier Worldwide business unit did not have the mechanisms for complete collection of the actual cost of the labor employed for internal projects. Time-centric earned value was developed for the Lanier Worldwide project office to fill the need for an earned value reporting tool.

Time-Centric Principles

The main idea behind the time-centric earned value system is to set a PMB based on planned work package starts and finishes over the course of the project. Time-centric earned value is very close to the concept of "work units" or "standard units of work" as a measure of accomplishment rather than a specific dollarized WBS cost account. Instead of a standard unit of work, however, time-centric earned value focuses on a completed task, with unknown actual cost, as the unit of value in the project.

Although a dollar value is not assigned to each work package start or finish, the total collection of starts and finishes, if executed completely, does represent the total scope (and value) of the project. The total scope of the project does have a dollar planned value (budget).

The historical reporting for purposes of determining variances remains a component of the time-centric system. Instead of earning a dollar value, what is earned is a start or a finish. The PMB is a set of planned starts and planned finishes. Therefore, there is a variance that can be defined thus:

$$\text{Variance (start)} = \text{Earned starts} - \text{Planned starts}$$

$$\text{Variance (finish)} = \text{Earned finishes} - \text{Planned finishes}$$

All the rules we have discussed about what constitutes a claim of credit apply. The definitions of start and finish used in the traditional method to gate the expenses for purposes of calculating the variances to the earned and planned value still apply, but apply to whether a task start can be claimed and not whether actual cost is to be applied. So too do the ideas of rebaselining, calculating the ETC, and the EAC still apply, but apply to the idea of finishing the project on a time basis and not a cost basis.

Time-centric indexes can also be defined and calculated:

$$\text{Task start performance index (TSPI)} = (\text{Earned starts})/(\text{Planned starts})$$

$$\text{Task finish performance index (TFPI)} = (\text{Earned finishes})/(\text{Planned finishes})$$

Figure 6-5 provides an illustration of a project wherein the PMB has 20 starts in the first three periods. We see in this figure that the project team has indeed started 20 tasks, but the starts are at a different pace than planned. We can calculate a variance for each period:

$$\text{Start variance}_1 = 3 - 5 = -2 \text{ starts}$$

$$\text{Start variance}_2 = 9 - 10 = -1 \text{ start}$$

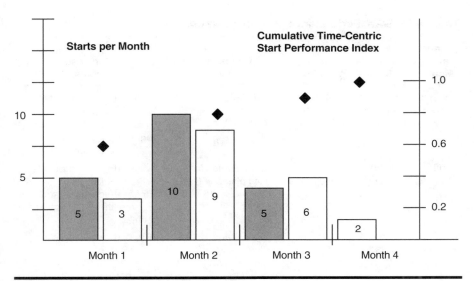

Figure 6-5 Time-Centric Project Start Example.

$$\text{Start variance}_3 = 6 - 5 = 1 \text{ start}$$

$$\text{Start variance}_4 = 2 - 0 = 2 \text{ starts}$$

$$\Sigma \text{ (All variances)} = 0 \text{ start}$$

At the end of four periods, the project is caught up on starts. The project manager can also forecast how soon the project will attain all the starts planned in the PMB using the performance indexes. Table 6-6 provides the start performance metrics. Similarly, we see in Figure 6-6 the finish performance for the example project. Variances similar to the start variances can be calculated; indexes can also be calculated as was done for the project starts. Table 6-7 provides those calculations.

Forecasting with the Time-Centric System

Just like in the traditional earned value system, forecasts can be made using the same formula as we developed for the forecast in that system:

Forecast = Actual performance + Remaining performance/Index

For example, in the first period the actual starts are 3, the remaining performance for the project is 17, and the index is 0.6. The forecast is therefore:

Table 6-6   Start Performance Project Example

Planned Starts by Month*	Actual Starts by Month	Monthly Index	Cumulative Index	Forecasted Finish
Month 1: 5 starts	Month 1: 3 starts	$TSPI_1 =$ $3/5 = 0.6$	Cum Starts = 3 Remaining = 17 Cum = 3/5 = 0.6	Adjusted remaining starts = 17/0.6 = 28 Forecast schedule remaining = 2 months * 28/17 = 3.3 months
Month 2: 10 starts	Month 2: 9 starts	$TSPI_2 =$ $9/10 = 0.9$	Cum Starts = 12 Remaining = 8 Cum = 12/15 = 0.8	Adjusted remaining starts = 8/0.8 = 10 Forecast schedule remaining = 1 month * 10/8 = 1.25 months
Month 3: 5 starts	Month 3: 6 starts	$TSPI_3 =$ $6/5 = 1.2$	Cum Starts = 18 Remaining = 2 Cum = 18/20 = 0.9	Adjusted remaining starts = 2/0.9 = 2.2 Forecast schedule remaining = 0 months * 2.2/2 = 0 months (no remaining schedule available)
Month 4: 0 starts	Month 4: 2 starts	$TSPI_4 = 2/0$ = indefinite	Cum Starts = 20 Remaining = 0 Cum = 20/20 = 1.0	Adjusted remaining starts = 0/1 = 0 Forecast schedule remaining = 0/0 = indefinite

* See related figure for a graphical presentation of this example.

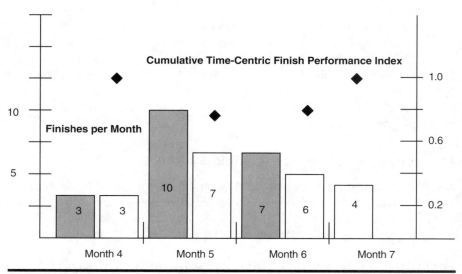

Figure 6-6 Time-Centric Project Finish Example.

Table 6-7   Finish Performance Project Example

Planned Finishes by Month*	Actual Finishes by Month	Monthly Index	Cumulative Index	Forecasted Finish
Month 4: 3 finishes	Month 1: 3 finishes	$TFPI_1 = 3/3$ = 1	Cum Finishes = 3 Remaining = 17 Cum = 3/3 = 1.0	Adjusted remaining finishes = 17/1 = 17 Forecast schedule remaining = 2 months * 17/17 = 2 months
Month 5: 10 finishes	Month 2: 7 finishes	$TFPI_2 =$ 7/10 = 0.7	Cum Finishes = 10 Remaining = 10 Cum = 10/13 = 0.77	Adjusted remaining finishes = 10/0.77 = 10.4 Forecast schedule remaining = 1 month * 10.4/10 = 1.04 months
Month 6: 7 finishes	Month 3: 6 finishes	$TFPI_3 = 6/7$ = 0.86	Cum Finishes = 16 Remaining = 4 Cum = 16/20 = 0.8	Adjusted remaining finishes = 4/0.8 = 5 Forecast schedule remaining = 0 months * 5/4 = 0 months (no remaining schedule available)
Month 7: 0 finishes	Month 4: 4 finishes	$TFPI_4 = 4/0$ = indefinite	Cum Finishes = 20 Remaining = 0 Cum = 20/20 = 1.0	Adjusted remaining finishes = 0/1 = 0 Forecast schedule remaining = 0/0 = indefinite

* See related figure for a graphical presentation of this example.

$$\text{First period index} = 3/5 = 0.6$$

$$\text{Actual starts} = 3$$

$$\text{Forecast} = 3 + 17/0.6 = 3 + 28.3 = 31.3 \text{ starts}$$

where 31.3 = "equivalent" starts.

How should the project manager interpret the forecast given above? The equivalent starts represent the length of the project as though the PMB were 31.3 starts rather than 20. In other words, based on the performance in the first period, the project is forecasted to be 11.3/20 = 56.5% longer in schedule than the PMB. Fortunately, by the second period the trend line turns more favorable:

$$\text{Cumulative index} = 12/15 = 0.8$$

$$\text{Cumulative starts} = 12$$

$$\text{Forecast} = 12 + 8/0.8 = 22 \text{ starts}$$

where 22 = "equivalent" starts.

As with the traditional earned value system, the most valuable contribution of the calculations is to stimulate the project team to take action necessary to deliver the value to the project sponsor as defined on the project balance sheet and specified in the project charter. Whether or not the time-centric or traditional system is used, the calculations should have the same effect and provide the requisite catalyst to correct whatever is not working well in the project.

SUMMARY OF IMPORTANT POINTS

Table 6-8 provides the highlights of this chapter.

Table 6-8 Summary of Important Points

Point of Discussion	Summary of Ideas Presented
The expense (P&L) statement	■ The two measures of budget and actual expenditures taken together as one pair of financial metrics do not provide a measure of value obtained and delivered for the actual expenditures.
	■ The P&L expense statement is one of the three most important financial statements that the controller will provide to the project manager.
	■ The other two financial statements useful to project managers are the cash flow statement and the balance sheet.
	■ The WBS can also serve as an important financial document, connecting as it does to the chart of accounts.
	■ Many expenses of the company are present whether or not there is a project; expenses such as these are called "indirect" or "overhead" expenses.
	■ Expenses can also be categorized as fixed or variable. Fixed expenses are not subject to the volume of work being done. Variable expenses track the workload: more work, more expense.
	■ There is one more way to show costs on the expense statement: record and manage to standard costs rather than actual costs. Simply put, standard costs are average costs.
Lean thinking	■ Lean thinking applied to project cost management has many potential benefits. If the cost to initiate the batch work could be made negligible, whether painting or writing software, project managers would plan the project exclusively around the requirements for deliverables and not around the deliverables as influenced by the requirements of the process itself.

Table 6-8 Summary of Important Points (continued)

Point of Discussion	Summary of Ideas Presented
Managing with three-point estimates	■ The P&L statement is deterministic. The P&L statement is a product of the business accounting department. The P&L is not based on statistics. ■ When doing the cost estimates leading up to the summarized project cost, three-point estimates and distributions should be applied to the WBS. ■ The ultimate cost summarization at the "top" of the WBS will be Normal regardless of the distributions applied within the WBS.
Earned value concept	■ The earned value concept is about focusing on accomplishment, called earnings or performance, and the variance between the dollar value of those accomplishments and the dollar cost of those accomplishments. ■ The variance of "accomplishment less cost < $0" is always reported as an unfavorable status. ■ Earned value also provides a means to forecast performance. The history measures by and large involve variances. Forecasts require performance indexes. ■ Three measures are needed to construct an earned value system of performance evaluation: (1) Planned value (PV): PV is the dollar value planned and assigned to the work or the deliverable in the WBS. (2) Actual cost (AC): The actual cost is the cost of performance to accomplish the work or provide the deliverable on the WBS. (3) Earned value (EV): Earned value is a measure of the project value actually obtained by the work package effort. ■ $Schedule variance = $Value variance = EV − PV. ■ Cost variance = EV − AC.
Dollar-sizing the cost accounts	■ The larger the account, the greater is the pessimistic–optimistic distance and the greater is the amount at stake in dollars. ■ Rolling wave planning simply means that the detail down to the cost account is done in "waves" or stages when the project activities, facilities, tools, staffing, risks, and approach become more known.
Time-centric earned value	■ The main idea behind the time-centric earned value system is to set a PMB based on planned work package starts and finishes over the course of the project. ■ The total collection of starts and finishes, if executed completely, does represent the total scope of the project. ■ Instead of earning a dollar value, what is earned is a start or a finish. The PMB is a set of planned starts and planned finishes. ■ As with the traditional earned value system, the most valuable contribution of the calculations is to stimulate the project team to take action necessary to deliver the value to the project sponsor as defined on the project balance sheet and specified in the project charter.

REFERENCES

1. Womack, James P. and Jones, Daniel T., *Lean Thinking,* Simon & Schuster, New York, 1996, Introduction, pp. 15–28.
2. Fleming, Quentin W. and Koppelman, Joel M., *Earned Value Project Management, Second Edition,* Project Management Institute, Newtown Square, PA, 2000, chap. 3, pp. 25–33.
3. Under Secretary of Defense (Acquisition), DoDI 5000.1 The Defense Acquisition System, Department of Defense, Washington, D.C., 1989; and its predecessor instruction: DoD Comptroller, DoDI 7000.2 Performance Measurement for Selected Acquisitions, Department of Defense, Washington, D.C., 1967.
4. Kemps, Robert R., *Project Management Measurement,* Humphrey's and Associates, Inc., Mission Viejo, CA, 1992, chap. 16, pp. 97–107.
5. Fleming, Quentin W. and Koppelman, Joel M., Appendix I, pp. 157–181 and Appendix II, pp. 183–188.
6. Goodpasture, John C. and Sumara, James R., *Earned Value — The Next Generation — A Practical Application for Commercial Projects,* PMI '97 Seminars and Symposium Proceedings, Project Management Institute, Newtown Square, PA, 1997.

7

QUANTITATIVE TIME MANAGEMENT

There is no "undo" button for oceans of time.
Tom Pike
Rethink, Retool, Results, 1999

QUANTITATIVE TECHNIQUES IN TIME MANAGEMENT

Time management is amply described in most texts on project management. In this chapter we will focus only on the quantitative aspects of time management and make a couple of key assumptions to begin with:

- The major program milestones that mark real development of business value are identified and used to drive the project at the highest level.
- The program logic is found in the detail project schedules. Lower level schedules are in network form, preferably the "precedence diagramming method (PDM)" and tie together the various deliverables of the work breakdown structure (WBS).

Major Program Milestones

The first assumption is essential, more so even than the second, because the program milestones tie business value to one of the most essential elements of quality: timeliness. It is almost without exception that the left side (or business side) of the project balance sheet expresses the business sponsor's timeliness needs. In fact, although it is usual to think of the "four-angle" of scope, quality, schedule, and resources as being somewhat equal partners, very often timeliness is far more important than project cost. The project cost is often small compared to overall life cycle costs, but the returns to the project may well be compromised if timeliness is not achieved.

The Program Logic

The second assumption speaks to the PDM diagram, sometimes also referred to as a PERT (Program Evaluation Review Technique) chart, although a PDM diagram and a PERT chart are actually somewhat different. However, suffice it to say at this point that these diagrams establish the detail "logic" of the project. By logic we mean the most appropriate linkage between task and deliverables on the WBS. We do not actually have a schedule at the point that a network diagram is in place; we merely have the logic of the schedule. We have the dependencies among tasks, we know which task should come first, we know the durations and efforts of each task, and from the durations and dependencies we know the overall length of the project. When all of this knowledge is laid on a calendar, with actual dates, then we have a schedule.

Presumably if the project team has scheduled optimally, the project schedule (network laid against calendar) will align with the milestones identified as valuable to the business. If only it were true in all cases! In point of fact, a schedule developed "bottom up" from the WBS task and deliverables almost always comes out too lengthy, usually missing the later milestones. There are many reasons why a too lengthy schedule occurs, but the chief reasons are:

- The project team members can think of a myriad of tasks that should be done that are beyond the knowledge or experience of the project sponsor. In fact, the project sponsor has not thought of such tasks because the sponsor is thinking in terms of what is required by the business and not what is required to execute the project.
- Each person estimating their task may not be using expected value and there may be excess pessimism accumulated in the schedule.

The difference between the network schedule and the program milestones represents risk. Such schedule risk in quantitative terms is the subject of this chapter and one of the main management tasks of the project manager. Addressing the risk in time between the requirements of the business and the needs of the project will occupy the balance of this chapter.

SETTING THE PROGRAM MILESTONES

The program milestones set the timeliness or time requirements of the project and come from the business case. The business case may be an internal requirement for a new product, a new or revised process or plant, or a new organizational rollout. The business case may come externally from agencies of government or from customers. The program milestones we speak of are not usually derived from the project side of the balance sheet but are the milestones that identify directly with business value. Some program milestones may include:

- Responding on time to Requests for Proposals (RFPs) from customers
- Product presentation at trade events
- Meeting regulatory or statutory external dates
- Hitting a product launch date
- Meeting certain customer deliveries
- Aligning with other and dependent projects of which your project is a component

Actually deciding on calendar dates for the business-case-related program milestones is very situational. Sometimes if they come from external sources, the milestone dates are all but given. Perhaps a few internal program milestones of unique interest to the business need to be added with the external milestones.

On the other hand, if the project is all internal, then the estimates may well come from other project experiences that are "similar to," or the project sponsor could let the project team "bottom up" the estimate and accept the inevitability of a longer schedule as a cost of doing business. Often, the project sponsor will simply "top down" the dates based on business need. If the latter is the case, the project sponsor must express conviction in the face of all-too-probable objections by the project team that the schedule is too aggressive.

In any event, the final outcome should be program milestones, defined as events of 0 duration, at which time a business accomplishment is measurable and meaningful to the overall objective. To be effective, there should not be more than a handful of such milestones or else the business accomplishments begin to look like ordinary project task completions.

Planning Gates for Project Milestones

The program milestones for certain types of "standard" projects may well be laid out in a prescribed set of planning gates, usually a half-dozen to a dozen at most, with well-specified criteria and deliverables at each gate. For our purposes, a gate is equivalent to a milestone, although technically a milestone has no duration and the event at a gate does take some time, sometimes a week or more. In such a case, there would then be a gate task with an ending milestone. Depending on the nature and risk of the project, such gated processes can themselves be quite complex, requiring independent "standing" teams of objective evaluators at each gate of the process. Taken to its full extent, the gated process may require many and extensive internal documents to support the "claims" that the criteria of the gate have been met, as well as documents for customers or users that will "survive" the project.

Program Milestones as Deterministic Events

Generally speaking, program milestones do not have a probabilistic character, which means that the time for the milestone is fixed and invariant. There is no uncertainty from a business value perspective when the milestone occurs. This is particularly so if the milestone is from an external source, like the day and time that an RFP is due in the customer's hands.

We will soon see that this deterministic characteristic does not carry over to the network schedule. Indeed, the idea of the network schedule is to have a series of linked estimates, one three-point estimate for each task, where the three estimated values are the most likely, the most optimistic, and the most pessimistic. Obviously, right from the beginning there is possible conflict between the business and its fixed milestones and the project with its estimated tasks. The differences in the timelines between the business and the project, as we have noted before, is a risk to be managed by the project manager and set onto the project side of the project balance sheet.

THE SCHEDULE NETWORK

As described in the opening of this chapter, the schedule network captures the logic of the project, reflecting in its structure the dependencies and relationships among tasks on the WBS. The network we will concern ourselves with is commonly referred to as the PDM. In a PDM network, the tasks of the WBS are represented as nodes or rectangles, and arrow-pointed links relate one task to another. In fact, we can think of the components of a network as consisting of building blocks.

Network Building Blocks

We will use the components shown in Figure 7-1 as the building blocks in our schedule network. As seen there, we have the simple task, the simple path

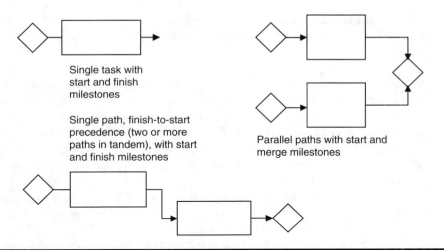

Single task with start and finish milestones

Single path, finish-to-start precedence (two or more paths in tandem), with start and finish milestones

Parallel paths with start and merge milestones

Figure 7-1   Schedule Building Blocks.

consisting of at least two tasks in tandem, the parallel paths consisting of two or more simple paths joined by a milestone, links between tasks, and milestones that begin, end, and join paths. To simplify illustrations, the milestones are often omitted and are simply implied by the logic of the network. For instance, as shown in Figure 7-2, we see the task itself serving as the starting, ending, and joining mechanism of tasks.

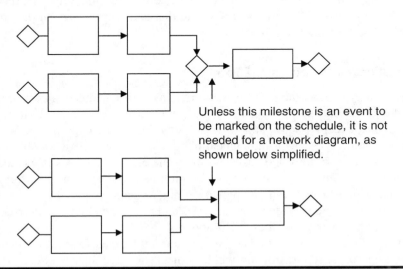

Unless this milestone is an event to be marked on the schedule, it is not needed for a network diagram, as shown below simplified.

Figure 7-2   Milestone Simplifications.

There are certain characteristics that are applied to each schedule task, represented by a rectangle in our network building blocks. These task characteristics are:

- Every task has a specific beginning and a specific ending, thereby allowing for a specific duration (ending date minus beginning date) measured in some unit of time (for instance, hours, days, weeks, or months). Rarely would a schedule task be shown in years because the year is too coarse a measure for good project planning.
- Every task has some effort applied to it. Effort is measured in the hours spent by a "full-time equivalent" (FTE) working on the task. By example, if the effort on a task is 50 hours, and a FTE is 40 hours, then there is 1.25 FTE applied to the task. If the task duration is 25 hours, then the 50 hours of effort must be accomplished in 25 hours of calendar time, requiring 2.5 FTE. Thus, we have the following equations:

$$\text{FTE applied to task} = (\text{Effort/Duration}) * (\text{Effort/Hours per FTE})$$

$$\text{FTE applied to task} = (50/25) * (50/40) = 2,500/1,000 = 2.5$$

- Every task has not only a specific beginning or ending, but also each task as an "earliest" or "latest" beginning or ending. The idea of earliest and latest leads to the ideas of float and critical path, which will be discussed in detail subsequently. Suffice it to say that the difference in "earliest" and "latest" is "float" and that tasks on the critical path have a float of precisely 0.

Estimating Duration and Effort

We can easily see that the significant metrics in every schedule network are the task durations and the task efforts. These two metrics drive almost all of the calculations, except where paths merge. We address the merge points in subsequent paragraphs. Now as a practical matter, when doing networks for some tasks it is more obvious and easier to apply the estimating ideas discussed in other chapters to the effort and let the duration be dependent on the effort and the number of FTE that can be applied. In other situations just the opposite is true: you have an idea of duration and FTE and the effort simply is derived by applying the equations we described above.

Most network software tools allow for setting defaults for effort-driven or duration-driven attributes for the whole project, or these attributes can be set task by task. For a very complex schedule, setting effort-driven or duration-driven attributes task by task can be very tedious indeed. Perhaps the best practical advice that can be given is to select the driver you are most comfortable with, and make selective adjustments on those tasks that are necessary. Consider this idea however: duration estimating ties your network directly to your program milestones. When a duration-driven network is developed, the ending dates or overall length of the network will fall on actual calendar dates. You will be able to see immediately if there is an inherent risk in the project network and the program milestones.

Perhaps the most important concept is the danger of using single-point estimates in durations and efforts. The PERT network was the first network system to recognize that the expected value is the best single estimate in the face of uncertainty, and therefore the expected value of the duration should be the number used in network calculations. The BETA distribution was selected for the PERT chart system and the two variables "alpha" and "beta" were picked to form a BETA curve with the asymmetry emphasizing the most pessimistic value.* Although the critical path method (CPM) to be discussed below started out using single-point estimates, in point of fact more often than not a three-point estimate is made, sometimes using the BETA curve and sometimes using the Triangular distribution. In effect, using three-point estimates in the CPM network makes such a CPM diagram little different from the PERT diagram.

THE CRITICAL PATH METHOD

One of the most common outcomes of the schedule network is the identification of one or more critical paths. Right at this point, let us say that the critical path, and in fact there may be more than one critical path through the network, may not be the most important path for purposes of business value or functionality. However, the critical path establishes the length of the network and therefore sets the overall duration of the project. If there is any schedule acceleration or delay along the critical path, then the project will finish earlier or later, respectively.

As a practical example of the difference between paths that are critical and functionally important, the author was once associated with a project to build an Intelsat ground station. The business value of the ground station was obviously to be able to communicate effectively with the Intelsat system and then make connectivity to the terrestrial communications system. However, the critical path on the project network schedule was the installation and operation of a voice intercom between the antenna pedestal and the ground communications

---

* More information on the BETA "alpha" and "beta" parameters is provided in Chapter 2.

control facility. The vendor selected for this intercom capability in effect set the critical path, though I am sure that all would agree that the intercom was not the most important functionality of the system. Nevertheless, the project was not complete until the intercom was delivered; any delay by the vendor (there was none) was a delay on the whole project.

Some Characteristics of the Critical Path

We have so far described the critical path as the longest path through the network. This is true and it is one of the clearest and most defining characteristics of the critical path.

A second idea is that there is no float or slack along the critical path. Having no float or slack means that if there is any change in durations along the critical path, then the overall schedule will be longer or shorter. In effect, such a characteristic means there is no schedule "reserve" that can isolate vagaries of the project with the fixed business milestones. In point of fact, almost no project is planned in this manner and the project manager usually plans a reserve task of time but not performance. We will see in our discussion of the "critical chain" concept that this reserve task is called a "buffer" and is managed solely by the project manager. Figure 7-3 illustrates this idea. For purposes of identifying and calculating the critical path, we will ignore the reserve task.

A third idea is that there can be more than one critical path through the network. A change in duration on any one of the critical paths will change the project completion date, ignoring any reserve task.

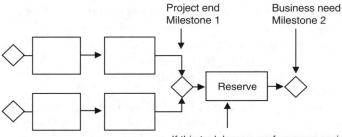

- If this task has no performance assigned to it but has time allocated to it by the project manager, then it is a "reserve" task.
- The project is intended to end at Milestone 1; the business requirement is to end at Milestone 2.

Figure 7-3 Reserve Task in Network.

Another notion is that of the "near-critical path." A near-critical path(s) is one or more paths that are not critical at the outset of the project, but could become critical. A path could become critical because the probabilistic outcomes of durations on one of these paths become longer than the identified critical path. Another possibility is that the critical path becomes shorter due to improved performance of its tasks and one of the "near-critical" paths is "promoted" to being the critical path. Such a set of events happens often in projects. Many project software tools have the capability of not only identifying and reporting on the near-critical path, but also calculating the probability that the path will become critical. Moreover, it is often possible to set a threshold so that the project manager sees only those paths on the report that exceed a set probability of becoming critical. In addition, it is possible to identify new paths that come onto the report or old paths that drop off the report because of ongoing performance during the course of the project.

Lastly, if there is only one connected path through the network, then there is only one critical path and that path is it; correspondingly, if the project is planned in such a way that no single path connects all the way through, then there is no critical path. As curious as the latter may seem, a network without a connecting path all the way through is a common occurrence in project planning. Why? It is a matter of having dependencies that are not defined in the network. Undefined dependencies are ghost dependencies. An early set of tasks does not connect to or drive a later set of tasks. The later set of tasks begins on the basis of a trigger from outside the project, or a trigger is not defined in the early tasks. Thus the latter tasks appear to begin at a milestone for which there is no dependency on the earlier tasks. In reality, such a network is really two projects and it should be handled as such. If addressed as two projects, then each will have a critical path. The overall length of the program (multiple projects) will depend on the two projects individually and the ghost task that connects one to the other. Such a situation is shown in Figure 7-4.

Calculating the Critical Path

Calculating the critical path is the most quantitatively intensive schedule management task to be done, perhaps more complicated than "resource leveling" and the calculation of merge points. Though intensive, critical path calculations are not hard to do, but on a practical basis critical path calculations are best left to schedule network software tools. The calculation steps are as follows:

■ For each path in the network that connects all the way through, and in our examples we will employ only networks that do have paths that

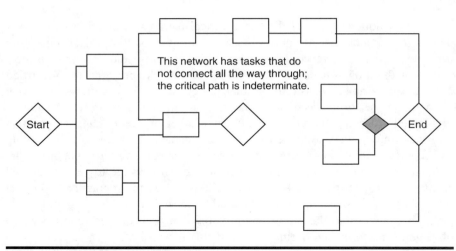

Figure 7-4   One Network as Two.

connect through, calculate the so-called "forward path" by calculating the path length using the earliest start dates.

■   Then for each path in the network, work in the opposite direction, using latest finish dates, and calculate the "backward path."

■   One or more paths calculated this way would have equal lengths, forward and backward. These are the critical paths. All other paths will have unequal forward and backward lengths. These paths are not critical.

■   The amount of forward–backward inequality in any path is the float or slack in the path. Overall, this path, or any one task on this path, can slip by the amount of the forward–backward inequality and not be more than critical and therefore not delay the project.

Calculating the Forward Path

Figure 7-5 shows a simple network with the forward path calculation.

We must adopt a notation convention. The tasks will be shown in rectangular boxes; the earliest start date will be on the upper left corner, and the earliest finish will be on the upper right corner. The corresponding lower corners will be used for latest start and finish dates, respectively. Duration will be shown in the rectangle.

In the forward path calculation, notice the use of the earliest start dates. The basic rule is simple:

$$\text{Earliest start date} + \text{Duration} = \text{Earliest finish date}$$

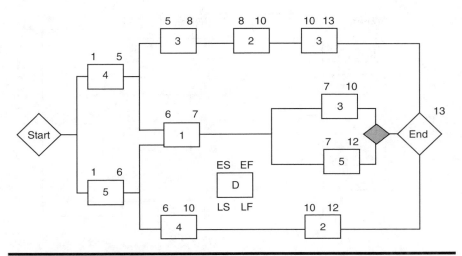

Figure 7-5 Forward Path Calculation.

Now we have to be cognizant of the various precedence relationships such as finish-to-start and finish-to-finish, etc. All but finish-to-start greatly complicate the mathematics and are best left to scheduling software. Therefore, our example networks will all use finish-to-start relationships. There is no loss in generality since almost every network that has other than only finish-to-start relationships can be redrawn, employing more granularity, and become an all finish-to-start network.

Working in the forward path with finish-to-start relationships, the rule invoked is:

Earliest start of successor task = Latest of the early finish dates of all predecessors

The final milestone from the forward path analysis is an "earliest" finish milestone. Again, unless explicitly shown, any final management reserve task of unallocated reserve task is not shown for simplicity. If it were shown, it would move out, or shift right, the final milestone to align with the program milestones from the business side of the balance sheet.

Calculating the Backward Path

Now let's calculate the backward path. The very first question that arises is: "What is the date for the latest finish?" The backward path is calculated with the latest finish dates and all we have at this point is the earliest finish date. The answer is that if there is no final reserve task in the network, the latest finish

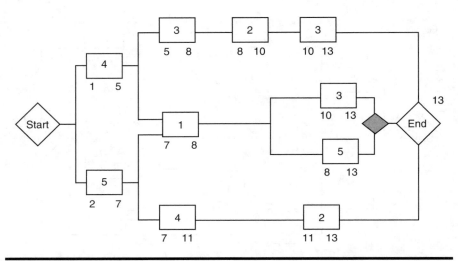

Figure 7-6 Backward Path Calculation.

date of the final milestone is taken to be the same as the earliest finish date calculated in the forward path. Having established a starting point for the backward path calculation, we then invoke the following equation:

$$\text{Latest start} = \text{Latest finish} - \text{Duration}$$

In calculating backward through the finish-to-start network, we use the earliest of the "latest start" dates of a successor task as the latest finish for a predecessor task. Figure 7-6 shows these calculations for our example network.

Finding the Critical Tasks

Figure 7-7 shows the critical path calculation in one diagram for our example network. To find the critical path, it is a simple matter of identifying every task for which either of the following equations is true:

$$\text{Earliest start (or finish)} = \text{Latest start (or finish)}$$

$$\text{Earliest start (or finish)} - \text{Latest start (or finish)} = 0 = \text{float or slack}$$

Those tasks that obey the equations just given have zero slack or float. Such zero-float tasks are said to be critical and they form the one or more critical paths through the network.

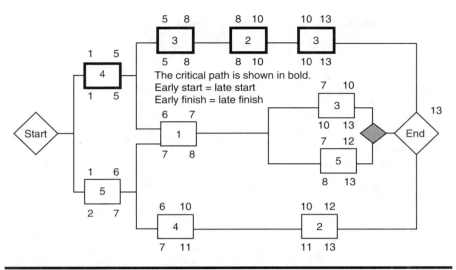

Figure 7-7   Critical Path Calculation.

THE CENTRAL LIMIT THEOREM APPLIED TO NETWORKS

Take notice that the critical path through the network always connects the beginning node or milestone and the ending node or milestone. The ending milestone can be thought of as the output milestone, and all the tasks in between are input to the final output milestone. Furthermore, if the project manager has used three-point estimates for the task durations, then the duration of any single task is a random variable best represented by the expected value of the task.* The total duration of the critical path from the input or beginning milestone to the output milestone, itself a 0-duration event, or the date assigned to the output milestone, represents the length of the overall schedule. The length of the overall schedule is a summation of random variables and is itself a random variable, L, of length:

---

* Actually, whether or not the project manager proactively thinks about the random nature of the task durations and assigns a probability distribution to a task does not change the fact that the majority of tasks in projects (projects we define as one-time endeavors never done exactly the same way before) are risky and tasks have some randomness to their duration estimate. Therefore, the fact that the project manager does not or did not think about this randomness does not change the reality of the situation. Therefore, the conclusions cited in the text regarding the application of the Central Limit Theorem and the Law of Large Numbers are not invalidated by the fact that the project manager may not have gone to the effort to estimate the duration randomness.

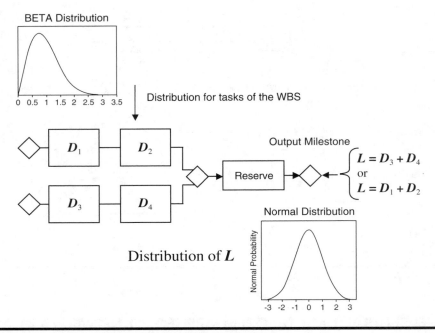

Figure 7-8 The Output Milestone Distribution.

$$L = \Sigma \, D_i = (D_1 + D_2 + D_i \; ...)$$

where D_i are the durations of the tasks along the critical path.

We know from our discussion of the Central Limit Theorem that for a "large" number of durations in the sum the distribution of L will tend to be Normal regardless of the distributions of the individual tasks. This statement is precisely the case if all the distributions are the same for each task, but even if some are not, then the statement is so close to approximately true that it matters little to the project manager that L may not be exactly Normal distributed. Figure 7-8 illustrates this point.

Significance of Normal Distributed Output Milestone

The significance of the fact that the output milestone is approximately Normal distributed is not trivial. Here is why. Given the symmetry of the Normal curve, a Normal distributed output milestone means there is just as likely a possibility that the schedule will underrun (complete early) as overrun (complete late). Confronted with such a conclusion, most project managers would say: "No! The schedule is biased toward overrun." Such a reaction simply means that either the schedule is too short and the Normal output milestone is too aggressive, or the project manager has not thought objectively about the schedule risk.

Consider this conclusion about a Normal output milestone from another point of view. Without even considering what the distributions of the individual tasks on the WBS might be, whether BETA or Triangular or Normal or whatever, the project manager remains confident that the output milestone is Normal in its distribution! That is to say that there is a conclusion for every project, and it is the same conclusion for every project — the summation milestone of the critical path is approximately Normal.*

Calculating the Statistical Parameters of the Output Milestone

What the project manager does not know is the standard deviation or the variance of the Normal distribution. It is quite proper to ask of what real utility it is to know that the output milestone is Normal with an expected value (mean value) but have no other knowledge of the distribution. The answer is straightforward: either a schedule simulation can be run to determine the distribution parameters or, if there is no opportunity to individually estimate the tasks on the WBS, then the risk estimation effort can be moved to the output milestone as a practical matter.

At this point, there really is not an option about selecting the distribution since it is known to be Normal; if expected values have been used to compute the critical path, or some reasonable semblance of expected values has been used, then the mean of the output milestone is calculable. It then remains to make some risk assessment of the probable underrun. Usually we calculate the underrun distance from the mean as a most optimistic duration. Once done, this underrun estimate is identically the same as the distance from the expected value to the most pessimistic estimate. Such a conclusion is true because of the symmetry of the Normal distribution; underrun and overrun must be symmetrically located around the mean.

The last estimate to make is the estimate for the standard deviation. The standard deviation estimate is roughly one-sixth of the distance from the most optimistic duration estimate to the most pessimistic estimate.

---

* Strictly speaking, the Law of Large Numbers and the Central Limit Theorem are applicable to linear sums of durations. The critical path usually qualifies as a linear summation of durations. Merge points, fixed dates, and PDM relationships other than finish-to-start do not qualify.

Next, the Normal distribution for the outcome milestone is normalized to the standard Normal distribution. The standard Normal curve has mean = 0 and $\sigma = 1$. Once normalized, the project manager can apply the Normal distribution confidence curves to develop confidence intervals for communicating to the project sponsor.

Statistical Parameters of Other Program Milestones

The Central Limit Theorem is almost unlimited in its handiness to the project manager. Given that there is a "large number" of tasks leading up to any program or project milestone, and large is usually taken to be ten or more as a working estimate, then the distribution of that milestone is approximately Normal. The discussion of the output milestone applies in all respects, most importantly the statements about using the Normal confidence curves or tables.

Therefore, some good advice for every project manager is to obtain a handbook of numerical tables or learn to use the Normal function in any spreadsheet program that has statistical functions. Of course, every project manager learns the confidence figures for ± 1, 2, or 3 standard deviations: they are, respectively, 68.26, 95.46, and 98.76.

MONTE CARLO SIMULATION OF THE NETWORK PERFORMANCE

The arithmetic of finding expected value, standard deviation, and variance, at least to approximate values suitable and appropriate to project management, is not hard to do when working with the most common distributions we have described so far in this book. Anyone with reasonable proficiency in arithmetic can do it, and with a calculator or spreadsheet the math is really trivial. However, the manual methodology applied to a network of many tasks, or hundreds of tasks, or thousands, or even tens of thousands of tasks, is so tedious that the number of hand calculations is overwhelming and beyond practicality. Moreover, the usual approach when applying manual methods is to work only with the expected value of the distribution. The expected value is the best single number in the face of uncertainty, to be sure, but if the probability distribution has been estimated, then the distribution is a much more rich representation of the probable task performance than just the one statistic of the distribution called the expected value. Sensibly, whenever more information is available to the project manager, then it is appropriate to apply the more robust information set to the project planning and estimating activities.

If you can imagine that working only with the expected values is a tedious undertaking on a complex network, consider the idea of working with many points from each probability distribution from each task on the network. You immediately come to the conclusion that it is not possible to do such a thing manually. Thus, we look to computer-aided simulation to assist the project manager in evaluating the project network. One immediate advantage is that all the information about task performance represented by the probability distribution is available and usable in the computer simulation. There are many simulation possibilities, but one very popular one in common use and compatible with almost all scheduling programs and spreadsheets is the Monte Carlo simulation.

The Monte Carlo Simulation

The concept of operations behind the Monte Carlo simulation is quite simple: by using a Monte Carlo computer simulation program,* the network schedule is "run" or calculated many times, something we cannot usually do in real projects. Each time the schedule is run, a duration figure for each task is picked from the possible values within the pessimistic to optimistic range of the probability distribution for the task. Now each time the schedule is run, for any given task, the duration value that is picked will usually be different. Perhaps the first time the schedule is calculated, the most pessimistic duration is picked. The next time the schedule is run, perhaps the most likely duration is picked. In fact, over a large number of runs, wherein each run means calculating the schedule differently according to the probabilistic outcomes of the task durations, if we were to look at a report of the durations picked for a single task, it would appear that the values picked and their frequency of pick would look just like the probability distribution we assigned to the task. The most likely value would be picked the most and the most pessimistic or optimistic values would be picked least frequently. Table 7-1 shows such a report in histogram form. The histogram has a segregation or discrete quantification of duration values, and for each value there is a count of the number of times a duration value within the histogram quantification occurred.

---

* There are many PC and larger system software packages that will run a Monte Carlo simulation on a data set. In this chapter, our focus is on the network schedule, so the easiest approach is to obtain a package that "adds in" or integrates with your scheduling software. Of course, Monte Carlo simulation is not restricted to just schedule analysis. Any set of distributions can be analyzed in this way. For instance, the cost data from the WBS whereon each cost account has a probability distribution are candidates for Monte Carlo simulation. For cost analysis, an add-in to a spreadsheet or a statistical programs package would be ideal for running a Monte Carlo analysis of a cost data set.

Table 7-1 Monte Carlo Outcome for Tasks

"Standard" Normal Distribution of Outcome Milestone		
Normalized Outcome Value[a] (As Offset from the Expected Value)	Histogram Value * 100[b]	Cumulative Histogram * 100[b] (Confidence)
−3	0.110796	0.110796
−2.75	0.227339	0.338135
−2.5	0.438207	0.776343
−2.25	0.793491	1.569834
−2	1.349774	2.919607
−1.75	2.156932	5.07654
−1.5	3.237939	8.314478
−1.25	4.566226	12.8807
−1	6.049266	18.92997
−0.75	7.528433	26.4584
−0.5	8.80163	35.26003
−0.25	9.6667	44.92673
0	9.973554	54.90029
0.25	9.6667	64.56699
0.5	8.80163	73.36862
0.75	7.528433	80.89705
1	6.049266	86.94632
1.25	4.566226	91.51254
1.5	3.237939	94.75048
1.75	2.156932	96.90741
2	1.349774	98.25719
2.25	0.793491	99.05068
2.5	0.438207	99.48888
2.75	0.227339	99.71622
3	0.110796	99.82702

[a] The outcome values lie along the horizontal axis of the probability distribution. For simplicity, the average value of the outcome (i.e., the mean or expected value) has been adjusted to 0 by subtracting the actual expected value from every outcome value: Adjusted outcomes = Actual outcomes − Expected value.

After adjusting for the mean, the adjusted outcomes are then "normalized" to the standard deviation by dividing the adjusted outcomes by the standard deviation: Normalized outcomes = Adjusted outcomes/σ.

After adjusting for the mean and normalizing to the standard deviation, we now have the "standard" Normal distribution.

[b] The histogram value is the product of the horizontal value (outcome) times the vertical value (probability); the cumulative histogram, or cumulative probability, is the confidence that a outcome value, or a lesser value, will occur: Confidence = Probability outcome ≤ Outcome value.

For better viewing, the cell area and the cumulative area have been multiplied by 100 to remove leading zeroes. The actual values are found by dividing the values shown by 100.

Monte Carlo Simulation Parameters

The project manager gets to control many aspects of the Monte Carlo simulation. Such control gives the project manager a fair amount of flexibility to obtain the analysis desired. A few of the parameters usually under project manager control follow. The software package actually used will be the real control of these parameters, but typically:

■ The distribution applied to each task, a group of tasks, or "globally" to the whole network can be picked from a list of choices.

■ The distribution parameters can be specified, such as pessimistic and optimistic values, either in absolute value or as a percentage of the most likely value that is also specified.

■ The task or milestone (one or more) that is going to be the "outcome" of the analysis can be picked.

■ The number of runs can be picked. It is usually hard to obtain good results without at least 100 independent runs of the schedule. By independent we mean that all initial conditions are reset and there is no memory of results from one run to the next. For larger and more complex networks, running the schedule 100 times may take some number of minutes, especially if the computer is not optimized for such simulations. Better results are obtained with 1,000 or more runs. However, there is a practical trade-off regarding analysis time and computer resources. This trade-off is up to the project manager to handle and manage.

Monte Carlo Simulation Outcomes

At the outcome task of the simulation, the usual simulation products are graphical, tabular, and often presented as reports. Figure 7-9 shows typical data, including a "critical path and near-critical analysis" on paths that might be in the example network. The usual analysis products from a Monte Carlo simulation might include:

■ A probability density distribution, with absolute values of outcome value and a vertical dimension scaled to meet the requirement that the sum of all probabilities equals 1

■ A cumulative probability distribution, the so-called "S" curve, again scaled from 0 to 1 or 0 to 100% on the vertical axis and the value outcomes on the horizontal axis

■ Other statistical parameters, such as mean and standard deviation

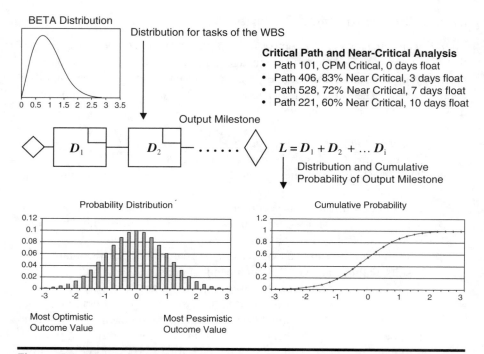

Figure 7-9   Monte Carlo Outcomes.

The Near-Critical Path

Identification of near-critical paths that have a reasonable probability of becoming critical is a key outcome of Monte Carlo simulation. For many project managers, the near-critical path identification is perhaps the most important outcome. In fact, during the course of the Monte Carlo simulation, depending on the distributions applied to the critical tasks and the distributions applied to other paths, there will be many runs, perhaps very many runs, where the critical path identified by straightforward CPM calculations will not in fact be critical. Some other path, on a probabilistic basis, is critical for that particular run. Most Monte Carlo packages optimized for schedule applications keep careful record of all the paths that are, or become, critical during a session of runs. Appropriate reports are usually available.

Project managers can usually specify a threshold for reporting the near-critical paths. For example, perhaps the report contains only information about paths that have a 70% confidence, or higher, of becoming critical. Setting the threshold helps to separate the paths that are nearly critical and should be on a "watch list" along with the CPM-calculated critical path. If the schedule network is complex, such threshold reporting goes a long way in conserving valuable management time.

Convergence of Parameters in the Simulation

During the course of the session of 100 or more runs of the schedule, you may be able to observe the "convergence" of some of the statistical parameters to their final values. For instance, the expected value or standard deviation of the selected "outcome" task is going to change rapidly from the very first run to subsequent runs as more data are accumulated about the outcome distribution. After a point, if the parameter is being displayed, the project manager may well be able to see when convergence to the final value is "close enough." Such an observation offers the opportunity to stop the simulation manually when convergence is obtained. If the computer program does not offer such a real-time observation, there is usually some type of report that provides figures of merit about how well converged the reported parameters are to a final value.

There is no magic formula that specifies how close to the final value the statistical parameters like expected value, standard deviation, or variance should be for use in projects. Project managers get to be their own judge about such matters. Some trial and error may be required before a project manager is comfortable with final results.

Fixed Dates and Multiple Precedences in Monte Carlo Simulations

Fixed dates interfere with the Monte Carlo simulation by truncating the possible durations of tasks to fixed lengths or inhibiting the natural "shift-right" nature of merge points as discussed in the next section. Before running a simulation, the general rule of thumb is to go through your schedule and remove all fixed dates, then replace them with finish-to-start dependencies of project outcomes.

The same is usually said for precedences other than finish-to-start: redefine all precedences to finish-to-start before running the simulation. Many Monte Carlo results may be strange or even incorrect, depending on the sophistication of the package, if there are other than finish-to-start dependencies in the schedule. Again, the general rule of thumb is to go through your schedule and remove all relationships other than finish-to-start and replace them with an alternative network architecture of all finish-to-start dependencies of project outcomes. Although objectionable at first, the author has found that few networks really require other than finish-to-start relationships if the proper granularity of planning is done to identify all the points for finish-to-start, which obviates the need to use the other relationships.

ARCHITECTURE WEAKNESSES IN SCHEDULE LOGIC

One of the problems facing project managers when constructing the logic of their project is avoiding inherently weak architectures in the schedule network. Certainly from the point of view of risk management, avoidance is a key strategy and well applied when developing the logic of the project. In this section we will address two architectural weaknesses that lend themselves to quantitative analysis: the merge point of parallel paths and the "long" task.

Merge Points in Network Logic

By merge point we simply mean a point in the logic where a milestone has two or more predecessors, each with the same finish date. Illustrations of network building blocks shown earlier in this chapter illustrate simple parallel paths joining at a milestone. Such a construction is exactly what we are talking about. Obviously, for all project managers such a logic situation occurs frequently and is really unavoidable entirely; the idea is to avoid as many merging points as possible.

Here is the problem in a nutshell. Let us assume that each of the merging paths is independent. By independent we mean that the performance along one path is not dependent on the performance along the other path. We must be careful here. If there are shared resources between the two paths that are in conflict, whether project staff, special tools, facilities, or other, then the paths are truly not independent. But assuming independence, there is a probability that path A will finish on the milestone date, p(*A* on time) = p(*A*), and there is a probability that path B will finish on the milestone date, p(*B* on time) = p(*B*). Now, the probability that the milestone into which each of the two paths merge will be achieved on time is the probability that both paths will finish on time. We know from the math of probabilities and from Bayes' Theorem that if *A* and *B* are independent, the probability of the milestone finishing on time is the product of the two probabilities:

$$p(\text{Milestone on time}) = p(A) * p(B)$$

Now it should be intuitively obvious what the problem is. Both p(*A*) and p(*B*) are numbers less than 1. Their product, p(*A*) * p(*B*), is even smaller, so the probability of meeting the milestone on time is less than the smallest probability of any of the joining paths. If there are more than two paths joining, the problem is that much greater. Figure 7-10 shows graphically the phenomenon we have been discussing.

Suppose that p(*A*) = 0.8 and p(*B*) = 0.7, both pretty high confidence figures.

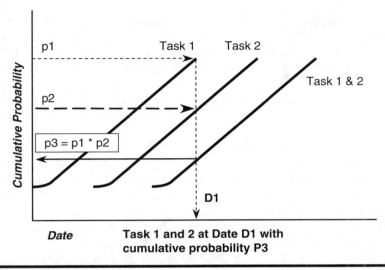

Figure 7-10 Merge Point Math.

The joint probability of their product is quite simply: 0.8 ∗ 0.7 = 0.56. Obviously, moving down from a confidence of 70% at the least for any single path to only 56% for the milestone is a real move and must be addressed by the project manager. To mitigate risk, the project manager would develop alternate schedule logic that does not require a merging of paths, or the milestone would be isolated with a buffer task.

We have mentioned "shift right" in the discussion of merge point. What does "shift right" refer to? Looking at Figure 7-10, we see that to raise the confidence of the milestone up to the least of the merging paths, in this case 70%, we are going to have to allow for more time. Such a conclusion is really straightforward: more time always raises the confidence in the schedule and provides for a higher probability of completion. But, of course, allowing more time is an extension, to the right, of the schedule. Extending the schedule to the right is the source of the term "shift right." The rule for project managers examining project logic is:

At every merge point of predecessor tasks, think "shift right."

Merging Dependent Paths

So far the discussion has been about the merging of independent paths. Setting the condition of independence certainly simplifies matters greatly. We know from our study of multiple random variables that if the random variables are not independent, then there is a covariance between them and a degree of correlation. We also know that if one path outcome is conditioned on the other path's outcome, then we must invoke Bayes' Theorem to handle the conditions.

$$p(A \text{ on time AND } B \text{ on time}) = p(A \text{ on time given } B \text{ is on time})$$
$$* \ p(B \text{ is on time})$$

We see right away on the right side of the equation that the "probability of *A* on time given *B* on time" is made smaller by the multiplication of the probability of "*B* on time." From what we have already discussed, making "probability of *A* on time given *B* on time" smaller is a shift right of the schedule. The exact amount is more difficult to estimate because of having to estimate "probability of *A* on time given *B* on time," but the heuristic is untouched: the milestone join of two paths, whether independent or not, will shift right. Only the degree of shift depends on the conditions between the paths.

Thinking of the milestone as an "outcome milestone," we can also approach this examination from the point of view of risk as represented by the variance of the outcome distribution. We may not know this distribution outright, although by the discussion that follows we might assume that it is somewhat Normal. In any event, if the two paths are not independent, what can we say about the variance of the outcome distribution at this point? Will it be larger or smaller?

We reason as follows: The outcome performance of the milestone is a combined effect of all the paths joining. If we look at the expected value of the two paths joining, and the paths are independent, then we know that:

$$E(A \text{ and } B) = E(A) * E(B), \text{ paths independent}$$

But if the paths are not independent, then the covariance between them comes into play:

$$E(A \text{ and } B) = E(A) * E(B) + Cov(A \text{ and } B)$$

where paths *A* and *B* are not independent.

The equation for the paths not independent tells us that the expected value may be larger (longer) or smaller (shorter) depending on the covariance. The covariance will be positive — that is, the outcome will be larger (the expected value of the outcome at the milestone is longer or shifted right) — if both paths move in the same direction together. This is often the case in projects because of the causes within the project that tend to create dependence between paths.

The chief cause is shared resources, whether the shared resource is key staff, special tools or environments, or other unique and scarce resources. So the equation we are discussing is valuable heuristically even if we often do not have the information to evaluate it numerically. The heuristic most interesting to project managers is:

Parallel paths that become correlated
by sharing resources stretch the schedule!

The observation that sharing resources will stretch the schedule is not news to most project managers. Either through experience or exposure to the various rules of thumb of project management, such a phenomenon is generally known. What we have done is given the rule of thumb a statistical foundation and given the project manager the opportunity, by means of the formula, to figure out the actual numerical impact. However, perhaps the most important way to make use of this discussion is by interpreting results from a Monte Carlo simulation. When running the Monte Carlo simulation, the effects of merge points and shift right will be very apparent. This discussion provides the framework to understand and interpret the results provided.

Resource Leveling Quantitative Effects

Resource leveling refers to the planning methodology in which scarce resources, typically staff with special skills (but also special equipment, facilities, and environments), are allocated to tasks where there is otherwise conflict for the resource. The situation we are addressing naturally arises out of multiple planners who each require a resource and plan for its use, only to find in the summation of the schedule network that certain resources are oversubscribed: there is simply too much demand for supply.

The first and most obvious solution is to increase supply. Sometimes increasing supply can work in the case of certain staff resources that can be augmented by contractors or temporary workers, and certain facilities or environments might likewise be outsourced to suppliers. However, the problem for quantitative analysis is the case where supply cannot be increased, demand cannot be reduced, and it is not possible physically to oversubscribe the resource. Some have said this is like the case of someone wondering if "nine women could have a baby in one month." It is also not unlike the situation described by Fredrick Brooks in his classic book, *The Mythical Man-Month*,[1] wherein he states affirmatively that the thought that a simple interchange of resources, like time and staff, is possible on complex projects is a myth! Interestingly enough, Brooks also states what he calls "Brooks Law":

Adding additional resources (increasing supply)
to a late project only makes it later![2]

For purposes of this book, we will limit our discussion of resource leveling to simply assigning resources in the most advantageous manner to affect the project in the least way possible. Several rules of thumb have been developed in this regard. The most prominent is perhaps: "assign resources to the critical path to ensure it is not resource starved, and then assign the remaining resources to the near-critical paths in descending order of risk." Certainly this is a sensible approach. Starving the critical path would seem to build in a schedule slip right away. Actually, however, others argue that in the face of scarce resources, the identification of the true critical path is obscured by the resource conflict.

Recall our discussion earlier about correlating or creating a dependency among otherwise independent paths. Resource leveling is exactly that. Most scheduling software has a resource leveling algorithm built in, and you can also buy add-in software to popular scheduling software that has more elaborate and more efficient algorithms. However, in the final analysis, creating a resource dependency among tasks almost certainly sets up a positive covariance between the paths. Recall that by positive covariance we mean that both path performances move in the same direction. If a scarce resource is delayed or retained on one path beyond its planned time, then surely it will have a similar impact on any other task it is assigned to, creating a situation of positive covariance.

Figure 7-11 and Figure 7-12 show a simple example. In Figure 7-11, we see a simple plan consisting of four tasks and two resources. Following the rule of thumb, we staff the critical path first and find that the schedule has lengthened as predicted by the positive covariance. In Figure 7-12, we see an alternate resource allocation plan, one in which we apparently do not start with the critical path, and indeed the overall network schedule is optimally shorter than first planned as shown in Figure 7-11. However, there is no combination of the two resources and the four tasks that is as short as if there were complete independence between tasks. Statistically speaking we would say that there is no case where the covariance can be zero in the given combination of tasks and resources.

Long Tasks

Another problem common to schedule network architecture is the so-called long task. What is "long" in this context? There is no exact answer, though there are many rules of thumb, heuristics. Many companies and some customers have built into their project methodology specific figures for task length that are not to be exceeded when planning a project unless a waiver is granted by the project

Rule #1: Begin the project by beginning to work on the longest path

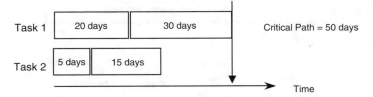

Rule #2: Apply resources first to the Critical Path; then check impact to Critical Path

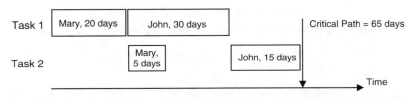

Figure 7-11   Resource Leveling Plan.

manager. Some common heuristics of "short" tasks are 80 to 120 hours of FTE time or perhaps 10 to 14 days of calendar time. You can see by these figures that a long task is one measured in several weeks or many staff hours.

What is the problem with the long task from the quantitative methods point of view? Intuitively, the longer the task, the more likely something untoward will go wrong. As a matter of confidence in the long task, allowing for more possibilities to go wrong has to reduce the confidence in the task. Can we show this intuitive idea simply with statistics? Yes; let us take a look at the project shown in Figure 7-13.

In Figure 7-13 we see a project consisting of only one task, and it is a long task. We have assigned a degree of risk to this long task by saying that the

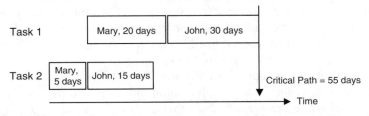

Figure 7-12   Resource Leveling Optimized.

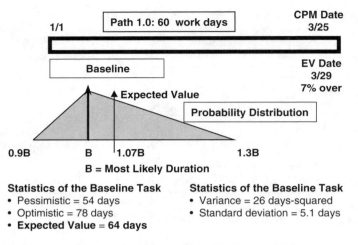

Figure 7-13   Long Task Baseline.

duration estimate is represented by a Triangular distribution with parameters as shown in the figure. We apply the equations we learned about expected value and variance and compute not only the variance and expected value but the standard deviation as well. It is handy to have the standard deviation because it is dimensioned the same as the expected value. Thus if the expected value is measured in days, then so will the standard deviation be. Unfortunately, the variance will be measured in days-squared with no physical meaning. Therefore the variance becomes a figure of merit wherein smaller is better.

The question at hand is whether we can achieve improvement in the schedule confidence by breaking up the long task into a waterfall of tandem but shorter tasks. Our intuition guided by the Law of Large Numbers tells us we are on the right track. If it is possible for the project manager and the WBS work package managers to redesign the work so that the WBS work package can be subdivided into smaller but tandem tasks, then even though each task has a dependency on its immediate predecessor, our feeling is that with the additional planning knowledge that leads to breaking up the long task should come higher confidence that we have it estimated more correctly.

For simplicity, let's apply the Triangular distribution to each of the shorter tasks and also apply the same overall assumptions of pessimism and optimism. You can work some examples to show that there is no loss of generality in the final conclusion. We now recompute the expected value of the overall schedule

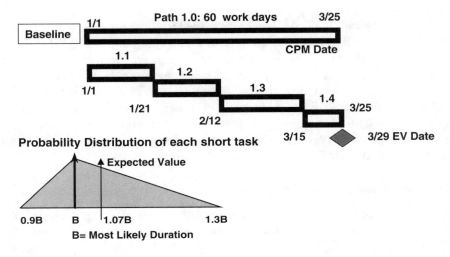

Statistics of the shorter tasks
Task 1.1, ML = 15, EV = 16, Var = 1.63
Task 1.2, ML = 15, EV = 16, Var = 1.63
Task 1.3, ML = 20, EV = 21.33, Var = 2.89
Task 1.4, ML = 10, EV = 10.67, Var = 0.72

Overall
- Sum of all **EV = 64 days** (*same as baseline*)
- Sum of all variances = 6.86 days-squared (*74% improved over baseline*)
- Standard deviation = 2.62 days (*49% improved over baseline*)

See the chapter that explains probability distributions for the formulas for variance and standard deviation for the Triangular distribution.

Figure 7-14   Shorter Tasks Project.

and the variance and standard deviation of the output milestone. We see a result predicted by the Law of Large Numbers as illustrated in Figure 7-14. The expected value of the population is the expected value of the outcome (summation) milestone. Our additional planning knowledge does not change the expected value. However, note the improvement in the variance and the standard deviation; both have improved. Not coincidentally, the (sample) variance has improved, compared to the population variance, by $1/N$, where N is the number of tasks into which we subdivided the longer task, and the standard deviation has improved by $1/\sqrt{N}$. We need only look back to our discussion of the sample variance to see exactly from where these results come.

ROLLING WAVE PLANNING

In Chapter 6 (in the discussion about cost accounting), we noted that it is not often possible to foresee the future activities in a project with consistent detail over the entire period of the project. Therefore, planning is often done in "waves" or stages, with the activities in the near term planned in detail and the activities in the longer distance of time left for future detail planning. There may in fact be several planning waves, particularly if the precise approach or resource requirement is dependent or conditioned on the near-term activities. Such a planning approach is commonly called rolling wave planning.

Rolling Wave Characteristics

The fact is that the distinguishing characteristic of the planning done now for a future wave is that both cost accounts and network tasks are "long" (or "large") compared to their near-term counterparts. We have already discussed the long task in this discussion. Project managers can substitute the words "large cost account" for "long task" and all of the statistical discussions apply, except that the principles and techniques are applied to the cost accounts on the WBS and not to the network schedule.

Monte Carlo Effects in the Rolling Wave

Whether you are doing a Monte Carlo analysis on the WBS cost or on the network schedule, the longer tasks and larger work packages have greater variances. The summation of the schedule at its outcome milestone or the summation of the WBS cost at the top of the WBS will be a Normal distributed outcome regardless of the rolling waves. However, the Monte Carlo simulation will show you what you intuitively know: the longer task and larger cost accounts, with their comparatively larger variances, will increase the standard deviation of the Normal distribution, flatten its curve, and stretch its tails.

As the subsequent waves come and more details are added, the overall variances will decrease and the Normal distribution of the outcome variable, whether cost or schedule, will become more sharply defined, the tails will be less extreme, and the standard deviation (which provides the project manager entrée to the confidence tables) will be more meaningful.

THE CRITICAL CHAIN

There is a body of knowledge in schedule and resource planning that has grown since 1997 when Eliyahu M. Goldratt wrote *Critical Chain*,[3] arguably one of the most significant books in project management. In this book, written like a novel rather than a textbook, Goldratt applies to project management some business theories he developed earlier for managing in a production operation or manufacturing environment. Those theories are collectively called the Theory of Constraints. As applied to project management, Goldratt asserts that the problem in modern project management is ineffective management of the critical path, because the resources necessary to ensure a successful critical path are unwittingly or deliberately scattered and hidden in the project.

The Theory of Constraints

In the Theory of Constraints, described in another Goldratt business novel, *The Goal*,[4] the idea put forward is that in any systemic chain of operations, there is always one operation that constrains or limits the throughput of the entire chain. Throughput is generally thought of as the value-add product produced by the operation that has value to the customer. If the chain of operations is stable and not subject to too many random errors, then the constraint is stable and identifiable; in other words, the constraint is not situational and does not move around from one job session, batch, or run to the next.

To optimize the operation, Goldratt recommends that if the capacity of the constraint cannot be increased, or the constraint cannot be removed by process redesign, then all activities ahead of the constraint should be operated in such a manner that the constraint is never starved. Also, activities ahead of the constraint should never work harder, faster, or more productively than the minimum necessary to keep the constraint from being starved. Some may recognize this latter point as a plank from the "just-in-time" supply chain mantra, and in fact that is not a bad way to look at it, but Goldratt's main point was to identify and manage the constraint optimally.

From Theory of Constraints to Critical Chain

When Goldratt carried his ideas to project management, he identified the project constraint as the critical path. By this association, what Goldratt means is that the project is constrained to a certain duration, and that constrained duration cannot be made shorter. The consequence of the critical path is that constrained throughput (valuable deliverables to the project sponsor) cannot be increased, and indeed throughput is endangered if the critical path cannot be properly managed.

Goldratt made several recommendations in his book *Critical Chain*, but the most prominent are:

- The tasks on the critical path do indeed require statistical distributions to estimate the range of pessimism to optimism. But, unlike PERT* or CPM,** Goldratt insists that the median value, the 50% confidence level, be used. Using the median value, the so-called 50-50 point, means that there is equal likelihood that the task will underrun as overrun.
- All task activity in the project schedule network that is not on the critical path should be made subordinate to the demands of the critical path.
- There should be "buffers" built into any path that joins the critical path. A buffer is a task of nonzero duration but has no performance requirement. In effect, buffer is another word for reserve. However, Goldratt recommends that these buffers be deliberately planned into the project.
- By using the median figure for each task on the critical path, Goldratt recognizes that the median figure is generally more optimistic than the CPM most likely estimate and is often more optimistic than the expected value. Goldratt recommends that the project manager "gather up" the excess pessimism and put it all into a "project buffer" at the end of the network schedule to protect the critical path.

We have already discussed Goldratt's point about a project buffer in our earlier discussion about how to represent the project schedule risk as calculated on the network with the project sponsor's business value dates as set in the program milestones. We did not call it a buffer in that discussion, but for all intents and purposes, that is what it is. Figure 7-15 illustrates the placement of buffers in critical chain planning.

The critical chain ideas are somewhat controversial in the project management community, though there is no lack of derivative texts, papers, projects with lessons learned, and practitioners that are critical chain promoters. The controversy arises out of the following points:

- Can project teams really be trained to estimate with the median value? If so, then the critical chain by Goldratt's description can be established.
- Can team leaders set up schedule buffers by taking away schedule "pad" from cost account managers, or does the concept of buffers simply lead to "pad" on top of "pad"? To the extent that all cost account managers and team leaders will manage to the same set of principles, the critical chain can be established.

---

* PERT uses the BETA distribution and requires that the expected value be used.
** CPM traditionally uses a single-point estimate and, more often than not, the single estimate used is the "most likely" outcome and not the expected value.

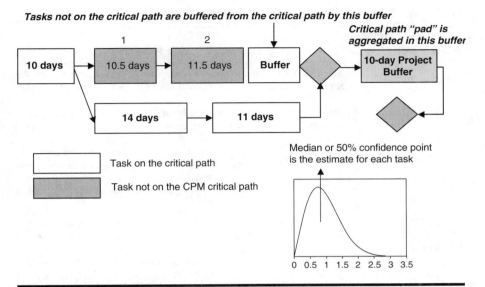

Figure 7-15 Critical Chain Buffers.

SUMMARY OF IMPORTANT POINTS

Table 7-2 provides the highlights of this chapter.

Table 7-2 Summary of Important Points

Point of Discussion	Summary of Ideas Presented
Quantitative time management	▪ The major program milestones that mark business value drive the project at the highest level.
	▪ The program milestones come from the business case.
	▪ Program milestones do not have a probabilistic character.
	▪ The program logic is found in the detail project schedules. Lower level schedules are in network form, preferably the precedence diagramming method, and tie together the various deliverables of the WBS.
	▪ The difference between the network schedule and the program milestones represents risk.
	▪ Every network schedule task has not only a specific beginning or ending, but each task also has an "earliest" or "latest" beginning or ending.
Critical path	▪ The most common outcome of the schedule network is the identification of the critical path.

214   Quantitative Methods in Project Management

Table 7-2   Summary of Important Points (continued)

Point of Discussion	Summary of Ideas Presented
	▪ The critical path, and in fact there may be more than one through the network, may not be the most important path for purposes of business value or functionality. ▪ The critical path establishes the length of the network and therefore sets the overall duration of the project. ▪ There is no float or slack along the critical path. ▪ The "near-critical path" is one or more paths that are not critical at the outset of the project, but could become critical due to performance differences along paths during the course of the project. ▪ The amount of forward–backward path inequality in any path that is the float or slack in the path.
Central Limit Theorem and schedules	▪ From the Central Limit Theorem, the distribution of the output milestone will be Normal regardless of the distributions of the individual tasks in the network. ▪ Given the symmetry of the Normal curve, there is just as likely a possibility that the schedule will underrun (complete early) as overrun (complete late).
Monte Carlo simulation	▪ By computer simulation using a Monte Carlo simulation program, the network schedule is "run" or calculated many times, something we cannot usually do in real projects. ▪ Outcome: a probability density distribution, with absolute values of outcome value and a vertical dimension scaled to meet the requirement that the sum of all probabilities equals 1. ▪ Outcome: a cumulative probability distribution, the so-called "S" curve, again scaled from 0 to 1 to 0 to 100% on the vertical axis and the value outcomes on the horizontal axis.
Architecture weaknesses	▪ At every merge point of predecessor tasks, think "shift right" about the schedule. ▪ Parallel paths that become correlated by sharing resources stretch the schedule! ▪ Another problem common to schedule network architecture is the so-called long task.
Critical chain	▪ The tasks on the critical path require statistical distributions to estimate the range of pessimism to optimism, but the median value, the 50% confidence level, should be used. ▪ All task activity in the project schedule network that is not on the critical path should be made subordinate to the demands of the critical path. ▪ There should be "buffers" built into any path that joins the critical path. A buffer is a task of nonzero duration but has no performance requirement. ▪ The project manager must "gather up" the excess pessimism and put it all into a "project buffer" at the end of the network schedule to protect the critical path.

REFERENCES

1. Brooks, Fredrick P., *The Mythical Man-Month,* Addison Wesley Longman, Inc., Reading, MA, 1995, p. 16.
2. Ibid., p. 25.
3. Goldratt, Eliyahu M., *Critical Chain,* North River Press, Great Barrington, MA, 1997.
4. Goldratt, Eliyahu M. and Cox, Jeff, *The Goal,* North River Press, Great Barrington, MA, 1985.

SPECIAL TOPICS IN QUANTITATIVE MANAGEMENT

It is common sense to take a method and try it.
If it fails, admit frankly and try another. But above all, try something.

Franklin Roosevelt[1]

REGRESSION ANALYSIS

Regression analysis is a term applied by mathematicians to the investigation and analysis of the behaviors of one or more data variables in the presence of another data variable. For example, one data variable in a project could be cost and another data variable could be time or schedule. Project managers naturally ask the question: How does cost behave in the presence of a longer or shorter schedule? Questions such as these are amenable to regression analysis. The primary outcome of regression analysis is a formula for a curve that "best" fits the data observations. Not only does the curve visually reinforce the relationship between the data points, but the curve also provides a means to forecast the next data point before it occurs or is observed, thereby providing lead time to the project manager during which risk management can be brought to bear on the forecasted outcome.

Beyond just the dependency of cost on schedule, cost might depend on the training hours per project staff member, the square feet of facilities allocated to each staff member, the individual productivity of staff, and a host of other

217

possibilities. Of course, there also are many multivariate situations in projects that might call for the mathematical relationship of one on the other, such as employee productivity as an outcome (dependency) of training hours. For each of these project situations, there is also the forecast task of what the next data point is given another outcome of the independent variable. In effect, how much risk is there in the next data set?

Single-Variable Regression

Probably the easiest place to start with regression analysis is with the case introduced about cost and schedule. In regression analysis, one or more of the variables must be the independent variable. The remaining data variable is the dependent variable. The simplest relationship among two variables, one independent and one dependent, is the linear equation of the form

$$Y = a * X + b$$

where X is the independent variable, and the value of Y is dependent on the value of X. When we plot the linear equation we observe that the "curve" is a straight line. Figure 8-1 provides a simple illustration of the linear "curve" that is really a straight line. In Figure 8-1, the independent variable is time and the dependent variable is cost, adhering to the time-honored expression "*time is money.*"

Those familiar with linear equations from the study of algebra recognize that the parameter "a" is the slope of the line and has dimensions of "Y per X," as in dollars per week if Y were dimensioned in dollars and X were dimensioned

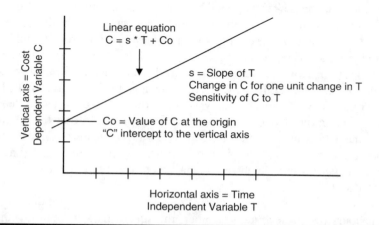

Figure 8-1   Linear Equation.

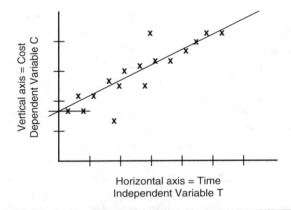

Figure 8-2   Random "Linear" Data.

in weeks. As such, project managers can always think of the slope parameter as a "density" parameter.* The "b" parameter is usually called the "intercept," referring to the fact that when X = 0, Y = b. Therefore, "b" is the intercept point of the curve with the Y-axis at the origin where X = 0.

Of course, X and Y could be deterministic variables (only one fixed value) or they could be random variables (observed value is probabilistic over a range of values). We recognize that the value of Y is completely forecasted by the value of X once the deterministic parameters "a" and "b" are known.

In Figure 8-2, we see a scatter of real observations of real cost and schedule data laid on the graph containing a linear equation of the form we have been discussing, C = a * T + b. Visually, the straight line (that is, the linear curve) seems to fit the data scatter pretty well. As project managers, we might be quite comfortable using the linear curve as the forecast of data values beyond those observed and plotted. If so, the linear equation becomes the "regression" curve for the observed data.

Calculating the Regression Curve

Up to this point, we have discussed single independent variable regression, albeit with the cart in front of the horse: we discussed the linear equation before we discussed the data observations. In point of fact, the opposite is the case in

---

* The word density used in a mathematical context refers to the incremental change in the dependent variable in response to an incremental change in the independent variable. We have already used the density concept when we referred to the probability distribution as the probability density curve.

real projects. The project team has or makes the data observations before there is a curve. The task then becomes to find a curve that "fits" the data.*

There is plenty of computer tool support for regression analysis. Most spreadsheets incorporate the capability or there is an add-in that can be loaded into the spreadsheet to provide the functionality. Beyond spreadsheets, there is a myriad of mathematics and statistics computer packages that can perform regression analysis. Suffice it to say that in most projects no one would be called on to actually calculate a regression curve. Nevertheless, it is instructive to understand what lies behind the results obtained from the computer's analysis.

In this book, we will constrain ourselves to a manual calculation of a linear regression curve. Naturally, there are higher order curves involving polynomial equations that plot as curves and not straight lines. Again, most spreadsheets offer a number of curve fits, not just the linear curve.

By now you might be wondering if there is a figure of merit or some other measure or criteria that would help in picking the regression line. In other words, if there is more than one possibility for the regression curve, as surely there always is, then which one is best? We will answer that question in subsequent paragraphs.

Our task is to find a regression curve that fits our data observations. Our deliverable is a formula of the linear equation type $Y = a * X + b$. Our task really, then, is to find or estimate "a" and "b". As soon as we say "estimate" we are introducing the idea that we might not be able to exactly derive "a" and "b" from the data. "Estimate" means that the "a" and "b" we find are really probabilistic over a range of value possibilities.

Since we are working with a set of data observations, we may not have all the data in the universe (we may have only a sample or subset), but nevertheless we can find the average of the sample we do have: we can find the mean value of X and the mean value of Y, and since we are now talking about random variables, we will use the notation already adopted, X and Y.

It makes some sense to think that any linear regression line we come up with that is "pretty good" should pass through, or very close to, the point on the graph represented by the coordinates of the average value of X and the average value of Y. For this case we have one equation in two unknowns, "a" and "b":

$$Y\text{av} = a * X\text{av} + b$$

where Xav is the mean or average value of the random variable.

---

* Of course, there is a place in project management for the "cart to come before the horse" and that is in hypothesis analysis and forecasting before the fact. In hypothesis analysis, the task is to validate that the data observed fit the forecast or hypothesis and that there is proper cause and effect and not just coincidence or other unidentified dependencies.

This equation can be rearranged to have the form

$$0 = a * X\text{av} + b - Y\text{av}$$

Students of algebra know that when there are two unknowns, two independent equations involving those unknowns must be found in order to solve for them. Thus we are now faced with the dilemma of finding a second equation. This task is actually beyond the scope of this book as it involves calculus to find some best-fit values for "a" and "b", but the result of the calculus is not hard to use and understand as our second equation involving "a" and "b" and the observations of X and Y:

$$0 = a * X^2\text{av} + b * X\text{av} - (X * Y)\text{av}$$

Solving for "a" and "b" with the two independent equations we have discussed provides the answers we are looking for:

$$a = [(X * Y)\text{av} - X\text{av} * Y\text{av}]/[X^2\text{av} - (X\text{av})^2], \text{ and } b = Y\text{av} - a * X\text{av}$$

Goodness of Fit to the Regression Line

We are now prepared to address how well the regression line fits the data. We have already said that a good line should pass through the coordinates of Xav and Yav, but the line should also be minimally distant from all the other data. "Minimally distant" is a general objective of all statistical analysis. After all, we do not know these random variables exactly; if we did, they would be deterministic and not random. Therefore, statistical methods in general strive to minimize the distance or error between the probabilistic values found in the probability density function for the random variable and the real value of the variable.

As discussed in Chapter 2, we minimize distance by calculating the square of the distance between a data observation and its real, mean, or estimated value and then minimizing that squared error. Figure 8-3 provides an illustration. From each data observation value along the horizontal axis, we measure the Y-distance to the regression line from that data observation point. Each such measure is of the form:

$$Y^2\text{distance} = \Sigma (Y\text{i} - Y\text{x})^2$$

where Yi is the specific observation, and Yx is the value of Y on the linear regression line closest to Yi.

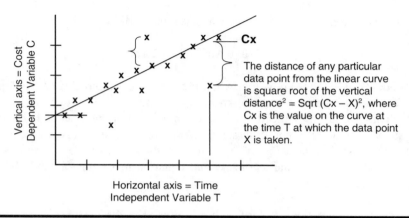

The distance of any particular data point from the linear curve is square root of the vertical distance^2 = Sqrt (Cx − X)^2, where Cx is the value on the curve at the time T at which the data point X is taken.

Horizontal axis = Time
Independent Variable T

Figure 8-3   Distance Measures in Linear Regression.

Consider also that there is another distance measure that could be made. This second distance measure involves the Yav rather than the Yx:

$$Y^2\mathrm{dAv} = \Sigma \ (Y\mathrm{i} - Y\mathrm{av})^2$$

Figure 8-4 illustrates the measures that sum to Y^2dAv. Ordinarily, this second distance measure is counterintuitive because you would think you would always want to measure distance to the nearest point on the regression line and not to an average point that might be further away than the nearest point on the line. However, the issue is whether or not the variations in Y really are

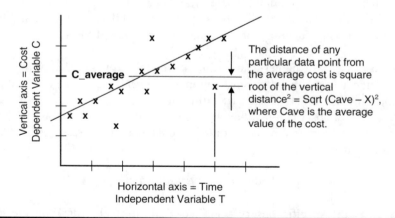

The distance of any particular data point from the average cost is square root of the vertical distance^2 = Sqrt (Cave − X)^2, where Cave is the average value of the cost.

Horizontal axis = Time
Independent Variable T

Figure 8-4   Distance Measures to the Average.

dependent on the variations in X. Perhaps they are strongly or exactly dependent. Then a change in Y can be forecast with almost no error based on a forecast or observation of X. If such is the case, then Y^2 distance is the measure to use. However, if Y is somewhat, but not strongly, dependent on X, then a movement in X will still cause a movement in Y but not to the extent that would occur if Y were strongly dependent on X. For the loosely coupled dependency, Y^2dAv is the measure to use.

The r² Figure of Merit

Mathematicians have formalized the issue about how dependent Y is on X by developing a figure of merit, r^2, which is formally called the *"coefficient of determination"*:

$$r^2 = 1 - (Y^2\text{distance}/Y^2\text{dAv})$$

$$0 \leq r^2 \leq 1$$

Most mathematical packages that run on computers and provide regression analysis also calculate the r^2 and can report the figure in tables or on the graphical output of the package. Being able to calculate r^2 so conveniently relieves the project manager of having to calculate all the distances first to the regression line and then to the average value of Y. Moreover, the regression analyst can experiment with various regression lines until the r^2 is maximized. After all, if $r^2 = 1$, then the regression line is "perfectly" fitted to the data observations; the advantage to the project team is that with a perfect fit, the next outcome of Y is predictable with near certainty. The corollary is also true: the closer r^2 is to 0, the less predictive is the regression curve and the less representative of the relationship between X and Y. Here are the rules:

$$r^2 = 1, \text{ then } Y^2\text{distance}/Y^2\text{dAv} = 0, \text{ or } Y^2\text{distance} = 0$$

where "Y^2distance = 0" means all the observations lie on the regression line and the fit of the regression line to the data is perfect.

$$r^2 = 0, \text{ then } Y^2\text{distance}/Y^2\text{dAv} = 1$$

where "Y^2distance/Y^2dAv = 1" means that data observations are more likely predicted by the average value of Y than by the formula for the regression line. The line is pretty much useless as a forecasting tool.

Figure 8-5 shows the r^2 for a data set.

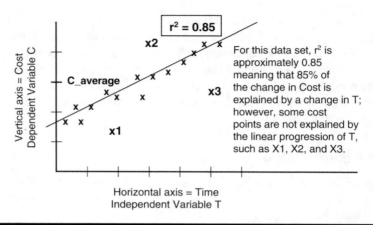

For this data set, r^2 is approximately 0.85 meaning that 85% of the change in Cost is explained by a change in T; however, some cost points are not explained by the linear progression of T, such as X1, X2, and X3.

Figure 8-5 r^2 of Data Observations.

Some Statistical Properties of Regression Results

There are some interesting results that go along with the analysis we have been developing. For one thing, it can be shown[2] that the estimate of "a" is a random variable with Normal distribution. Such a conclusion should not come as a surprise since there is no particular reason why the distribution of values of "a" should favor the more pessimistic or the more optimistic value. All of the good attributes of the Normal distribution are working for us now: "a" is unbiased maximum likelihood estimator for the true value of "a" in the population. In turn, the expected value of "a" is the true value of "a" itself:

$$\text{Mean value of "a"} = \text{expected value of "a"}$$
$$= \text{true value of "a" in the population}$$

$$\text{Variance (a)} = \sigma^2 / \Sigma \ (X\text{i} - X\text{av})^2$$

Looking at the data observations of X for a moment, we write:

$$\Sigma \ (X\text{i} - X\text{av})^2 = \text{n} * \text{Variance } (X)$$

where n = number of observations of X in the population.

Now we have a couple of interesting results: as the sample size, n, gets larger, the variance of "a" gets smaller, meaning that we can zero in on the true value of "a" all that much better. Another way to look at this is that as the variance of X gets larger, meaning a larger spread of the X values in the

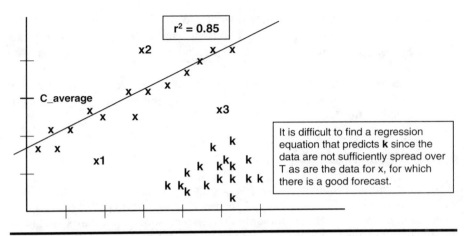

Figure 8-6 Spread of X.

population, again the variance of "a" is driven smaller, making estimate all the better. In effect, if all the X data are bunched together, then it is very difficult to find a line that predicts Y. We see that the ks in Figure 8-6 do not provide a sufficient spread to develop a regression curve.

Multiple Independent Variables

Having more than one independent variable complicates calculations immediately. The dependent variable, say cost, now depends on two different and independent variables, say schedule and worker productivity. Much of the conceptual ground is the same. Indeed, the r^2 becomes R^2, but the idea remains the same: the measure in a figure of merit of how the dependent data are driven by the independent data.

For the more complex projects there may be a need to do multiple variate regression. The only practical approach is to apply a computer program to do the calculations. The more challenging problem for the project manager is to actually deduce the contributing independent variables and make observations simultaneously of all the contributions under the same conditions. Either of a few things may be at work if R^2 is not as expected:

■   The project manager has deduced incorrectly what the contributing data are to the dependent outcome. For example, does project cost really depend on schedule and productivity or schedule and something else not recognized?

■ The independent data really do not predict the dependent data. There simply is not a strong cause-and-effect relationship even though on the surface there appears to be a strong correlation of one data item with another.

■ The data observations of the multiple variables were not made at the same time under the same conditions, thereby tainting the cause-and-effect influences.

HYPOTHESIS TESTING

Another common problem facing project managers is hypothesizing what is going to happen in their projects and then evaluating the hypothesis outcomes analytically. The letter H is commonly used to represent a hypothesis, and there is always more than one hypothesis: the true outcome and false outcome, or the null outcome and the alternative outcome, denoted H(0) and H(1). For instance, a project manager working in the environmental area is often faced with the null hypothesis that an additional regulation will not be passed that impacts the project or the alternative hypothesis that additional legislation will be passed and some impact to the project will occur. In this section, we examine some of the quantitative aspects of evaluating hypotheses that might occur in projects.

The Type 1 and Type 2 Error

Right from the outset, we are faced with what the statistical community calls the Type 1 and Type 2 error. The Type 1 error is straightforward: the hypothesis is true but we reject or ignore the possibility. Grave consequences could occur in making the Type 1 error, and the project manager seeks to avoid this mistake. For example, in our environmental example, we reject the possibility of a new regulation that impacts the project, ignoring the possible ramifications, but indeed the hypothesis is true and a new regulation is issued. "Now what?" asks the project sponsor.

The Type 2 error is usually less risky: we falsely believe the alternate hypothesis, H(1), and make investments to protect against the outcome that never happens. It is easy to see how a Type 2 error could be made in the environmental project, spending money to thwart the impact of a new regulation that never happens. Though no project manager or project sponsor wants to waste resources, perhaps a project cost impact is the only consequence of making a Type 2 error.

Interval of Acceptance

In testing for the outcome of the hypothesis, especially by simulation, we will "run" the hypothesis many times. The first few times may not be representative of the final outcome since it takes many runs to converge to the final and ultimate outcome. For a number of reasons, we may not have the luxury of waiting for or estimating the convergence. We may have to establish an interval around the likely outcome, called the interval of acceptance, within which we say that if an outcome falls anywhere in the interval of acceptance, then that outcome is "good enough." Now, if the objective is to avoid the Type 1 error, then we must be careful about rejecting a hypothesis that really is true. Thus we are led by the need to risk-manage the Type 1 error to widen the interval of acceptance. However, the wide acceptance criterion lets in the Type 2 error! Remember that Type 2 is accepting a hypothesis that is really false. There is no absolute rule here. It is all about experience and heuristics. Some say that the interval of acceptance should never be greater than 10%, or at most 20%. Each project team will have to decide for itself.

In many practical situations there is no bias toward optimism or pessimism. Our environmental example could be of this type, though regulatory agencies usually have a bias one way or the other. Nevertheless, if there is no bias, or it is "reasonably" small, then we know the distribution of values of H(0) or H(1) is going to be symmetrical even though we do not know the exact distribution. However, we get some help here as well. Recall the Central Limit Theorem: regardless of the actual distribution, over a very large number of trials the average outcome distribution will be Normal. Thus, the project manager can refer to the Normal distribution to estimate the confidence that goes along with an acceptance interval and thereby manage the risk of the Type 1 error. For instance, we know that only about 4% of all outcomes lie more than $\pm 2\sigma$ from the mean value of a Normal distribution. In other words, we are about 96% confident that an outcome will be within $\pm 2\sigma$ of the mean. If the mean and variance (and from variance the standard deviation can be calculated) can be estimated from simulation, then the project manager can get a handle on the Type 1 error (rejecting something that is actually true). Figure 8-7 illustrates the points we are making.

Testing for the Validity of the Hypothesis

Having constructed a null hypothesis and its alternative, H(0) and H(1), and made some assumptions about the outcomes being Normal because of the tendency of a large number of trials to have a Normal distribution, the question

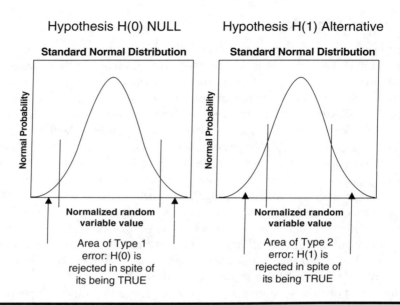

Hypothesis H(0) NULL   Hypothesis H(1) Alternative

Figure 8-7   Type 1 and 2 Errors.

remains: Can we test to see if the H(0) is valid? In fact, there are many things we can do.

The common approach to hypothesis testing is to test the performance of a test statistic. For example, with the Normal distributions of H(0) and H(1) normalized to the standard Normal plot, where the value of $\sigma = 1$ and $\mu = 0$, then if an outcome were any normalized number greater than about three, you would suspect that outcome did not belong to the H(0) since the confidence of a normalized outcome of three or more is only about a quarter of a percent, 0.26% to be more precise. We get this figure from a table of two-sided Normal probability density values or from a statistical function in a mathematics and statistical package.

t-Statistic Test

The other common test in hypothesis testing is to discover the true mean of the distribution for H(0) and H(1). For this task, we need a statistic commonly called the "t statistic" or the "Student's t" statistic.* The following few steps

---

* The "t statistic" was first developed by a statistics professor to assist his students. The professor chose not to associate his name with the statistic, but named it the "Student's t" instead.

show what is done to obtain an estimate of the mean of the distribution of the hypothesis:

- From the data observations of the outcomes of "n" trials of the hypothesis, calculate the sample average. Sample average = $H\mathrm{av} = (1/n) * \Sigma\ H\mathrm{i}$, where $H\mathrm{i}$ is the ith outcome of the hypothesis trials.
- Calculate the sample variance, $\mathrm{Var}H = [1/(n\text{-}1)] * \Sigma\ (H\mathrm{i} - H\mathrm{av})^2$.
- Calculate a statistic, $\mathrm{t} = \sqrt{n} * (H\mathrm{av} - \mu)/\sqrt{\mathrm{Var}H}$, where μ is an estimate of the true mean for which we are testing the validity of the assumption that μ is correct.
- Look up the value of t in a table of t statistics where n-1 = "degrees of freedom." If the value of t is realistic from the lookup table, then μ is a good estimate of the mean. For example, using a t-statistics lookup table for n-1 = 100, the probability is 0.99 that the value of t will be between ±2.617. If the calculated value of t for the observed data is not in this range, then the hypothesis regarding the estimate of the mean is to be rejected with very little chance, less than 1%, that we are committing a Type 1 error.

RISK MANAGEMENT WITH THE PROBABILITY TIMES IMPACT ANALYSIS

It is good practice for the project management team to have a working understanding of statistical and numerical methods to apply to projects. Most of what we have discussed has been aimed at managing risk so that the project delivers business value and satisfies the business users and sponsors. Experienced project managers know that the number of identified risks in projects can quickly grow to a long list, a list so long as to lose meaning and be awkward and ineffective to manage. The project manager's objective is to filter the list and identify the risks that have a prospect of impacting the outcome of the project. For this filtering task, a common tool is the P * I analysis, or the "probability times impact" analysis.

Probability and Impact

To this point we have spent a good deal of time on the probability development and analysis as applied to a project event, work breakdown structure (WBS) work package, or other project activity. We have not addressed to any great extent the impact of any particular risk to the project. Further, the product of impact and probability really sets up the data set to be filtered to whittle down the list. For example, a risk with a $1 million impact is really a $10,000 risk to manage if the probability of occurrence is only 1%. Thus, the attitude of the project manager is that what is being managed is a $10,000 problem, not $1 million.

The $10,000 figure is the weighted value of the risk. Take note that in other chapters we have called the weighted value the expected value (outcome times probability of outcome). When working with weighted values, it is typical to sum all the weighted values to obtain the dollar value of the expected value of the risks under management. On a weighted basis, it is reasonable to expect that some risks will occur in spite of all efforts to the contrary and some risks will not come true. But on average, if the list of risks is long enough, the weighted value is the best estimate of the throughput impact.

$$\text{Risk under management} = \Sigma \, (\text{Risk \$value} * \text{Risk probability})$$
$$(\text{dollar value})$$

$$\text{Average risk under management} = (1/N) * \Sigma \, (\text{Risk \$value} * \text{Risk probability})$$
$$(\text{dollar value})$$

$$\text{Risk under management} = \text{Throughput \$impact to project}$$

From the Central Limit Theorem, if the list of risks is "long enough," we know that the probability distribution of the average of the risks under management will be Normal, or approximately so. This means that there is equal pessimism and optimism about the ultimate dollar value of risks paid. We also know that the variance of the average will be improved by a factor of $1/N$, where N is the number of risks in the weighted list.

Throughput is a concept from the Theory of Constraints applied to project management. As in the critical chain discussion, throughput is the portion of total activity that makes its way all the way to project outcomes. The constraint in this case is risk management. The risks that make it through the risk management process impact the project. The dollar value of those impacts is the throughput of the risk possibilities to the project.

Obviously, the risk under management must be carried to the project balance sheet on the project side. If the expected value of the project plus the risk under management does not fit within the resources assigned by the business, then the project manager must take immediate steps to more rigorously manage the risks or find other offsets to bring the project into balance.

Probability Times Impact Tools

There are plenty of ways to calculate and convey the results of a P * I analysis. A simple multicolumn table is probably the best. Table 8-1 is one such example. As there are multiple columns in a P * I analysis, so are there multiple decisions to be made:

■ First, follow the normal steps of risk management to identify risks in the project. However, identified risks can and should be an unordered list without intelligence as to which risk is more important. The ranking of risks by importance is one of the primary outcomes of the P * I analysis.

■ Second, each identified risk, regardless of likelihood, must be given a dollar value equal to the impact on the project if the risk comes true. Naturally, three-point estimates should be made. From the three-point estimates an expected value is calculated.

■ The expected value is adjusted according to the risk attitude of the management team. The value of the risk if the risk comes true is the so-called "downside" figure of which we have spoken in other chapters. If the project or the business cannot afford the downside, then according to the concept of utility, the value of the risk is amplified by a weighting

Table 8-1   P * I Display

Risk Event	Probability of Occurrence	Impact to Project if Risk Occurs	P * I
Vendor fails to deliver computer on time	50% chance of 5-day delay	$10,000 per day of delay	P * I = 0.5 * 5 * 10,000 = $25,000
New environmental regulations issued	5% chance of happening during project development	$100,000 redesign of the environmental module	P * I = 0.05 * $100,000 = $5,000
Assembly facility is not available on time	5% chance of 10-day delay	$5,000 per day of delay	P * I = 0.05 * 10 * 5,000 = $2,500
Truck rental required if boxes exceed half a ton*	30% chance of overweight boxes	$200 per day rental, 10 days required	P * I = 0.3 * 200 * 10 = $600

* Truck rental risk may not be of sufficient consequence that it would make the list of risks to watch. Project manager may set a dollar threshold of P * I that would exclude such minor risk events.

factor to reflect the consequences of the impact. The dollar value should be in what might be called "utility dollars"[3] that reflect the risk attitude of the project, the business, or executives who make "bet the business" decisions.*

■ All risk figures are adjusted for the present value. Making a present value calculation brings into play a risk adjustment of other factors that are summarized in the discount factor.

■ An estimate of probability of risk coming true is made. Such an estimate is judgmental and subject to bias if made by a single estimator. Making risk assessments of this type is a perfect opportunity for the Delphi method of independent evaluators to be brought into play.

■ Finally, the present value of the impact utility dollars is multiplied by the probability of occurrence in order to get the final expected value of the risk to the project.

Once the P ∗ I calculations are made, the project team sets a threshold for risks that will be actively managed and are exposed to the project team for tracking. Other risks not above the threshold go on another list of unmanaged risks that are dealt with as circumstances and situations bring them to the forefront.

Unmanaged Risks

Project managers cannot ordinarily devote attention to every risk that anyone can think of during the course of the project life cycle. We have discussed several situations where such a phenomenon occurs: the paths in the network that are not critical or near critical, the risks that have very low P ∗ I, and the project activities that have very low correlation with other activities and therefore very low r^2 figures of merit. The fact is that in real projects, low-impact risks go on the back burner. The back burner is really just another list where the activities judged to be low threats are placed. Nothing is ever thrown away,

---

* Various types of utility factors can be applied to different risks and different cost accounts in the WBS. For instance, the utility concepts in software might be quite different from the utility concepts in a regulatory environment where compliance, or not, could mean shutting down company processes and business value. Generally, if the downside is somehow deemed unaffordable or more onerous than the unweighted impact of the risk, then a weight, greater than 1, is applied to the risk. The utility dollars = real dollars ∗ risk-averse factor. For instance, if the downside of a software failure is considered to have 10 times the impact on the business because of customer and investor relationships than the actual dollar impact to the project, then the equation for the software risk becomes utility dollars = real dollars ∗ 10.

but if a situation arises that promotes one of these unmanaged risks to the front burner, then that situation becomes the time and the place to confront and addresses these unmanaged risks.

SIX SIGMA AND PROJECT MANAGEMENT

Six Sigma is just making its appearance in project management. Six Sigma is the name coined by Motorola in the 1980s for a process and throughput improvement strategy it developed from some of the process control work done originally in the Bell Laboratories in the 1920s and later taken to Japan in the 1950s by W. Edwards Deming. Six Sigma's goal is to reduce the product errors experienced by customers and to improve the quality of products as seen and used by customers. Employing Six Sigma throughout Motorola led, in part, to its winning the prestigious Malcolm Baldrige National Quality Award 1988.

The name "Six Sigma" has an origin in statistics. The word "sigma" we recognize as the Greek letter "s" which we know as σ. From our study of statistics, we know that the standard deviation of a probability distribution is denoted by σ. Furthermore, we know that the confidence measures associated with a Normal distribution are usually cast in terms of so many σ from the mean: for example, as said many times before in this book, $\pm 1\sigma$ from the mean includes about 68.3% of the possible values of a random variable with a Normal distribution. Most project managers are comfortable with "2σ" estimating, which covers over 95% of all outcomes, and some project managers refine matters to "3σ", which encompasses a little over 99.7% of all outcomes. Six Sigma seems to be about going $\pm$"6σ" from the mean and looking at the confidence that virtually all outcomes are accounted for in the analysis. In reality only $\pm 4.5\sigma$ is required and practiced in the Six Sigma program, as we will see.

Six Sigma and Process Capability

Six Sigma is a process capability (Cp) technique. What is meant by process capability? Every man-made process has some inherent errors that are irreducible. Other errors creep in over time as the process is repeated many times, such as the error that might be introduced by tool wear as the tool is used many times in production. The inherent errors and the allowable error "creep" are captured in what is called the "engineering tolerance" of the process. Staying within the engineering tolerances is what is expected of a capable process. If the Normal distribution is laid on a capable process, as shown in Figure 8-8, in such manner that the confidence limits of the Normal distribution conform to the expectations of the process, then process engineers say with confidence that the process will perform to the required specification.

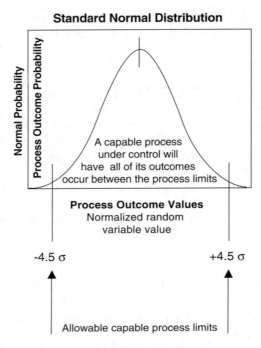

Standard Normal Distribution

A capable process
under control will
have all of its outcomes
occur between the process limits

Process Outcome Values
Normalized random
variable value

-4.5 σ   +4.5 σ

Allowable capable process limits

Beyond the capable process limits any outcome
would be considered an "error" or "an out of
tolerance" event that would have characteristics
that would not be acceptable to a customer.

Figure 8-8   Capable Process and Normal Distribution.

A refinement of the process capability was to observe and accommodate a bias in position of the process mean. In other words, in addition to small natural random effects that are irreducible, and the additional process errors that are within the engineering tolerance, there is also the possibility that the mean of the process will drift over time, creating a bias. A capable process with such a characteristic is denoted Cpk.

3.4 Parts Per Million

In the Motorola process, as practiced, the process mean is allowed to drift up to 1.5σ in either direction, and the process random effects should stay within an additional $\pm 3\sigma$ from the mean at all times. Thus, in the limit, the engineering tolerance must allow for a total of $\pm 4.5\sigma$ from the mean. At $\pm 4.5\sigma$, the confidence is so high that speaking in percentages, as we have done to this point, is very awkward. Therefore, one interesting contribution made by the promoters of Six Sigma was to move the conversation of confidence away from the idea of percentages and toward the idea of "errors per million opportunities for error." At the limit of ±4.5σ, the confidence level in traditional form is 99.9993198% or, as often said in engineering shorthand, "five nines."

However, in the Six Sigma parlance, the process engineers recognize that the tails of the Normal distribution, beyond 4.5σ in both directions, hold together only $6.8 * 10^{-6}$ of the area under the Normal curve:

$$\text{Total area under the Normal curve} = 1$$

$$1 - 0.999993198 = 0.00000680161 = 6.8 * 10^{-6}$$

Each tail, being symmetrical on each side, holds only $3.4 * 10^{-6}$ of the area as shown in Figure 8-9.* Thus, the mantra of the Six Sigma program was set at having the engineering tolerance encompass all outcomes except those beyond 4.5σ of the mean. In effect, the confidence that no outcome will occur in the forbidden bands is such that only 3.4 out-of-tolerance outcomes (errors) will occur in either direction for every 1 million opportunities. The statement is usually shortened to *"plus or minus 3.4 parts per million,"* with the word "part" referring to something countable, including an opportunity, and the dimension that goes with the word "million" is silently implied but of course the dimension is "parts."

The move from 4.5σ to Six Sigma is more marketing and promotion than anything else. The standard remains 3.4 parts per million.

Six Sigma Processes

In one sense, Six Sigma fits very well with project management because it is a repeatable methodology and the statistics described above are the outcome of a multistep process not unlike many in project management. Summarizing Six Sigma at a high level:

- Define the problem as observed in the business or by customers and suppliers
- Define the process or processes that are touched by the problem

---

* A notation common with very small numbers, $3.4 * 10^{-6}$ means "3.4 times 1/1,000,000" or "3.4 times one millionth." In many other venues, including computer spreadsheets, the letter E is used in place of the "10" and the notation would be "3.4 E-6." Another way to refer to small numbers like this is to say "3.4 parts per million parts," usually shortened to "3.4 parts per million." A "part" is anything countable, and a part can be simply an opportunity for an event rather than a tangible gadget.

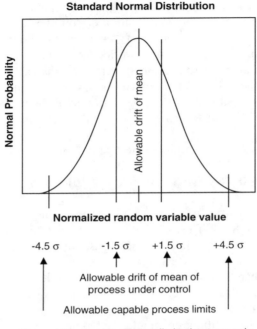

Standard Normal Distribution

Normal Probability

Allowable drift of mean

Normalized random variable value

-4.5 σ   -1.5 σ   +1.5 σ   +4.5 σ

Allowable drift of mean of
process under control

Allowable capable process limits

Beyond the capable process limits there are only
$3.4 * 10^{-6}$ opportunities in each tail of the curve.
The confidence the process will be within the
process limits exceeds "5 9s."

Figure 8-9   3.4 Parts Per Million.

- List possible causes and effects that lead toward or cause the problem within the process
- Collect data according to an experiment designed and developed to work against the causes and effects in the possible cause list
- Analyze what is collected
- Exploit what is discovered in analysis by designing and implementing solutions to the identified problem

Project Management and Six Sigma

Looking at the project management body of knowledge, especially as set forth by the Project Management Institute®, virtually every process area of project management has a multistep approach that is similar in concept to the high-level Six Sigma steps just described. Generally, project management is about defining the scope and requirements, developing possible approaches to implementing the scope, estimating the causes and effects of performance, performing, measuring the performance, and then exploiting all efforts by delivering product and services to the project sponsor.

The differences arise from the fact that a project is a one-time endeavor never to be exactly repeated, and Six Sigma is a strategy for repeated processes. Moreover, project managers do a lot of work and make a lot of progress at reasonable cost with engineering-quality estimates of few parts per hundred (2σ) or perhaps a few parts per thousand (3σ). However, even though projects are really only done once, project managers routinely use simulation to run projects virtually hundreds and thousands of times. Thus, there is some data collection and analysis at the level of few parts per thousand though there may be many millions of data elements in the simulation.

The WBS and schedule network on very large projects can run to many thousands of work packages, perhaps even tens of thousands of work packages, and thousands of network tasks, but rare is the project that would generate meaningful data to the level of 4.5σ.

The main contribution to projects is not in the transference to projects of process control techniques applicable to highly repetitive processes, but rather the mind-set of high quality being self-paying and having immeasurable good consequences down the road. In this sense, quality is broadly dimensioned, encompassing the ideas of timeliness, functional fit, environmental fit, no scrap, no rework, and no nonvalue-added work.

Six Sigma stresses the idea of high-quality repeatability that plays well with the emerging maturity model standards for project management. Maturity models in software engineering have been around for more than a generation, first promoted by the Software Engineering Institute® in the early 1980s as means to improve the state of software engineering and obtain more predictable results at a more predictable resource consumption than heretofore was possible. In this same time frame, various estimating models came along that depended on past projects for historical data of performance so that future performance could be forecast. A forecast model coupled with a repeatable process was a powerful stimulus to the software industry to improve its performance.

In like manner, the maturity model and the concepts of quality grounded in statistical methods will prove simulative to the project management community and will likely result in more effective projects.

QUALITY FUNCTION DEPLOYMENT

Quality Function Deployment (QFD) is about deployment of project requirements into the deliverables of the WBS by applying a systematic methodology

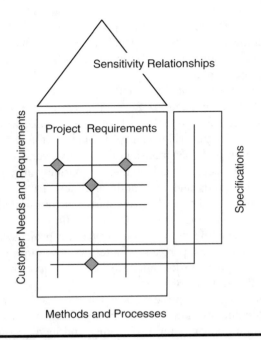

Figure 8-10   The House of Quality.

that leads to build-to and buy-to specifications for the material items in the project. QFD is a very sophisticated and elegant process that has a large and robust body of knowledge to support users at all levels. One only need consult the Internet or the project library to see the extent of documentation.

QFD is a process and a tool. The process is a systematic means to decompose requirements and relate those lower level requirements to standards, metrics, development and production processes, and specifications. The tool is a series of interlocked and related matrices that express the relationships between requirements, standards, methods, and specifications. At a top level, Figure 8-10 presents the basic QFD starting point.

Phases of Quality Function Deployment

Although there are many implementations and interpretations of QFD that are industry and business specific, the general body of knowledge acknowledges that the deployment of requirements down to detailed specifications requires several steps called phases. Requirements are user or customer statements of need and value. As such, customer requirements should be solution free and

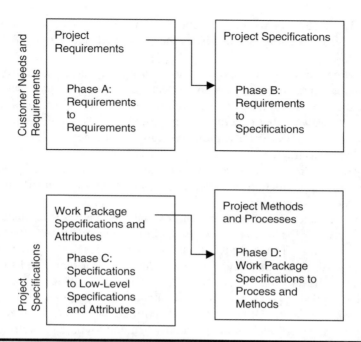

Figure 8-11   QFD Phases.

most often free of any quantitative specifications that could be construed as "buy-to" or "build-to." Certainly the process limits discussed in the section on Six Sigma would not ordinarily be in the customer specification. Thus, for example, the Six Sigma process limits need to be derived from the requirements by systematic decomposition and then assignment of specification to the lowest level requirements.

Figure 8-11 presents a four-phase model of QFD. Typically, in a real application, the project manager or project architect will customize this model into either more or fewer steps and will "tune" matrices to the processes and business practices of the performing organization. We see in Phase A that the customer's functional and technical requirements are the entry point to the first matrix. The Phase A output is a set of technical requirements that are completely traceable to the customer requirements by means of the matrix mapping. Some project engineers might call such a matrix a "cross-reference map" between "input" and "output." The technical requirements are quantitative insofar as is possible, and the technical requirements are more high level than the specifications found in the next phase. Technical requirements, like functional requirements, are solution free. The solution is really in the hardware and software and process deliverables of the cost accounts and work packages of the WBS. As such, technical requirements represent the integrated interaction of the WBS deliverables.

Following Phase A, we develop the specifications of the build-to or buy-to deliverables that are responsive to the technical and functional requirements. We call the next step Phase B. The build-to or buy-to deliverables might be software or hardware, but generally we are looking at the tangibles in the work packages of the WBS. Specifications typically are numerical and quantitative so as to be measurable.

Subsequent phases link or relate the technical specifications to process and methodology of production or development, and then subsequently to control and feedback mechanisms.

Project managers familiar with relational databases will see immediately the parallels between the matrix model of QFD and the relational model among tables in a database. The "output" of one matrix provides the "input" to the next matrix; in a database, the "outputs" are fields within a table, and the output fields contain the data that are the "keys" to the next table. Thus, it is completely practical to represent QFD in a relational database, and there are many software tools to assist users with QFD practices. Practitioners will find that maintenance of the QFD model is much more efficient when employing an electronic computer-based database rather than a paper-based matrix representation.

Quantitative Attributes on the Quality Function Deployment Matrix

Looking in more detail at the house of quality in Figure 8-12, we see that there are a number of quantitative attributes that can be added to and carried along with the matrices. The specific project to which QFD is applied should determine what attributes are important.

Symbols are sometimes added to the QFD chart; the symbols can be used to denote importance, impact, or probability of occurrence. Symbols could also be used to show sensitivity relationships among matrix entries. Sensitivity refers to the effect on attribute, parameter, or deliverable caused by a change in another attribute, parameter, or deliverable. The usual expression of sensitivity is in the form of a density: "X change per unit of change in Y."

Validating the Quality Function Deployment Analysis

A lot of effort on the part of the project team often goes into building the QFD house of quality matrices; more effort is required to maintain the matrices as more information becomes available. Some project teams build only the first

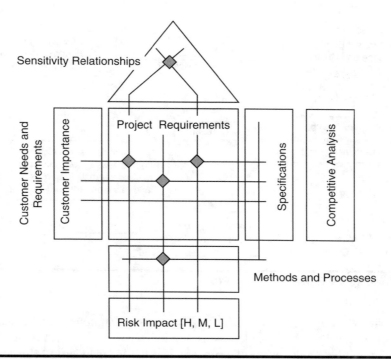

Sensitivity Relationships

Customer Needs and Requirements

Customer Importance

Project Requirements

Specifications

Competitive Analysis

Methods and Processes

Risk Impact [H, M, L]

Figure 8-12 QFD Details.

matrix linking customer and project requirements, while others go on to build a second matrix to link project requirements with either key methods, processes, or specifications.

It is imperative that the project efforts toward QFD be relevant and effective. In part, achieving a useful result requires validation of the QFD results by business managers (Phase A) and by other subject matter experts (SMEs) on the various phases. Validation begins with coordination with the business analysis documented on the balanced scorecard, Kano analysis, or other competitive, marketing, or risk analysis. Validation often follows the so-called "V-curve" common in system engineering. An illustration of the "V-curve" applied to the QFD validation is shown in Figure 8-13.

Once validated to external drivers, such as the balanced scorecard or Kano analysis, the project team can validate the QFD matrices by examining the internal content. For instance, there should be no blank rows or columns. At least one data element should be associated with every row or column. Attributes that are scored strongly in one area should have strong impacts elsewhere and, of course, document all the assumptions and constraints that bear

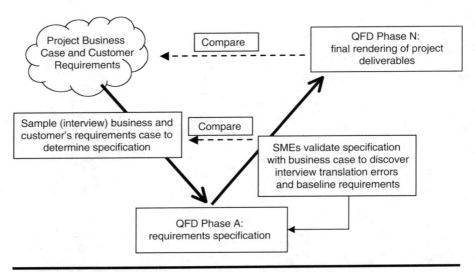

Figure 8-13   V-Curve Validation Process.

on attribute ratings and relationships. Examine the assumptions and constraints for consistency and reasonableness as applied across the project. Independent SMEs could be employed for the process, and the independent SMEs could be employed in a Delphi-like strategy to make sure that nothing is left behind or not considered.

Affinity and Tree Diagrams in Quality Function Deployment

Affinity diagrams are graphical portrayals of similar deliverables and requirements grouped together, thereby showing their similarity to or affinity for each other. Tree diagrams are like the WBS, showing a hierarchy of deliverables, but unlike the WBS, the QFD tree diagrams can include requirements, specifications, methods, and processes. Tree diagrams and affinity diagrams are another useful tool for identifying all the relationships that need to be represented on the QFD matrices and for identifying any invalid relationships that might have been placed on the QFD matrix.

SUMMARY OF IMPORTANT POINTS

Table 8-2 provides the highlights of this chapter.

Table 8-2 Summary of Important Points

Point of Discussion	Summary of Ideas Presented
Regression analysis	■ Regression analysis is a term applied by mathematicians to the investigation and analysis of the behaviors of one or more data variables in the presence of another data variable. ■ The primary outcome of regression analysis is a formula for a curve that "best" fits the data observations. ■ In regression analysis, one or more of the variables must be the independent variable. ■ Statistical methods aim to minimize the distance or error between the probabilistic values and the real value of the variable. ■ If $r^2 = 1$, then the regression line is "perfectly" fitted to the data observations; if r^2 is 0, the regression curve is less representative of the relationship between X and Y.
Hypothesis testing	■ The Type 1 error is straightforward: the hypothesis is true but we reject or ignore the possibility. ■ The Type 2 error is usually less risky: we falsely believe the alternate hypothesis and make investments to protect against the outcome that never happens. ■ We have to establish an interval around the likely outcome, called the interval of acceptance, within which we say "good enough." ■ Regardless of the actual distribution, over a very large number of trials the average outcome distribution will be Normal. ■ A common test in hypothesis testing is to discover the true mean of the distribution for H(0) and H(1) using a statistic commonly called the "t statistic."
Risk management with P * I	■ The project manager's objective is to filter the list and identify the risks that have a prospect of impacting the outcome of the project. For this filtering task, a common tool is the P * I analysis, or the "probability times impact" analysis. ■ Risk under management (dollar value) = Σ (Risk \$value * Risk probability). ■ The average of the risks under management will be Normal or approximately so.
Six Sigma	■ Six Sigma's goal is to reduce the product errors experienced by customers; in other words, to improve the quality of products as seen and used by customers. ■ In the Motorola process, the process mean is allowed to drift up to 1.5σ in either direction, and the process random effects should stay $\pm3\sigma$ from the mean at all times. ■ The confidence that no outcome will occur out of tolerance is such that only 3.4 out-of-tolerance outcomes (errors) will occur in either direction for every 1 million opportunities. ■ The differences between project management and Six Sigma arise from the fact that a project is a one-time endeavor never to be exactly repeated and Six Sigma is a strategy for repeated processes.

Table 8-2 Summary of Important Points (continued)

Point of Discussion	Summary of Ideas Presented
	■ Six Sigma stresses high-quality repeatability that plays well with the emerging maturity model standards for project management.
Quality function deployment	■ QFD is about deployment of project requirements into the deliverables of the WBS by applying a systematic methodology that leads to build-to and buy-to specifications for the material items in the project.
	■ QFD is a process and a tool.
	■ The process is a systematic means to decompose requirements and relate those lower level requirements to standards, metrics, development and production processes, and specifications.
	■ The tool is a series of interlocked and related matrices that express the relationships between requirements, standards, methods, and specifications.
	■ Achieving a useful QFD result requires validation of results by business managers and by other subject matter experts.

REFERENCES

1. Brooks, Fredrick P., *The Mythical Man-Month,* Addison Wesley Longman, Inc., Reading, MA, 1995, p. 115.
2. Downing, Douglas and Clark, Jeffery, *Statistics the Easy Way,* Barron's, Hauppauge, NY, 1997, pp. 264–269.
3. Schuyler, John, *Risk and Decision Analysis in Projects, Second Edition*, Project Management Institute, Newtown Square, PA, 2001, pp. 35 and 52.

QUANTITATIVE METHODS IN PROJECT CONTRACTS

Now this is not the end. It is not even the beginning of the end.
It is perhaps the end of the beginning.

Sir Winston Churchill
London, 1942

PROJECT CONTRACTS

Contracts between suppliers and the project team are commonly employed to accomplish two objectives:

- **Change the risk profile of the project** by transferring risk from the project team to the supplier. Presumably, a due diligence examination of the supplier's ability to perform confirms that the supplier has a higher probability of accomplishing the scope of work in acceptable time at reasonable cost than does the project team. The decision-making processes discussed in this book provide a method and tool for making contracting decisions.
- **Implement policy** regarding sharing the project opportunity with participants in the supply chain. If the contract is related to a public sector project, public policy regarding small business and minority business participation may be operative on the project team. In the private sector, there may be policy to involve selected suppliers and customers in

projects, or there may be policy to not involve selected participants in the project.

In this chapter, we will address project contracting as an instrument of risk management.

The Elements of a Contract

A contract is a mutual agreement, either oral or written, that obligates two or more parties to perform to a specific scope for a specified consideration, usually in a specified time frame. The operative idea here is *mutual* agreement. A contract cannot be imposed unilaterally on an unwilling supplier. In effect, as project manager you cannot declare the project to be in contract with a supplier, have an expectation of performance, and then return later and claim the supplier is in breach for not performing. Therefore, it is generally understood in the contracting community that the following five elements need to be in place before there is a legal and enforceable contract:

- There must be a true *offer to do business* with a supplier by the project or contracting authority.
- There must be a corresponding *acceptance of the offer to do business* by the supplier's contracting authority.
- There must be a specified *consideration* for the work to be performed. Consideration does not need to be in dollar terms. Typical contract language begins: "In consideration of _____, the parties agree......"
- The supplier must have the legal capacity to perform. That is, the supplier may not materially misrepresent the supplier's ability to perform.
- The statement of work (SOW) must be for a legal activity. It is not proper to contract for illegal activity.

Project and Supplier Risks in Contracts

Contracts are used largely to change the risk profile of the project. Project managers contract for skills, staff, facilities, special tools and methods, and experience not available or not available at low enough risk in the project team itself. Some contracts begin as "team agreements" wherein two companies agree to work together in a prime contractor–subcontractor role, whereas other contracts are awarded to a sole source, selected source, or competitive source.*

---

* Sole source: there is only one contractor known to have the ability to perform the SOW. Selected source: a contractor selected without competition to perform the SOW. Competitive source: a contractor selected from among a peer group of competent offerors on the basis of competition.

Regardless of how the two parties come together with a contract, the fact is that both parties assume some of the risk of the endeavor. Contracting cannot eliminate project risk; project risk can simply be made manageable by transference to a lower risk supplier. For the project manager, the primary residual risk, once the contract is in place, is performance failure on the part of the supplier. The supplier may run into unforeseen technical problems, experience business failures elsewhere that affect the project, or be subject to external threats such as changes in regulations or uncontrollable acts of God. Of course, depending on the type of contract selected, the project manager may choose to retain some or most of the cost risk of the SOW and only transfer the risk of performance to the supplier.

The supplier is on the receiving end of the risk being transferred out of the project. If the supplier is competent and experienced, and has the staff, tools and methods, facilities, and financial backing to accept the SOW, then the supplier's risk is minimized and the contract is a viable business opportunity for the supplier. Further, as mentioned above, the project manager may elect to retain the cost risk and thereby transfer only performance risk to the supplier. But, of course, in all contracting arrangements, the project is the supplier's customer. Customers in a contracting relationship are a source of risk. The project (customer) could breach the contract — by failing to provide specified facilities, information, technical or functional assistance — or could fail to pay or could delay payments.

Both parties seek to minimize their risk when entering into a contract. The supplier will be inclined to identify risks early enough so that provisions in the contract can cover the risks: more money, more time, and assistance in various forms. The project team will be inclined to seek performance guarantees and the means to reward upside achievement or punish downside shortfalls. Each party invokes its risk management plan when approaching a contract opportunity.

Contracting Vehicles

Contracts used to convey the SOW from the project to the supplier fall into two broad categories:

- **Fixed price (FP) contracts** that transfer both the cost and performance risk to the supplier. FP contracts require the contractor to "complete" the SOW. In this sense, *FP contracts are "completion" contracts.* FP contracts are appropriate when the scope of the SOW is sufficiently defined that a price and schedule can be definitely estimated and "fixed" for the required performance. FP contracts are inappropriate for many R&D activities where the scope of work is indefinite.

- **Cost plus (CP) or cost-reimbursable contracts** that transfer only a portion of the cost risk to the contractor (supplier) and require only a contractor's "best effort" toward completing the SOW. *CP contracts are not completion contracts.* CP contracts are the appropriate vehicle for R&D and other endeavors where the scope is not defined to the point that definitive estimates can be made. Although CP contracts have an estimated scope of work, the contractor is only bound to perform in a reasonable and competent manner. The contractor is not bound to "complete" the SOW since the true scope is unknown. Projects with large "rolling wave" plans are best accomplished with CP contracts.

In addition to the FP and CP categories that broadly define which party has the cost and scope risk in the arrangement, there are categories for handling the amount of profit that a supplier can make on a contracted scope of work:

- The profit (fee) could be built into the contract price and not visible to the project manager. Firm fixed price (FFP) contracts have only one dollar parameter: price. Only the supplier knows the potential profit in the deal; the profit is a combination of a risk premium to cover the supplier's assumed risk and a profit amount to earn the contractor's required return on cost.
- The fee could be fixed by mutual negotiation (fixed fee, FF). FF is appropriately combined with cost-reimbursable contracts.
- The fee could be variable depending on performance. Variable fees could be combined with either FP or CP contracts. Two fee types are typically employed: (1) an incentive fee that is paid according to a formula based on performance of either cost or schedule or both and (2) an award fee that is paid according to criteria of performance attributes. Award fee is not necessarily formula driven and the amount paid is always subject to the judgment and opinion of the award fee authority in the project.

THE MATHEMATICS OF PROJECT CONTRACTS

Mathematical formulas enter the picture when the project manager seeks to dollar-quantify the risk transferred or retained by a contracting activity. Each contract type, whether FP or CP, has a set of mathematical parameters. Table 9-1 provides a summary of the major contract types and the principal financial parameters for each. In the following paragraphs, we

Table 9-1   Financial Parameters in Contracts

Contract Type	Contract Parameters
Firm fixed price (FFP)	Total price
Fixed price incentive fee (FPIF)	Target cost, target fee, target price, price ceiling, share ratio
Fixed price award fee (FPAF)	Total price, award fee, fee criteria
Cost plus fixed fee (CPFF)	Estimated target cost, fixed fee
Cost plus incentive fee (CPIF)	Target cost, target fee, target price, share ratio
Cost plus award fee (CPAF)	Target cost, target fee, target price, award fee, fee criteria
Cost plus percentage of costs (CPPC)	Actual cost, % uplift on cost
Time and materials (T&M)	Labor rates by labor categories, uplift fee on materials if any

will present examples of how these parameters are applied to various contracts. Let's begin with FFP.

Fixed Price Contract Math

Firm Fixed Price Example

Scenario: A supplier is awarded an FFP contract for a special facility with
certain specified features and functions. The contracted price is $100,000 and
the schedule is 120 days. The facility is ready in time with all required features
and functions. The supplier announces that the actual cost was only $80,000.

Question: How much does the project owe the supplier on obtaining a
certificate of occupancy?

Answer: $100,000. The price is firm and fixed regardless of whether the
supplier overran or underran the estimates.

Let us move to another form of FP contract, one with an incentive fee, called
FPI (fixed price incentive). In an incentive fee arrangement, some of the cost
risk is retained by the project, but the supplier is given the opportunity to earn
more or less fee commensurate with performance. There are several financial
parameters in the FPI calculation.

Fixed Price Incentive Example

Scenario: A supplier is awarded an FPI contract to build a special facility with
certain specified features and functions. The contract cost (risk) sharing param-

eters are negotiated between the project and the contractor. In this example the parameters are as follows: the contracted *target price* (TP) is $100,000, the *target cost* (TC) is $85,000, the *target fee* (TF) is $15,000, the *target return on cost* (ROC) is equal to 15/85 = 17.6%, the *ceiling price* (CPr) is $110,000, and the *sharing ratio* (SR) is 80%/20% applied to cost. The schedule is 120 days.

In this example, the facility is ready in time with all required features and functions. Actual cost is denoted AC, the contractor's share is denoted SRc, and in this example SRc is equal to 20%.

The FPI formula is:

$$\text{Contractor payable} = (\text{TC} - \text{AC}) * \text{SRc} + \text{AC} + \text{TF} \leq \text{CPr}$$

Case 1. The supplier announces that the actual cost was only $80,000, $5,000 *below* target cost; the supplier is paid according to the formula

$$\text{Contractor payable (\$000)} = (\$85 - \$80) * 0.2 + \$80 + \$15 = \$96 \leq \$110$$

$$\text{ROC} = (96 - 80)/80 = 20\%$$

Case 2. The supplier announces that the AC = $95,000, $10,000 *above* TC:

$$\text{Contractor payable (\$000)} = (\$85 - \$95) * 0.2 + \$95 + \$15 = \$108 \leq \$110$$

$$\text{ROC} = (108 - 95)/80 = 16.25\%$$

Case 3. The supplier announces that the AC = $105,000, $20,000 *above* TC:

$$\text{Contractor payable (\$000)} = (\$85 - \$105) * 0.2 + \$105 + \$15 = \$116 \leq \$110$$

In this case, the *ceiling price is exceeded*. The project's cost risk is capped at $110,000, so the contractor is paid only $110,000.

$$\text{ROC} = (110 - 105)/105 = 4.8\%$$

It is instructive to understand what supplier cost, adjusted for incentive sharing, exactly equals the risk cap of the project. For this case, the contract situation has reached the point of total assumption (PTA). Costs above the cost at PTA are borne exclusively by the supplier, as shown in Figure 9-1. Below the PTA, costs are shared by the project according to the sharing ratio. The cost at PTA is defined by the formula

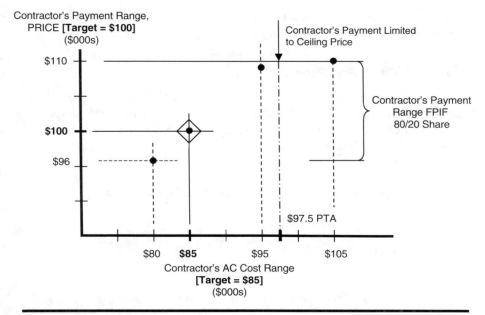

Figure 9-1   FPIF Risk.

Cost at PTA: $(TC - AC) * SRc + AC + TF = CPr$

Solving for AC: AC at PTA $= (CPr - TF - TC * SRc)/(1 - SRc)$

In the example that we have been discussing, the AC at PTA is ($000):

AC at PTA $= (\$110 - \$15 - \$85 * 0.2)/(1 - 0.2) = \$97.5$

Cost Plus Contract Math

Let us look at the CP contract vehicle and see how the project manager's cost risk is handled. Recall that the CP contract is primarily applied in situations where scope is indefinite and a cost estimate cannot be made to the precision necessary for an FP contract. In all CP contracts, the cost risk (as different from the fee) is largely retained by the project. On the other hand, the fee can either be fixed (no risk to the project) or made an incentive fee, usually on cost. With an incentive fee, the project assumes some of the risk of the total fee paid.

The simplest example of CP contracts is the CPFF (cost plus fixed fee), wherein the contractor is reimbursed cost* and receives a fixed fee that is negotiated and set before work begins.**

Cost Plus Fixed Fee Example

Scenario: A software program is to be developed for which the estimated cost is $100,000. A fixed fee of $8,000 is negotiated before the work starts. The estimated ROC is 8%. What is the contractor paid under the following cases?

 Case 1: AC = $90,000.
 Answer:

$$\text{Contractor payment} = \$90,000 + \$8,000 = \$98,000$$

$$\text{ROC} = 8/90 = 8.9\%$$

Case 2: AC = $110,000.
Answer:

$$\text{Contractor payment} = \$110,000 + \$8,000 = \$118,000$$

$$\text{ROC} = 8/110 = 7.3\%$$

 To reduce the risk to the project, the project manager decides to create an incentive on cost such that on a 70%/30% share ratio, the contractor participates in any cost savings. Let's see how this might work in the example just discussed.

---

* In cost-reimbursable contracts, the contractor's costs consist of three components: direct costs of performance for labor and material (nonlabor) applied exclusively to the contract; overhead costs attendant to the direct costs, usually for managers, buildings, general supplies like pencil and paper, utilities, and so forth; and general and administrative costs (G&A) that cover marketing and sales, general management, finance and accounting, independent R&D, and human resources. Overhead and G&A are applied through multiplying the direct costs by a rate that recovers the overhead and G&A proportionately. For instance, if the overhead rate is 110% and the G&A rate is 35%, then for every direct dollar of cost, the project is charged $1.10 additional for overhead and $0.35 for G&A, making the *burdened cost* to the project of a direct dollar of cost equal to: $1 direct + $1.10 overhead + $0.35 G&A = $2.45.

** For organizations that routinely engage in CP contracting, guidelines are developed for calculating fee. Normally these guidelines are published for both parties, the contractor and the project. The guidelines help identify the fee rate given the fact that the contractor's cost risk is all but zero. Without risk, the fee represents more of an opportunity cost wherein the project is seeking to attract the contractor's assets rather have some other opportunity capture the contractor's capability.

Cost Plus Incentive Fee Example

Scenario: A software program is to be developed for which the estimated *target cost* is $100,000. An *incentive fee* (IF) of $8,000 is negotiated before the work starts; the *target price* is $108,000; there is *no* ceiling price. The project's cost liability is unlimited, as in all CP contracts, regardless of incentives. The sharing ratio is 70%/30%. SRc = 30%. The estimated *target ROC* is 8% = 8,000/100,000. What is the contractor paid under the following cases ($000)?
  Case 1: AC = $90, $10 *under* the estimated cost.

$$\text{Contractor paid} = AC + (TC - AC) * SRc + IF$$

$$\text{Contractor paid (\$000)} = \$90 + (\$100 - \$90) * 0.3 + \$8 = \$101.3$$

$$ROC = 11.3/90 = 12.6\%$$

Case 2: AC = $110, $10 *over* the estimated cost.

$$\text{Contractor paid (\$000)} = \$110 + (\$100 - \$110) * 0.3 + \$8 = \$113.7$$

$$ROC = 3.7/110 = 3.4\%$$

Now compare the two CP examples to see how the risk to the project manager changed with the introduction of the incentive fee on cost ($000). The cases are illustrated in Figure 9-2:

- *Case 1*: AC = $90. With the CPFF, the project paid $98, whereas on the CPIF the project paid $101.3.
- *Case 2*: AC = $110. With the CPFF, the project paid $118, whereas on the CPIF the project paid $113.7.
- The risk range for the CPFF is from $98 to $118, a range of $20; on the CPIF, the risk range is from $101.3 to $113.7, a range of a lesser figure of $12.4. The risk range has been reduced by employing incentives:

$$\text{Risk range improvement} = (20 - 12.4)/20 = 38\%$$

Time and Materials Contract Math

A commonly employed contract vehicle for obtaining the services of temporary staff or to engage in highly speculative R&D is the time and materials (T&M) contract. The usual form of this contract is that the time charges are at a standard

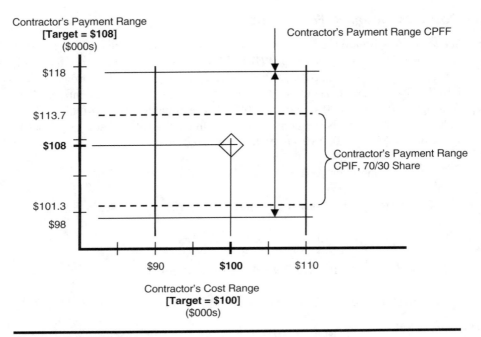

Figure 9-2   CPIF Risk.

and fixed rate for a labor category, but there may be many different labor categories, each with a different labor rate, that are chargeable to the contract. Nonlabor items for all manner of material, travel, subsistence, and other things are charged at actual cost, or actual cost plus a small percentage uplift for administrative handling.

The T&M contract is somewhat of a hybrid, having FP rates but CP materials. In addition, the total charges for labor are wholly dependent on how much of what kind of labor is actually used in the contract. The T&M contract shares the CP problem of no limit to the dollar liability of the project. The contractor need only provide a "best effort" toward the SOW. There is no fixed or incentive fee. The fee is fixed on a labor rate, but the total fee paid is dependent on what labor rates are employed and how much of each is used in the performance of the tasks on the work breakdown structure.

Time and Materials Example 1

Scenario: Two labor categories are chargeable to the contract, developer at $75/hour and tester at $50/hour; 50 hours of the former and 100 hours of the latter are employed on the work breakdown structure. In addition, $500 in tool rental and $300 in training expense are chargeable to the contract. A 2% fee is assessed for material handling.

Question: What is the contractor paid at the end of services rendered?

Answer:

Contractor paid = $75 * 50 + $50 * 100 + ($500 + $300) * 1.02 = $9,566

The supplier is at some risk on T&M contracts, but compared to FFP, the supplier's risk is pretty minimal. The supplier's risk is in the difference between the actual salaries and benefits paid to the employees and the standard rates charged in the contract. If salaries are higher than the standard rates for the specific individuals provided, the supplier will lose money. Consider the following example.

Time and Materials Example 2

Scenario: For the T&M scenario given above, assume that two developers, Tom and Mary, are provided for 25 hours each. Including benefits, Mary makes $76/hour, more than the standard rate, and Tom makes $65/hour, less than the standard rate. Each billable hour by Mary is a loss for the supplier, but each billable hour by Tom is profitable. Susan is provided as the tester and her salary is $48/hour, again profitable at the standard rate.

Question: What is the contractor's ROC on this deal, considering only the labor (time) component?

Answer:

$$Cost = 25 * 76 + 25 * 65 + 100 * 48 = \$8,325$$

$$Revenue\ on\ labor = \$75 * 50 + \$50 * 100 = \$8,750$$

$$ROC = (\$8,750 - \$8,325)/\$8,325 = 5.1\%$$

SUMMARY OF IMPORTANT POINTS

Table 9-2 provides the highlights of this chapter.

Table 9-2   Summary of Important Points

Point of Discussion	Summary of Ideas Presented
Project contracts	■ Contracts between suppliers and the project team are commonly employed to accomplish two objectives: *change the risk profile* of the project and implement *policy* regarding sharing the project opportunity. ■ Five elements are required to have a contract: offer to do business, acceptance of offer, consideration, legal capacity, legal purpose.
Project and supplier risks	■ Contracts do not eliminate risk. ■ Contracts transfer risk among parties. ■ All parties have a risk even after the contract is signed.
Contract vehicles	■ Fixed price contracts transfer the cost risk to the supplier and require the contractor to "complete" the SOW. ■ Cost plus or cost-reimbursable contracts transfer only a portion of the cost risk to the contractor (supplier) and require only a "best effort" toward completing the SOW. ■ T&M contracts are minimum risk for the supplier and maximum risk for the project; however, if not managed properly, the supplier can lose money.
Fees in contracts	■ The fee could be fixed by mutual negotiation (fixed fee). ■ The fee could be variable depending on performance. ■ CPIF formula: Contractor paid $= AC + (TC - AC) * SRc + IF$. ■ FPIF formula: Contractor payable $= (TC - AC) * SRc + AC + TF \leq CP_r$. ■ PTA formula: $AC\ (PTA) = (CP_r - TF - TC * SRc)/(1 - SRc)$.

INDEX